EARLY CHILDHOOD EDUCATION

EARLY CHILDHOOD EDUCATION

A Guide for Observation and Participation
second edition

Lucile Lindberg
Rita Swedlow

Department of Education
Queens College of The City University of New York

Allyn and Bacon, Inc.   *Boston   London   Sydney*

Library of Congress Cataloging in Publication Data

Lindberg, Lucile.
   Early childhood education.

   Includes index.
     1. Education, Preschool. I. Swedlow, Rita,
1928–   joint author. II. Title.
LB1140.2.L55 1979   372.21   79–13535
ISBN 0-205-06720-4 pbk.
ISBN 0-205-06724-7 spiral bound

Printed in the United States of America.

CONTENTS

Because many knowledges, skills and attitudes are learned during the early years, we are concerned with the quality of programs that are developed for young children in nursery schools, kindergartens, and day care centers. Research in human development indicates that children learn as they interact with other children, adults, and things in their environment. Good programs for young children provide for such interactions.

This book is intended to serve as a supplementary text for courses in early childhood education where students examine content and methodology that provide for interactive experiences. It focuses on activities and behaviors of three-, four-, and five-year-old children, either in interage groups or in classes where children are separated according to age.

Worksheets have been developed to focus attention on the specific components of an early childhood program. The observer's attention is directed toward the ways in which a classroom for young children functions, how materials and equipment are used, what children can learn in such a setting, and how a teacher helps children. This book has been field-tested with undergraduate students enrolled in methods courses and with student teachers. Both graduate students and paraprofessionals enrolled in day care courses have used these worksheets as a basis for analysis and discussion.

It is assumed that those who use this book will have had a basic foundations course. There is no attempt to present all points of view concerning programs for young children. While this book is particularly appropriate to an open classroom setting, it is also appropriate for other types of programs.

Listings of additional resources are included so that the reader can acquire further background in the area being studied.

ACKNOWLEDGMENTS

Many people have lent their support as we prepared this volume. We are very appreciative of the interest they have shown in this approach to the study of an early childhood program.

The worksheets were field-tested by teachers at the Queens College Early Childhood Center. Dorothy Benardos, Catalina Fortino, Richard Gordon, Stella Kearse, Diana Shelto, Carol Stevenson, and Judit Taylor conducted seminars and tutorials in conjunction with the worksheets.

We thank Nina Ambrosino, consulting psychologist, and other members of the staff, Mary Chazin, Nancy Cimilluca, John Dell Italia, Agnes Kritzer, Wilma Otto, and Engelina Vega for their help in adjusting schedules and routines. We appreciate the cooperation of the children and their parents.

The faculty of the Queens College Elementary-Early Childhood Education Department, Dean Marvin Taylor, Associate Dean Arthur Carin, and Assistant Dean Janet Ezair; Chairpersons Dan Brovey, Nancy Dill, Paul Longo, and Alan Simon have encouraged us in our efforts to develop a program that would be in keeping with current developments in teacher education.

Queens College students from the Early Childhood Integrated Year Program and the School of General Studies have made helpful suggestions as they worked with the observation forms.

To our colleague Mary W. Moffitt we give special thanks for her continuing support and her valuable recommendations, so graciously made.

We appreciate the suggestions made by educators in the field who have used the first edition These suggestions and recommendations have been useful in the preparation of this revised edition.

L.L. and R.S.

PREFACE

Systematic observation and participation make it possible for students of early childhood education to study in depth the kinds of activities that take place in most schools for young children.

The content of this book is arranged both according to the components of an early childhood education program and the curriculum areas of social studies, communication arts, mathematics, and science. Student observers may focus on either or both, depending upon their course of study. Chapter 2 states the philosophical framework of this book, and Chapter 3 gives a rationale for observation.

This book may be used either in a field-based, modular teacher education program or in a course-oriented program. It can be used in competency-based teacher education programs as well. The worksheets may be used in live classrooms, in simulated classroom situations, or with videotaped classroom episodes. The worksheets have been developed to focus attention on the specific components of an early childhood program.

Each chapter includes objectives, behavioral indicators, pretests and posttests, worksheets, and resource materials that give both theoretical and practical background. The objectives are stated in general terms. Specifics of the objectives will vary from situation to situation, according to the types of settings and the needs of students. Space has been provided for additional objectives. The term "satisfactorily," as used in the behavioral indicators, is meant to be defined by each institution or instructor, since there is no way of determining who the students will be in any given situation.

The worksheets, the core of the book, are constructed to help students learn what to focus on in a classroom. They provide for a nonthreatening type of observation: nonthreatening to the supervisor, the teacher, the child, and the observer. The basic premise is that a bit of directed observation is more valuable than a great

INTRODUCTION

deal of random watching. The background information at the beginning of each chapter may serve as an orientation. There are times when an instructor can assign more than one worksheet to a student for the same observation periods. It is not intended that any one student shall complete all worksheets.

If a worksheet is used near the beginning of a course, the actual process of observing will be sharpened. Using the same worksheet after a student has had more experience may help the student to apply more theoretical knowledge to the real-life situation being observed.

The worksheets have been planned so that a student, with the help of an instructor, may select the appropriate ones to be used. Due to their individual nature, it is expected that the order in which worksheets will be selected will differ from student to student. In some instances there may be overlap; classification and problem solving, for example, appear in different chapters. There has been no attempt to create mutually exclusive categories of activities because play is an interactive process.

No matter who the children are or what the location or size of the school, appropriate worksheets can be used, since the skills of observation are the same for all situations. Each instructor can adapt the worksheets according to the special nature of the classroom in which observations will be made and to the emphases of each course.

The values of the activities to be observed may be enhanced by a seminar. When arrangements can be made for a classroom teacher, director, or principal to meet with students and discuss their observation, this can lend greater understanding to the experience and can clarify misconceptions and answer questions.

The young of all species play. It is their way of learning to live in society. When children play, they learn a multiplicity of concepts, skills, understandings, and attitudes simultaneously, and they draw relationships among concepts. For example, when children build with blocks, they are concerned with shapes, sizes, and relationships. They measure, match, and classify. They face problems of construction. They share materials with others and communicate their ideas and feelings.

Since more knowledge exists than people can ever learn, there is no rational way of deciding which facts are most important for each child. Because facts are not usually used in isolation, they should not be learned in isolation, but rather in context.

When a child learns through play, the learning becomes internalized and remains a part of his or her being. Many activities in play require observation, inquiry, and problem solving, all of which can lead to a high level of thinking. How can anyone claim that his goal is to develop thinking people, and then deny children the opportunity for a full play experience? When a parent complains, "All they do is play!" a teacher's response might be, "How fortunate you are. A child who plays hard is learning to work hard. He is establishing the work habits and values of a lifetime."

Since play is a young child's medium for learning, it is important that it be spontaneous rather than structured to meet adult goals. As society has become increasingly complex and competition has become intense, there has been a tendency to replace children's play with structured activities. Aware of children's natural tendency to play, adults often simulate play with programmed exercises. For example, because children enjoy playing with cars, some programs use this interest to teach concepts of movement and force. They require children to do exercises in which this interest is used for teaching prescribed content. By directing a child to place a car in and

AN APPROACH TO TEACHING AND LEARNING

out of a box, they create a formal lesson on the concepts of "in" and "out."

In order to acquire maximal learning, children need to be able to play for the sake of playing. Play is its own reward. Imagination flourishes when children play. Play is equally valuable for cognitive, physical, social, and emotional development. The involvement helps a child explore his thoughts and feelings about himself both as a person and as a learner. It helps him find different ways of dealing with social situations. He learns about the world he is in and the roles people play in that world. As he learns how to interact with others, he must strike a balance between dependent and independent behaviors. As a child learns to function within established limits, he will be able to use materials in his own creative ways, interact with others, and at the same time learn to control his own behavior. Gaining self-control in interaction with others and in dealing with both success and frustration is an important part of living.

When a child is seriously interested in play, she observes carefully and becomes familiar with the properties of the materials she is using. She plays with them long enough to know how they can be used. In her play a child collects all kinds of valuable things; for example, rocks, shells, twigs, and leaves. She takes a real interest in organizing and classifying things, creating her own systems of classification that go beyond the simplistic labeling often called for in structured exercises. Giving a child a supply of beads to sort according to size is not likely to result in as much learning as permitting a child to sort the beads on any basis he devises, partially because the ideas are his own and partially because he is then free to try various other forms of classification. A child learns more when he sets his own challenges than when challenges are set for him. Each child has his own way of learning and should be allowed to proceed at his own pace.

When a child makes discoveries through play, his personal involvement adds intensity to the experience. He learns what questions to ask and identifies problems that are important to him. A careful listener will hear a child stating his problem and hypotheses even while he is moving on to test these predictions through more play. A child trying to transport sand from one end of the sandpit to the other complains, "It keeps spilling. I'll get that truck to move it over." Placing the pail in the truck, the child successfully maneuvers the vehicle and the cargo to the other side. He begins to understand the relationship between cause and effect, and he begins to identify and set for himself more complex problems, gaining a sense of power as he is able to cope more efficiently with his environment. As a child develops skills through his play, he sets up his own drills.

Before children can experience enriched play, they need to have past experiences to draw upon. Children who have had limited experiences do not have as much substance in their play as those who have had richer experiences. If a teacher provides an environment with interesting materials and equipment, then children are stimulated in their play. As children play with others, they can increase their vocabularies and develop facility with language.

Some materials, such as puzzles, have their own intrinsic order. Sand, water, clay, and paint permit a child to make her own order. A teacher does not need a great number of extraordinary materials. Many so-called junk items hold a child's interest better than specially manufactured materials. However, there is always the danger of overstocking these materials and perhaps overstimulating children. An overabundance of materials is confusing and sometimes disconcerting to children.

A teacher plays a very important role if she makes materials available in such a way that inquiry is the way of life. She shows her interest in and gives support to children's self-initiated investigations. She helps clarify concepts and correct misconceptions. She provides for individual differences in both learning style and rate.

Of necessity, there are some limits that must be set. Children cannot be permitted to hurt each other. Equipment must be used in a safe way. However, where possible, the limitations should be set by the materials and not by the teacher.

Although a teacher has a definite role in children's play, that role does not always require intervention. If a teacher is alert and is observing the children carefully, he will know how or when to make his contributions. One appropriate question may add a whole new dimension to a child's play. "What kind of shampoo do you have in this beauty shop?" "Is your baby sick?" A brief-case, strategically placed in a room, might stimulate different play.

Parents have a right to expect their children to learn in school, and the school is obligated to inform parents of the concepts and skills their children are developing through play. It is a teacher's responsibility to interpret the values of play to parents.

ADDITIONAL RESOURCES

Almy, Millie. "Spontaneous Play: An Avenue for Intellectual Development." In *Foundations of Early Childhood Education*, Michael S. Auletta (ed.), pp. 150–166. New York: Random House, 1969.

Association for Childhood Education International. *Play: Children's Business*. Washington, D.C., 1974.

Cohen, Dorothy H., and Rudolph, Marguerita. *Kindergarten and Early Schooling*. Englewood Cliffs, N.J.: Prentice-Hall, 1977. Chapter 7, "The Meaning of Play in Children's Lives," pp. 97–112; Chapter 8, "Play in the Curriculum," pp. 113–124.

Ellis, M.J. *Why People Play*. Englewood Cliffs, N.J.: Prentice-Hall, 1973.

Leeper, Sarah Hammond; Skipper, Dora Sikes; and Witherspoon, Ralph. *Good Schools for Young Children*. 4th ed. New York: Macmillan, 1979. Chapter 18, "Play Activities," pp. 392–418.

Moffitt, Mary W. "Does Play Make a Difference?" Part 3 in *Leisure Today*. Washington, D.C.: American Association for Health, Physical Education and Recreation, June 1972.

Moffitt, Mary W., and Omwake, Eveline. *The Intellectual Content of Play*. New York: New York State Association for the Education of Young Children, 1967.

Read, Katherine H. *The Nursery School: Human Relationships and Learning*. 6th ed. Philadelphia: W.B. Saunders Co., 1976. Chapter 12, "The Role of Play," pp. 196–207.

Rudolph, Marguerita. *From Hand to Head: A Handbook for Teachers of Preschool Programs*. New York: McGraw-Hill, 1973. Chapter 13, "The Threshold of Literacy," pp. 121–131; Chapter 15, "Striving for Concepts in Preschool Education," pp. 141–148.

Spodek, Bernard. *Teaching in the Early Years*. Englewood Cliffs, N.J.: Prentice-Hall, 1972. Chapter 10, "Child's Play as Education," pp. 199–217.

Film (16mm). *Outdoor Play—A Motivating Force for Learning*. New York: Campus Films, 1973.

Observation provides a way of becoming acquainted with how children interact with materials and people, and also with the arrangement of equipment. Through observation it is possible to identify differences in the ways children learn. The tentativeness or decisiveness of a child's movements as he approaches an easel or a ball of clay provide important clues. When a child is observed playing at a workbench, his physical coordination and other aspects of his physical development can be seen. Because the planning done in any classroom is dependent upon an awareness of these factors, a good teacher must use observation skills daily.

While there are times when an observer will focus on an individual child, often he or she will observe more than one child when focusing on activities in certain areas of a room or specific curriculum content. This book is intended for use in observations of individuals and small-group activities. Attention will be given to how children behave in their relationships and in their interactions in given situations. Some worksheets focus the observations on the teacher's role. These worksheets are offered only after numerous observations of children's behavior have been made. As the observer focuses on an activity, he becomes aware of the clues in children's behavior that prompted a teacher's action.

The observer can then also determine to what extent a teacher's behavior enhanced the play or interfered with it. (If an observer focuses too much attention on a teacher, however, he is likely to miss the clues provided by the children.)

There are many observation scales and checklists available that provide in-depth information on children's behavior. In this book the emphasis will be both on children's behavior and on its relationship to planning and classroom management.

An observer becomes aware of what is important as he focuses on specific behaviors, which may be missed if his observations are too global. Since it is not possible to observe everything at

OBSERVATION AS A STUDY TOOL

once, an attempt is made here to help the observer isolate specifics to focus on. Even when zeroing in on a particular activity, an observer can gain a perspective of the whole room. If an observer's attention wanders, he is not likely to form an accurate appraisal of what has been taking place.

Many students and teachers have difficulty entering and participating in an ongoing classroom. This is partially due to the fact that they have not taken time to observe the situation long enough to make intelligent decisions. An observer becomes familiar with a child's reactions to peers, materials, and adults and is more likely to understand his behavior.

When a teacher has had time to observe and assess a situation, he can take his cues from what he knows about a child, and is then not likely to make decisions about arranging materials or intervening on the basis of a single incident.

ARRANGEMENTS FOR OBSERVATION

If an observer is to get to the heart of what is happening, he must give his full attention to an observation. Observing is such a concentrated activity that an observer cannot concentrate for a long period of time.

There will be times when an observer will listen for the meanings of what children say. The exact words will sometimes be recorded. He will be interested in the voice quality, body posture, facial expressions, gestures, muscle tension, and the ways a child walks or runs. Whenever possible, the age of a child should be included in an observation because it helps the observer to understand a child's behavior.

In some instances, it may be helpful to use the same worksheets in three different rooms in order to observe three-, four-, and five-year-old children. In programs where there is interage grouping, a student may be assigned to observe children of different ages in the same room in order to sharpen her awareness of developmental differences. And, since all children do not develop at the same rate, it is also a valuable experience for students to observe children of the same age in order to identify these developmental differences.

While it is important to be comfortable when observing, using a small chair may make an observer less conspicuous. An observer should be near enough to see and, if possible, to hear what is going on. If a child speaks to him, a brief answer will do. If a child asks, "What are you doing?" an honest answer is called for: "I am writing down what you are doing." Sometimes a child might ask, "Why?" "Because I am interested" is a sufficient answer. Children do not object to observers if the adults in the situation are not upset by an observer's presence. A child might sometimes say to an observer, "You didn't write down what I said."

A good observer is a silent observer. When engaged in a thorough observation, there will be no time to talk to others.

OBJECTIVITY IN OBSERVATION

It is impossible to be completely objective. The very decision of what to record and what not to record is subjective. However, it is important to write down what actually is happening as objectively as possible, rather than to incorporate what one thinks should be happening. An observer should try to be aware of the difference between what is happening and his interpretation of it. No one has the right to draw sweeping generalizations from brief observations, but some generalizing is helpful in gaining some insight into the teaching-learning situation.

ETHICAL CONSIDERATIONS

Statements about a child should never be made in front of him or other children. It is equally important to refrain from talking about any classroom observations or other school business outside the school, however great the temptation. Talking to a colleague about a child on a bus or in other public places is unethical and unprofessional.

ADDITIONAL RESOURCES

Almy, Millie. *Ways of Studying Children*. New York: Teachers College Press, 1959.

Cartwright, Carolyn, and Cartwright, Philip. *Developing Observation Skills*. New York: McGraw-Hill, 1974.

Cohen, Dorothy H., and Stern, Virginia. *Observing and Recording the Behavior of Young Children*. New York: Teachers College Press, 1970.

Hildebrand, Verna. *Introduction to Early Childhood Education*. 2nd ed. New York: Macmillan, 1971. Chapter 1, "So You Are Going to Teach Young Children," pp. 3–27; Chapter 3, "Getting to Know Children," pp. 45–65.

Leeper, Sarah Hammond; Skipper, Dora Sikes; and Witherspoon, Ralph L. *Good Schools for Young Children*. 4th ed. New York: Macmillan, 1979. Chapter 3, "The Young Child as a Person," pp. 46–69.

Medinnus, Gene R. *Child Study and Observation Guide*. New York: John Wiley & Sons, 1976.

Pitcher, Evelyn G.; Miriam G. Lasker; Sylvia G. Feinberg; and Linda A. Braun. *Helping Young Children Learn*. Columbus, Ohio: Charles E. Merrill, 1974.

Rowan, Betty. *The Children We See: An Observational Approach to Child Study*. New York: Holt, Rinehart and Winston, 1973.

Todd, Vivian Edmiston, and Heffernan, Helen. *The Years Before School*. 3rd ed. New York: Macmillan, 1977. Chapter 2, "Understanding Preschool Children," pp. 33–78.

Objectives	Behavior Indicators	Worksheets
To have knowledge of the value of block building in the total program.	Complete Post Test 1 satisfactorily.	4.1 through 4.16
To have knowledge of the kinds of physical activity involved in block building. To have the ability to utilize the environment in order to provide for this activity.	Complete Post Test 2 satisfactorily. During participation, allow for physical activity; for example, children stretching to build high, crawling to clean up, carrying loads of blocks.	4.5, 4.11, 4.12
To identify types of blocks. To identify names of unit blocks. To evaluate types of blocks.	Complete Post Test 3 satisfactorily.	4.1
To have knowledge of appropriate arrangement and storage and management, including cleanup.	Complete Post Tests 4 and 5 satisfactorily.	4.1, 4.2, 4.3, 4.10
To demonstrate an awareness of the affective component of block building.	Complete Post Test 6 satisfactorily. During participation, demonstrate supportive behavior; for example, encourage and recognize accomplishments.	4.1, 4.8, 4.9, 4.11, 4.13, 4.14
To recognize the possibilities for social interaction.	Complete Post Test 7 satisfactorily.	4.1, 4.3, 4.8, 4.9, 4.11, 4.12, 4.14.
To recognize the cognitive learnings that can be gained through block building.	Complete Post Test 8 satisfactorily.	4.3, 4.4, 4.6, 4.7, 4.9, 4.11, 4.13, 4.15, 4.16
To analyze roles of the teacher in planning for and supervising block-building activities.	Complete Post Test 9 satisfactorily. During participation, demonstrate a predetermined degree and quality of intervention; for example, ask a question, introduce material, make a comment, act as silent observer.	4.2, 4.8, 4.15, 4.16

Other(s).

BLOCK BUILDING

Pre/Post Tests

1. List as many objectives in block building as you can. Number them in order of importance.

2. Name the kinds of physical activities that are involved in block building.

3. List three types of blocks available and give a short evaluation of if, where, and how you would use each type.

4. Draw an arrangement of blocks as you think they should be stored in the block area. What is your rationale for placing the blocks in that order?

5. Describe a cleanup period and explain why the approach used is appropriate.

6. Describe ways in which children can develop positive self-concepts as they work with blocks.

7. Identify ways in which block play provides for the following kinds of grouping: solitary, parallel, associative, cooperative.

8. List the experiences a child might have in the block area that could be categorized as part of the following curriculum areas: mathematics, science, social studies, language arts, aesthetics.

9. List five roles a teacher might assume in order to provide opportunities for children in the block area.

From childhood to adulthood, people in many cultures build with blocks. Adults put bricks or concrete blocks together in building a house or a barbeque pit in the back yard. They lay tiles for a terrace. Many educators consider blocks the most versatile learning material for children. The open-ended quality of blocks lends itself to individual differences. Therefore, children of all ages and at every stage of development find playing with blocks a satisfying and challenging experience. Both boys and girls like to play with blocks and will spend long periods of time block-building if the adults supervising them do not have the preconceived idea that blocks are for boys only. Some children will work in a very simple way, while others will use blocks in a very complicated manner. Working with blocks integrates many kinds of learnings.

SELF-CONCEPT

As children develop control of blocks, they develop their own internal self-controls as well. As a child creates her own constructions, she feels a sense of mastery. She is a person of worth. When a child creates something that pleases him, he wishes to make it again and again and, as he repeats the construction and becomes more adept, he gains self-confidence. Because it is his own creation, it is possible for him to gain a sense of power. ("This is mine, all mine. I built it myself.")

Since there is no one correct way of building, even the simplest construction has worth. The nature of the material permits a certain amount of risk-taking that may not be as possible with more fragile or expendable materials. If a child makes a mistake, he can try again.

A child may build vertically or horizontally with blocks. He may build an enclosure with blocks and crawl into it. This would help him develop an awareness of himself in space. As he becomes more accurate in judging the size of blocks in relation to a distance to be spanned, he is on the way to discovering his relationship to other things. Sharing block-building experiences with other children provides an avenue for discovering himself in relation to others.

Blocks are one of the few materials that can be built up and torn down without a child having a feeling of guilt. They provide a legitimate way for releasing energy and diverting aggressive behavior; rather than attacking others, a child can pit his strength against the weight and volume of the blocks.

A child's ability to balance objects becomes

more precise as he seeks ways to make a block structure more solid, and, in the process, he develops a positive self-concept. Completing even a simple project may give a child a sense of power. As he builds more and more extensive constructions, often higher than himself, he can feel a sense of mastery.

SOCIAL INTERACTION

As children play in a block area, they arrange themselves in different social groups. A child may be in the block area building alone (solitary play), or he may be building his structure beside another child who is also building a structure (parallel play). Other children work and talk together about their common activity without dividing their labor or organizing activities to accomplish a common goal (associative play). Or, children may plan and work together on a building (cooperative play). There will be children who engage only in parallel play and those who play cooperatively most of the time. A child may engage in cooperative play one day and build by himself the next day. Children try out different types of interactions depending upon their states of readiness, their experiences both in and out of school, and their own feelings about themselves at the time.

PHYSICAL DEVELOPMENT

As a child plays with blocks, he becomes more aware of what he can do and develops his physical skills. He uses gross motor skills as he lifts, stretches, and crawls. And, as he handles and places each block, he develops fine muscle control.

In the beginning, many children will remove every block on the shelf for the sheer joy of handling them. They may have no intention of building anything. This manipulative experience helps children become familiar with the properties of blocks (their size, weight, shape) while, at the same time, providing for rigorous activity. A child also gets exercise as he reaches for blocks and stands on tiptoe to place them high. Putting the blocks away provides for a great deal of physical exercise. As a child gains continued experience in handling blocks, his eye-hand and hand-hand coordination become refined.

CONCEPTS AND SKILLS

Many concepts and skills are developed as children play with blocks. If blocks are placed on shelves in categories according to size and shape, children will become aware of this ordering. Since classification is basic to the disciplines of mathematics, science, social studies, and language arts, this awareness is an important part of mastering cognitive processes.

As children build with blocks, they arrange them in patterns, which they make more and more complex. Seeing the outline of a structure can develop an awareness of configuration in a two-dimensional context. For example, in reading, a child uses configurational clues in decoding words and sentences. Whether a child is creating a roadway, a tower, or a bridge, the figure he produces stands out against the background.

As a teacher helps children put materials away, blocks are sorted, matched, and classified according to size and shape. When there is a pictorial representation of each shape on the shelves, children have the experience of relating a three-dimensional object to a two-dimensional form. And, if the shelves are labeled with the appropriate block names, children will learn to identify a block with a symbol.

As boys and girls play with blocks, they are learning concepts basic to the curriculum areas that they will study throughout their school careers. In handling blocks, children become aware of similarities and differences. Certain blocks stack more easily than others because they are the same shape. As a child becomes a bit more sophisticated in stacking and builds a series of stacks, he practices one-to-one correspondence in keeping the stacks equal; one-to-one correspondence is basic to any study of mathematics.

Blocks that make up a tower are parts of a whole structure. The concept of the whole and its relationship to its parts is important for a child's understanding of the basic mathematical processes of addition, subtraction, multiplication, and division.

As a child gains experience, he is not daunted when he runs out of blocks. If there are no double-unit blocks to complete his construction, he can seek for their equivalents in smaller shapes, thus recognizing the equivalency relationship. He adds block to block to block, sometimes by ones or twos, and later on by threes and more.

If a child makes a structure higher than expected, he subtracts one or two blocks from the whole. As he carries blocks, he deals with multiples. When he decides to make his single-lane road into two lanes, he is practicing division.

In building a tower, a child gains experience with sets. Seeing a stack of half-unit blocks with a pillar on top, a child builds another tower using a similar set of blocks. As he builds columns using the same grouping of blocks, he is establishing a set relationship. Using concrete materials to create sets will help him later as he uses sets in more abstract forms.

There are many quantitative concepts that a child acquires as he works with blocks, concepts such as more blocks, less blocks, and the comparative relationships of big stack, bigger stack, and biggest stack, or the tallest building and the shortest building.

When a child is extending a track across the floor, he is concerning himself with linear measure. When he is building a garage, he is involved with volume. The nature of the blocks lends itself to the development of both of these concepts.

The constant sizes and shapes of the blocks permit a child to establish his own units of measure. He can use the blocks to measure the distance between two supports as he completes a bridge, for example.

In referring to blocks, a teacher uses special terminology—pillar, unit, double unit, or triangle. Although children are not expected to use these terms, many do begin to incorporate into their vocabularies both these terms and those related to the mathematical processes. After hearing these terms used by the teacher, many children eventually begin to talk about subtracting three blocks from their building or adding four triangles to their garage.

The precision with which the blocks are cut contributes to a child's understanding of mathematical concepts. If a child runs out of unit blocks, there are many ways he can duplicate the unit; for example, two half units or squares equal a whole unit; two small ramps equal a whole unit; and two small triangles equal a whole unit. In performing these operations, the child is working with fractional components in a concrete way. As he practices these concepts, they become part of his basic knowledge.

PROBLEM SOLVING

The steps involved in any kind of problem solving are the steps used in scientific inquiry. When sufficient and varied experiences are available for children, they initiate their own problems that are in keeping with their needs.

A child states his problem when he says, "I am going to make a superhighway." Problems may be simple or complex, depending upon a child's level of thinking. One child's superhigh-

way may be two parallel rows of blocks extending across the classroom, ending when he runs out of blocks or out of room. Another child visualizes his highway with curves, corners, bridges, and tunnels. His problem is to arrange the structure so that his car will move along the whole highway. He tests his structure as he runs his car along various parts of the road. He finds that the bridge is so high that the car will not go over it. He may solve the problem by lifting the car up to the bridge. Another child defines the problem in a different way and tries several solutions. Finally, he discovers that a ramp will do the job. Each child has worked out his own solution.

As children have more and more experiences, there will be less trial and error, and their approaches will become more scientific. Outcomes are anticipated before a decision is made about which solution to try first. Previous experiences and successes enable a child to take calculated risks in seeking a solution to a problem. A child who has had success with problems is able to take chances and make mistakes, thus engaging in more testing. As a block structure becomes more complex, the problems of construction become more complex. A child becomes aware of what happens when an object goes up or down an inclined plane, and the pull of gravity is demonstrated as an object gains or loses momentum in the process. A child experiments with weight and distance to see what will happen as he places objects on a balanced structure. He is amazed at the asymmetric arrangement that is sometimes necessary to achieve balance.

A systematic process evolves as a child learns what a given formation of blocks will accomplish for him. A child who has successfully worked through a systematic approach for solving problems begins to look for ways of applying this approach to new problems that arise in the block area.

Problem-solving activities are also an important foundation for social studies. Children set their own problems, make their own decisions, evaluate their own results, and then move on to other problems. Suddenly the car on the road is headed for the airport, but there is no airport. Then comes the problem, where and how shall it be built? Once accomplished, how can it be enlarged to house additional airplanes? Thinking through such problems makes a child more aware of his world. As he clarifies concepts he gains further understanding.

Background for map making is developed as children enclose space—in making the foundation of a building, for example. Children define a body of water by putting blocks around an area; they define a house in the same manner, just as a geographer outlines land or water forms, such as an island or a seashore. As they do this again and again, they become familiar with using the blocks to indicate boundaries.

As children build, they sometimes play together. Often this community of effort brings an interplay that leads to very elaborate and imaginative creations. A group interacting cooperatively as they plan, execute their plans, and use their structures, constitutes a society in microcosm.

Handling blocks provides experience with language, both written and spoken. Blocks have shapes and are put together to form larger shapes or constructions—just as letters have shapes and are put together to form larger shapes or words. Block structures have definite outlines or configurations, as do words.

Sometimes children lack information they need to complete the building they have in mind. A teacher may be their resource, helping by asking questions, introducing new vocabulary, or calling their attention to the pictures in a book.

As children play with their constructions, they may ask for or make labels to identify them. They may quickly improvise additional arrangements as needed for their play. All of this stimulates conversation that can lead to further creative thinking.

Children use their block structures to reenact experiences. In the process, they clarify concepts and develop understanding of roles. As children play, they share vocabulary, as well as the experiences they have had at school, at home, and in the larger community.

If a teacher has access to a camera that develops pictures on the spot, a child can see his own three-dimensional structure in a two-dimensional form.

ARRANGEMENT

The amount of space given to a block-building area will depend upon the size of the room and the importance a teacher places on block play in his planning. If children are to get maximum use out of the blocks, they need enough space to expand their structures. A block area should be out of the line of traffic so that other children do not interfere with the block building and so that the block building does not inhibit other activities in the room.

Block building needs to be done in a care-fully defined area, which can be designated by the arrangement of cabinets. In many rooms the block-building area is further defined by a large piece of carpet. It is important for any carpet used in this area to be very flat, for children are likely to become frustrated if the pile of the carpet does not provide for a firm building base. An indoor-outdoor type of carpet has proved to be satisfactory. An additional value of carpet is that it decreases the noise level.

The cabinets in which blocks are stored should be low so that children can take the blocks out and put them away without difficulty. There should be a sufficient number of shelves so that there is enough space to organize the blocks according to shape and so that a child can see the varied lengths and shapes of the blocks as he faces the shelves. For example, the length of a double-unit block should be in full view, and the three edges of a triangle should be visible.

Cabinets should be of a sturdy construction so that there is no danger of their falling over. When they are on casters (that can be locked), it is easy to enlarge the block area or move it to another section of the room when a rearrangement is desired. Many commercially made cabinets are constructed with a back panel so that, if a teacher chooses to use only some of the shapes, the cabinet may be turned around so that the other shapes are not in view.

EQUIPMENT

If a school cannot afford commercially made cabinets, parents can be involved in building storage space. Some parents are skilled enough to construct shelves according to specifications. In other instances, parents or teachers have laid wooden crates on their sides and reinforced, sanded, and painted them for use as makeshift storage space. Crates are much more satisfactory than boxes. When blocks are stored in a box, children usually throw the blocks in, often damaging them. When a box is used to store blocks, children do not get experience in classification nor do they see whole-part relationships, both of which are important learnings possible through arranging blocks on a shelf.

Unit blocks are the most popular blocks used in classrooms. There are good reasons for this. Their precise construction allows children to discover equivalencies and other mathematical relationships as they handle them. Because of this precision in construction, children can build sturdy structures. A single shape may be used for very complex structures, or many shapes may be used for greater elaboration. The types of constructions that can be made are unlimited because of the open-ended quality of the material. The basic shape (the unit block) is twice as wide as it is thick, and twice as long as it is wide. With most companies, the units measure 1 3/8″ × 2 3/4″ × 5 1/2″. The square (half unit), double unit, and quadruple unit are exactly what their names imply.

Commercial sets of unit blocks are constructed of nonsplitting hardwood and are extremely sturdy and durable. The natural wood color is pleasing to the eye, and the blocks are satisfying to the touch. If used on a carpet, they even make a pleasant sound as they fall. These qualities are lost if the blocks are painted. Damaged blocks should be sanded. This requires adult precision. Children do not have the control needed for such careful sanding.

Because blocks are costly, teachers are tempted not to buy them. However, because there are so many learning possibilities, blocks are among the most important pieces of equipment in a room. Their durability makes them one of the few materials that do not need to be replaced. They may be purchased in complete sets (about 760 blocks), half sets (about 380 blocks), or individual shapes. Too few blocks tend to limit play. A set of blocks is designed so that children of different levels of ability can use them with satisfaction.

In some schools, blocks have been cut from lumber using the specifications mentioned above. When accurately cut, these can be very satisfying. However, unless a school has a source of lumber, this is an expensive project.

After children have had many opportunities to play with blocks, they can be given accessories to enhance play. These are usually familiar objects such as cars, trucks, signs, and figures of animals and people. Some of these are commercially produced especially for this purpose. However, in many settings where accessories are not available, materials in the room can be used. Children are often encouraged to exercise their imaginations by using a block as a car or person. If accessories are available all of the time, they may detract from the improvising that children can do while working with blocks.

With large hollow blocks, children can quickly build houses, garages, and airports that are incorporated into dramatic play. These blocks vary in size but the commercially produced blocks usually are 6″ × 6″ × 12″, 6″ × 12″ × 12″, and 6″ × 6″ × 24″. While these blocks can be used both indoors and outdoors, because of the space required they are more frequently used out-

doors, and they are usually stored outside the classroom. A dolly can be used to transport all of them together. A great deal of physical exercise is involved as children remove them from the dolly, build with them, and put them back.

When hollow blocks are used outdoors, they often need painting after a season's wear. Sanding may be required to prevent splintering. Auxiliary boards, barrels, and cable spools increase the possibilities for play. When commercial blocks are not available, packing boxes may serve as a substitute.

It is usually best not to use hollow blocks and unit blocks together because the unit blocks, being so much smaller, tend to become the accessories. When children are involved with the hollow blocks, they are likely to lose sight of the proportions or equivalencies of the unit blocks, and thus much of their value is lost.

Block forms are available in both Styrofoam and cardboard. These are light and easily moved. However, there is no challenge to lifting or carrying them. They do not wear well, and the children become frustrated when buildings do not stand in place. In settings where no other blocks are available, it is better to have these blocks than no blocks at all. Some teachers have made blocks by sealing the lids of shoe boxes and painting them. (Table blocks will be discussed in Chapter 9, on manipulative materials.)

ROLE OF THE TEACHER

How a teacher values block play in his scale of priorities will determine the time allotted for this activity, the location and size of the area, the quantity of blocks made available, and the quality of play that results.

If there is to be purposeful play with blocks, a teacher's strong support is required. This may be given in many ways. Often this means that a teacher observes in the block area. His mere physical presence shows his interest in what is happening. In a room where no block play is going on, children usually begin to build if a teacher sits down in the area. It will probably not be necessary for the teacher to say anything because his presence says so much.

Silent support is an important role of a teacher. However, he may need to find a way to direct a child toward a project; for example, he may raise a question about procedure or involvement, such as "May Alice help you with your firehouse?" "Can you find a place for the garage?" If a child begins to destroy the buildings of others, a teacher should be ready to redirect the child's energies either within the block area or elsewhere in the room. As children become more experienced with blocks, and as a teacher through observation becomes aware of the children's stages of development, he may help them understand the problem-solving tasks in which they are engaged. Toward this end the teacher may ask, "What are you trying to do?" (*stating the problem*), "How can you do it?" (*assessing resources and planning procedure*), "Can you get the bridge to stand?" (*testing*), "How did you get it to stay up?" (*recapitulation of process*), "How did it work?" (*evaluation*).

Because there are many facets to a teacher's role, it is often difficult to determine the difference between a positive form of intervention and interference. If comments are never made, children may lack challenge. If comments are made too often, children may become dependent, sometimes stopping play when a teacher is not there. On the other hand, children lose interest in the play if it is not truly theirs. Any question asked should be open-ended and any comment made should extend learning, encourage thinking, or clarify concepts. When a teacher mentions an individual block, he calls it by its proper name, thus enriching the language experience of the child. It is not expected that children will use the name but some will pick it up quickly.

If the number of blocks provided and the space available are adequate, there need be no formal selection of children who will play in the block area. Instead, there can be freedom of movement in and out. When children are in an early manipulative stage, their attention span in block building is short. As they gain greater experience, they may work for longer periods of time.

When a teacher provides sufficient time for children to become thoroughly familiar with a single shape, they can see more things to do with the shape. Some teachers begin a school year by having one or two sizes of blocks available, leaving those shapes out for a period of time so that children may discover the many ways in which they can be combined. As a new shape is introduced, the nature of play changes and the structure becomes more elaborate. When cylinders were introduced after one group of children had been playing for several weeks with the units and double units, they "rediscovered" the wheel and designed huge automobiles and airplanes.

UNIT BLOCKS

Square

Unit

Double Unit

Quadruple Unit

Ellipse

Curve

1/4 Circle

Gothic Door

Large Switch

Small Switch

Large Buttress

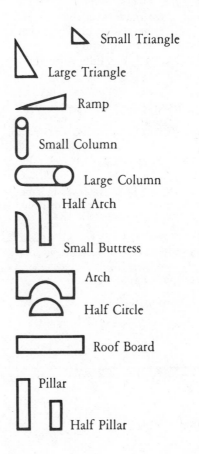

Small Triangle

Large Triangle

Ramp

Small Column

Large Column

Half Arch

Small Buttress

Arch

Half Circle

Roof Board

Pillar

Half Pillar

Putting blocks away is as much a part of block play as the actual construction and selection of blocks. The children who build need not be the same children who put the blocks away. For the child who played with them, some other part of the cleanup may be a more valuable experience. If a teacher initiates cleanup and is active in the process, the children will join. A teacher might take this opportunity to encourage children who ordinarily do not use blocks to handle them and become familiar with them as they put them back on the shelves.

Children put the blocks away in stacks of twos, threes, and fours. If the positions of the blocks on the shelves are marked with a two-dimensional representation of the forms and with the block name, some children will match the picture with the block form and others will associate the printed name with the block.

As children take risks in block building, some of their structures crash. This is an important part of the learning process. A teacher can take advantage of valuable problem-solving opportunities in helping children to find an orderly way to take down a block structure without having the structure crash.

A heap of blocks is not enticing to children, so it is important that blocks be returned to the shelves and floor space made available for the next group. Orderly arrangement on the shelves is in itself a stimulus for construction.

When a block area is carefully supervised, blocks are a very safe medium and can be used in a variety of ways. Sometimes children build structures higher than themselves or test strength by carrying big stacks. If a teacher is aware of these kinds of testing, there is no danger. These are the times when he must be near the area.

Although blocks are sturdy and long-lasting, care must be taken in handling them so that they remain in good condition. Children learn to value blocks when they develop the habit of not stepping on or throwing them.

Blocks should be reserved for the block area. If there is need for using blocks for other purposes, such as cargo for a truck, then scrap lumber should be secured from the local lumber yard.

Sometimes children create a structure that is so important for them that they cannot bear to take it down, or they are engaged in dramatic play that they wish to continue at another time. If a room is not shared with another group, a teacher can easily arrange to keep a structure standing. A sign can be prepared, such as "please do not knock down our building." Or, "this is a house. Please save it." If a room is shared with a second group, arrangements can be made so that the two groups take turns using the space. Children soon learn to respect the structures that others have made and realize that this area of the room is temporarily off limits. When a building is left standing, children may add to it the next day.

ADDITIONAL RESOURCES

Hildebrand, Verna. *Introduction to Early Childhood Education.* 2nd ed. New York: Macmillan, 1976. Chapter 9, "Structured Learning Activities," pp. 225–230.

Hirsch, Elisabeth S., ed. *The Block Book.* Washington, D.C.: National Association for the Education of Young Children, 1974.

Rudolph, Marguerita. *From Hand to Head—A Handbook for Teachers of Preschool Programs.* New York: McGraw-Hill, 1973. Chapter 10, "The Child as a Multimedia Artist," pp. 80–96.

Starks, Esther B. *Block Building.* Washington, D.C.: Department of Elementary, Kindergarten, Nursery, N.E.A., 1965.

Film (16mm). *Blocks: A Medium for Perceptual Learning.* New York: Campus Films, 1970.

Filmstrip and Audiotape. *Block Building, Early Childhood Curriculum Series I.* New York: Campus Films, 1976.

Slides and Audiotape. *Block Building.* Washington, D.C.: Childhood Resources, 1971.

Worksheet 4.1   Block Building

(This worksheet is appropriate for use when an observer can observe only once in this area.)
Unit blocks provide children with opportunities for many types of learning. You will be studying the materials, their use, and the role of a teacher in a block area. You will be identifying both cognitive and perceptual learnings. You will be observing grouping, materials, and space arrangement.

The ways in which children use materials will vary according to stages of development and previous experiences. In parentheses indicate the age of each child that you describe.

Time	No. of children	Grouping: solitary, parallel, associative, cooperative	Identify shapes and accessories used	Describe how they were used	Describe care and handling of materials	Draw and describe storage arrangement and accessibility of blocks
					Describe cleanup process	

No. of children	Materials used	Children's conversation	Observer's reaction	Role of teacher: verbal and nonverbal	What activities did you see that contribute to the following learnings?
					Mathematics
					Science
					Social Studies
					Language Arts

Did some children appear to be more familiar with the materials than others? If so, indicate in what ways.

Worksheet 4.2   Space and Arrangement

Blocks have long been recognized as an important medium for learning. The nonspecific nature of the medium lends itself to a wide range of learning possibilities. The way the materials are arranged is an important determinant in learning.

Draw and describe the storage arrangement and accessibility of the blocks.

What appears to be the rationale for this arrangement?

If you feel some other arrangement would be more suitable, indicate the changes you might make in a diagram below. State your rationale.

Worksheet 4.3   Use of Materials

Block building is an open-ended activity. A child can build simple or intricate structures according to his interest and skill. A child may work alone or with others. The dramatic play that evolves encourages conversation. It provides challenges for children at all levels. Even putting blocks away provides challenges.

Observe a child playing with blocks. Indicate his age. Was the child working alone or with a group? What did he do? What did he say?

What learning possibilities did you observe during the cleanup period?

Repeat this observation with an older or a younger child. How did their play differ?

Worksheet 4.4   **Cognitive Components of Block Play**

Below are listed some of the components involved in learning to read and write. Observe in the block area.
Do you see evidences of any of the learnings listed below? Draw or describe the behavior that illustrates
each type of learning. In parentheses indicate the ages of the children.

Component	Description
Configuration	
Figure-ground	
Matching	
Classification	
Left-to-right progression	
Vocabulary development	
Directionality	
Other	

Worksheet 4.5   Physical Activity

Physical activity is an important part of a child's total development. Block building is a medium that lends itself to much physical activity. Observe one child for five minutes. Describe as many movements as you can capture. Do not forget to include both gross and fine movements.

Description of child:

Movements:

Repeat the observation with an older or younger child. How did this observation differ from the other?

Worksheet 4.6   Curriculum Areas

Observe children in the block area. What activities did you observe that contributed to learnings in the following curriculum areas?

Social Studies

Language Arts

Mathematics

Science

Aesthetics

Worksheet 4.7   Problem Solving

When given an opportunity, children engage in problem solving at a very early age. Block building lends itself to different kinds of problem-solving activities. Describe the problem situations you see as you watch children playing with blocks (e.g., forming a corner, creating a ramp, or stacking). If possible observe children of different ages and compare kinds of problems and approaches to solving them.

Description of problem:

How was the problem resolved? Was the resolution child-initiated or teacher-initiated?

Description of problem:

How was the problem resolved? Was the resolution child-initiated or teacher-initiated?

Description of problem:

How was the problem resolved? Was the resolution child-initiated or teacher-initiated?

Worksheet 4.8   Social Interaction

The block area is a place where a child can play constructively regardless of his social development or how he feels on a given day. He may play alone, near others, or with others. Observe children working with blocks and describe the types of social interactions that you see. Indicate the ages of the children.

TYPES OF GROUPING

Solitary (Child plays by himself.)

Parallel (Children are near each other but engaged in independent play. They may or may not be talking to each other. Each child's talk is related to his own frame of reference.)

Associative (Children are talking together as they work with the same type of materials, but they do not organize their activity to accomplish a common goal.)

Cooperative (Children plan and build together; they may or may not talk.)

Worksheet 4.9   Dramatic Play

As children play with blocks, they frequently engage in dramatic play. They assume a variety of roles, some of which are part of their home and school environments, and some of which originate in books or television programs, and some of which are purely imaginative. List the roles children take while playing in the block area. Suggest concepts that might be clarified through playing such roles.

Roles	Concepts

Worksheet 4.10   Accessories

Anything that children wish to create or play in the block area can be accomplished without any additional materials. Children improvise easily with blocks. However, there are situations in which a teacher finds that the addition of accessories will further dramatic play. Observe the children in the block area and list the accessories and the ways in which they enhance play.

Accessory used	Way in which it enhances the play

What other accessories might you introduce?

Commercially produced block accessories	Teacher-made accessories such as tickets or labels	Improvised materials from the surrounding environment, such as fire fighter's hat, tool chest, etc.

Worksheet 4.11   Putting Blocks Away

In some classrooms children who participate may not be the same ones who clean up. Cleanup can be an exciting adventure in itself. Observe a cleanup period and identify the learnings in physical, social, affective, and cognitive domains.

Physical	Social	Affective	Cognitive

Worksheet 4.12   Large Hollow Blocks I

On many playgrounds, arrangements have been made for the use of large hollow blocks (which may be used indoors in some places). Their weight and size make it possible to build usable constructions. In order to use them a child must exert tremendous physical energy. Observe children at play with these blocks and describe the kinds of activities you see according to the categories listed below.

Physical activity	Social interaction

Worksheet 4.13   Large Hollow Blocks II

(This worksheet may or may not be used with worksheet 4.12.) As children play with blocks, there are many opportunities for cognitive learnings. There is no right or wrong approach. Therefore children can achieve success. Observe and describe the cognitive and affective aspects of children's play.

Cognitive	Affective

Worksheet 4.14   Large Hollow Blocks III

Children playing with large hollow blocks frequently engage in dramatic play. Observe children playing with blocks. Record the conversations they engage in. Draw a line after each completed conversation.

Conversation: Identify children by name, code letter, or descriptive phrase.

How did the materials contribute to the dramatic play?

Worksheet 4.15   Role of the Teacher I

A teacher's attitude toward blocks is reflected in the ways in which he gets involved. This involvement can be either verbal or nonverbal. Observe children in the block area and describe the roles the teacher played.

Support through physical presence:

Extending learnings through questions:

Extending learnings by adding materials:

What concepts were involved?

Worksheet 4.16   Role of the Teacher II

What the teacher does can help a child become independent or dependent. It can intensify or thwart a child's imagination. It can encourage or discourage problem solving. Observe children as they play with blocks. List the instances when a teacher intervened. Beside each listing, place the number from the right-hand column that indicates the type of intervention.

Type of teacher intervention	Code no.	Child's apparent response to the intervention
		1. Exhibited independent behavior.
		2. Intensified the imagination.
		3. Set new challenge.
		4. Raised a question.
		5. Engaged in repetition of the behavior.
		6. Other.

Objectives	Behavior Indicators	Worksheets
To have knowledge of the value of woodworking in the total program.	Complete Post Test 1 satisfactorily.	5.1 through 5.5
To demonstrate an awareness of physical development in woodworking.	Complete Post Tests 8 and 9 satisfactorily.	5.4, 5.7
To have knowledge of criteria necessary to evaluate the tools used in a woodworking area.	Complete Post Tests 3 and 4 satisfactorily.	5.1
To have knowledge of criteria for use in evaluating the location and arrangements for woodworking.	Complete Post Test 3 satisfactorily.	5.8
To demonstrate an awareness of the affective components of woodworking.	Complete Post Test 5 satisfactorily. During participation, encourage development of self-concept (e.g., recognize accomplishments and provide for independence).	5.3, 5.4
To recognize the cognitive learnings that can be gained through woodworking.	Complete Post Tests 2 and 6 satisfactorily.	5.1, 5.2, 5.4, 5.5
To analyze the roles of the teacher in planning for and supervising woodworking activities.	Complete Post Test 7 satisfactorily. During participation, demonstrate a predetermined degree and quality of intervention (e.g., ask a question, introduce material, make a comment, be a silent observer).	5.1, 5.6, 5.9

Other(s).

WOODWORKING

Pre/Post Tests

1. List as many objectives for woodworking activities as you can. Number them in order of importance.

2. List academic learnings that might be developed through woodworking experiences.

3. Draw an arrangement for a woodworking area in a classroom. What is your rationale for this arrangement?

4. What tools would you consider important for a woodworking area? What criteria would you consider in selecting these tools?

5. What opportunities might you find for a child to enhance his self-concept while working with wood?

6. What opportunities might you find in the woodworking area that could be categorized in the following curriculum areas: mathematics, social studies, language arts, science?

7. List five roles that the teacher might assume in order for children to have effective woodworking experiences.

8. What parts of his body does a child use while working with wood?

9. State the ways in which woodworking activity contributes to a child's total physical development.

Children have a wide variety of experiences and gain many learnings as they work with wood. Many teachers neglect this medium because of their own lack of experience with tools and their concerns for children's safety. Many are bothered by the noise.

Youngsters, however, enjoy hearing the sounds they make as they pound with a hammer. "I can make a loud noise. What a powerful person I am!" They release stored-up energy that might otherwise be expressed in less acceptable ways. A child can legitimately make noise at a workbench. It takes considerable effort and concentration for a child to control woodworking tools. When tools of high quality are used, what a satisfying feeling it is for a child to gain control of them. Children must master tools all by themselves; such mastery promotes independent behavior. They test their strength as they wield hammers. Self-concepts are enhanced as children gain feelings of importance from their mastery of the tools. As a child becomes more adept with a hammer, the hammer, as an extension of his arm, becomes an instrument for the expression of his own internal rhythm. His imagination knows no bounds as a piece of wood becomes an airplane, a bird house, a doll bed. When adults do not stereotype woodworking as a male activity, both boys and girls make use of a workbench.

Wood has an aesthetic appeal. It can be a medium for artistic expression. When a child puts two pieces of wood together, he sees and feels the grain of the wood, smells the aroma of the sawdust, and touches the smooth surface after it has been sanded, noting differences in texture of sanded and unsanded pieces.

Woodworking provides many opportunities for manipulative experiences. It is an area in which children use their muscles, bones, and nerves. A child uses every part of his body, large and small muscles, and he uses bodily force as he conquers the resistance of the wood.

As a child saws, he builds foundations in mathematics—for example, he learns division as he cuts a board into pieces, and addition as he nails them together. A child sorts nails and classifies them into long, longer, longest, or thick ones and thin ones, and places them into appropriate containers.

He explores ways of working with wood over a period of time, and discovers that by measuring a nail against the thickness of two pieces of wood he can select the correct length of nail for a job. He searches in the woodbox for pieces of wood and becomes aware of similarities and differences in size, shape, texture, and weight. A child acquires a very concrete sense of whole-part relationships in dealing with this three-dimensional material.

Children add to their vocabularies as they speak about the length, softness, and smoothness of wood. These are some of the foundations of learning, which can later be applied to reading and writing, that a child can acquire at a workbench.

In order to hammer a nail into wood, a child experiments with many ways of holding the hammer and positioning his body. As he tries again and again to hit the nail with the head of the hammer, he develops eye-hand coordination. Often through his interest in nailing, he notes that the position of the nails form a pattern, and he proceeds to create his own special configurations. He sets up more complex problems. He may nail two pieces of wood so that the top piece will be movable, or make a boat-shaped piece of wood even more boatlike. As he completes each step in his construction, he examines it and tests it to find out whether or not he has accomplished his objectives; for example, he sees if two pieces of wood will stay together.

A child may be so enthralled with his creation that he engages in dramatic play. He becomes a pilot as he holds his airplane high above him, or a captain as his boat sails along the floor. While a child can hold, enjoy, and play with a finished product, the end result is not the most important thing. The processes of selecting, testing, elaborating, and evaluating are the really meaningful ingredients—what learning is all about.

ARRANGEMENT

A workbench should be placed so that children will have access to the area and the noise will not interfere with the quieter activities in the room. In order to ensure safety, it is necessary to arrange the woodworking area out of the line of traffic.

A special place needs to be provided for the tools. Usually a pegboard attached to the wall serves the purpose. If outlines of the tools are drawn on the board, children can learn to be independent as they put tools away, developing a sense of order through this organization. This kind of arrangement helps a teacher know whether tools are safely in place when not in use. Children learn to match the tool to the configuration on the board in a one-to-one correspondence.

A sturdy box, placed beside a workbench, is a suitable storage space for wood scraps. Children can then independently select wood as needed, and a teacher can control the amount of wood used by the quantity placed in the woodbox. A working area of 2½′ × 4′ allows two children to work at the same time. If climate permits, a workbench placed out of doors in a sheltered area can be used even during inclement weather.

EQUIPMENT

A workbench must be heavy and solid; if it is not, it is unsafe. Suitable benches are commercially made. While these are costly, they are usually a one-time expense. If this expense is not feasible, good workbenches can be improvised by using a heavy table with the legs sawed off to an appropriate height, or by using a sawhorse with a C-clamp.

With young children, a workbench of approximately 24 inches in height should be used. In order to adapt this height to smaller children, a platform 3 to 4 inches high may be constructed for them to stand on.

While tools should be appropriate to the size of a child, especially to the length of the arm and the size of the hand, they must be adult tools. Those sold in commercial toolchests for children are usually of poor quality. And, because children cannot do what they would like to do with these toy tools, they become frustrated.

They do not endure hard use and they are dangerous. Heads may come off hammers, and flimsy saws do not stay set and are difficult to keep on course. While high-quality tools are essential, it is not necessary to have many. A child needs time to find out what a tool can do. There are many discoveries a young child can make using a hammer and a saw.

A bent-claw hammer with drop-forged head, approximately 11 to 13 ounces in weight, is desirable. When a hammer is too light, a child does not use his strength to good advantage, and when it is too heavy, he tends to place his hand so close to the head of the hammer that he does not get good leverage or power. Since there is room for only two children at most workbenches, two hammers should be sufficient.

It is advisable to select wire or box nails that will not cause splitting to the degree of heavier gauged common nails. Nails in sizes 12, 14, and 16, and in lengths from ½ inch to 1¼ inches, serve most purposes. Cups or small cans are handy storage containers and are useful in matching and sorting.

A ten-point saw (ten teeth to the inch) of high quality steel and 12 to 16 inches long is best for use with young children. A dull saw or one that has lost its set is far more dangerous than a sharp one because it is likely to slip. Also, it requires greater force to push the saw. Other saws, such as coping saws, hack saws, or keyhole saws, are not recommended for children. The coping saw blades may snap with extra pressure, and the other saws are too difficult to control.

Sandpaper, when wrapped and thumbtacked around a small wood block, permits uniform pressure on wood and is easy for children to handle. They enjoy using a rasp to shape wood. A medium wood rasp, 10 inches long, will serve the purpose.

A plane is not necessary for use with three-, four-, and five-year-old children. Hands are not developed enough to grasp it securely. Furthermore, the cutting blade is difficult to set for satisfactory use. Screwdrivers are not necessary. They are dangerous because in maintaining pressure on the head of a screw, the screwdriver may slip and puncture the fingers holding the screw. If a brace and bit is used at all, it should be introduced late in the year.

White pine is a soft wood that is ideal for construction. It does not splinter easily. Because it is not too hard and is fine grained, children are not easily frustrated in sawing and nailing. It presents a challenge but one that a child can handle. Hardwoods and plywood are too difficult for young children to work with. Hardwoods are resistant to nailing, while plywood splinters.

Lumber is costly, so there is a temptation not to purchase it. There was a time when it was easy to acquire scrap lumber. Now scrap pieces are usually sold by the bag. Wood that is found in scrap heaps or boxes should be carefully tested before it is placed in the woodbox because much of it is either too hard or too thin to be a satisfying medium.

ROLE OF THE TEACHER

A teacher who values wood as a medium sets a tone by providing a setting that encourages working with this medium. When a teacher's behaviors and attitudes show respect for tools and what tools can do, children adopt these attitudes. Children who observe a teacher handling tools with care sense that they should, too. Tools are used only for the purposes intended and are put away properly when not in use.

Some teachers do not introduce wood or tools early in the year. Since the woodworking area requires close supervision, especially in the beginning, they prefer to establish routines in other areas first. However, when there is more than one adult in the room, there can be a real advantage to setting up the woodworking area in the very beginning of the year. Woodworking provides a place where children's aggressions and anxieties can be expressed in nondestructive ways through hammering and sawing and may even keep some discipline problems from arising.

A woodworking area is a good place for observing physical development and coordination.

A teacher who observes children regularly is aware of the level of self-control of each child. Some children must never be left alone in the workworking area.

A teacher observes and gives support while permitting children to try and try again. Discovery is the name of the game. Sometimes it is a temptation to show children how to handle the materials or to make suggestions, but if a child is shown how to do things, he does not have an opportunity to discover them for himself. However, one intervention that is important is making certain that the wood is securely placed in the vise when a child is sawing.

In woodworking, more than in other activities, adult expectations may go beyond children's capacities. This is possibly due to the nature of the tools. Just holding a hammer can be a valuable experience for a young child. Some teachers do not introduce nails until children have had many opportunities to pound on pieces of wood, making indentations as they get the feel of what a hammer can do. Children do not always have to be making something, although sometimes their explorations lead them to do so.

Woodworking is usually a very popular activity. Although the space often accommodates no more than two children, a teacher should not put pressure on a child to finish his explorations quickly. When he is at the workbench, he should be able to feel that one project may lead to another and then another. Wood has a great appeal for both boys and girls when appropriate provisions are made for its use.

ADDITIONAL RESOURCES

Baker, Katherine Read, ed. *Ideas That Work with Young Children.* Washington, D.C.: National Association for the Education of Young Children, 1972. Lillian Burke, "It Goes On and On," pp. 56–58.

Cohen, Dorothy H., and Rudolph, Marguerita. *Kindergarten and Early Schooling.* Englewood Cliffs, N.J.: Prentice-Hall, 1977. Chapter 10, "The Many Purposes of Blockbuilding and Woodworking," pp. 168–179.

Moffitt, Mary W. *Woodworking for Children*. New York: Early Childhood Education Council of New York, 1972.

Rudolph, Marguerita. *From Hand to Head—A Handbook for Teachers of Preschool Programs*. Chapter 10, "The Child as a Multimedia Artist," pp. 80–96.

Film (16mm). *Concept Development in Outdoor Play*. New York: Campus Films, 1974.

Filmstrip and Audiotape, *Woodworking*, Early Childhood Curriculum Series I, New York: Campus Films, 1976.

Worksheet 5.1   Woodworking

(This worksheet is appropriate for use when only one observation can be made in this area.)
Children develop many skills, both cognitive and physical, as they work with tools. Due to the nature of the materials, this area requires special attention on the part of the teacher. Observe children in the classroom. Indicate the materials used, the teacher's role, and the learnings.

No. and sex of children	Materials used	Description of teacher's role: verbal, with materials; nonverbal but present; other contact.

Worksheet 5.2   Cognition

The use of tools and wood encourages many kinds of learning in all areas of the curriculum.
Observe children in the woodworking area. What activities do you observe and what curriculum areas are they related to? Describe each activity under the appropriate rubrics. (An activity may be listed in more than one curriculum area.)

Mathematics

Science

Social Studies

Language Arts

Aesthetics

Worksheet 5.3   Self-Concept

A child learns with his whole being. When engaged in woodworking activities, his senses are stimulated. Mastery of the materials enhances his self-concept. Observe a child working with wood and tools. List the ways in which these senses are stimulated.

Smelling

Touching

Seeing   •

Hearing

Which parts of the experience seemed to enhance the child's self-concept?

Record children's conversations.

Worksheet 5.4   Developing Coordination

Working with tools requires the coordination of eye and hand, which is important in reading and writing. Children refine this skill at the workbench. As they develop coordination, they meet with success and find satisfaction in what they do. What actions do you observe at the workbench that require eye-hand coordination?

Movements requiring eye-hand coordination	Relationship to reading and/or writing

Did you note any children's reactions that indicated satisfaction in what they were doing? Explain.

Record children's language.

Worksheet 5.5   Problem Solving

As children work with materials, they encounter problems that they attempt to solve. Working with wood provides opportunities for many challenges; for example, nailing two pieces of wood together or selecting the correct nail for a particular thickness of wood. As you observe children at a workbench, list the problems that they attempt to solve and the ways in which they attempt to solve them.

Problem	Attempt at solution

How might these problems have differed if the children were less experienced? More experienced?

Worksheet 5.6   Safety

Woodworking is a medium that makes it possible for children to develop skills in the use of their imaginations. It has an open-ended quality. Children can enjoy a sense of power in just handling tools or in creating objects. Dangers are minimized when this activity is closely supervised and the tools are of superior quality. The nature of the supervision when children are being initiated into the activity differs from the supervision after they have gained experience with the materials.

   Observe a child at the workbench. Describe the nature of the supervision, the quality of the tools, and the care and handling of the materials.

Nature of the supervision	Description of the tools	Care and handling of the tools

What criteria do you think should be used in selecting woodworking equipment?

Worksheet 5.7   Physical Development

While the child is at the workbench, he uses every part of his body. Describe how and under what circumstances the child uses the parts of his body listed below.

Head:

Neck:

Shoulder:

Arm:

Wrist:

Hand:

Fingers:

Trunk:

Legs:

Feet:

Worksheet 5.8   Arrangement

It is important for the teacher to select a place for the workbench that is out of the line of traffic. The tools and the woodbox should be conveniently located near the workbench. Describe the woodworking area in the classroom. Diagram the arrangement of the equipment. What reasons might the teacher have had for this arrangement?

Arrangement of the equipment:

Rationale for the arrangement:

Worksheet 5.9   Role of the Teacher

Children develop many skills as they work with tools. Due to the nature of the materials, the woodworking area requires attention on the part of the teacher. Observe a child at the woodworking area.

Describe the materials and the provisions made to facilitate their use:

Record any conversation between the children and the teacher:

Record any conversation between child and child.

Did both boys and girls use the workbench?

What evidence was there that the teacher encouraged this?

Objectives	Behavior Indicators	Worksheets
Describe the properties of graphic art materials that lend themselves to the affective dimension of a child's development.	Complete Post Test 1 satisfactorily.	6.3, 6.8, 6.9, 6.11
Describe the ways in which the graphic arts contribute to cognitive learnings in reading, writing, social studies, and science.	Complete Post Test 2 satisfactorily.	6.1, 6.2, 6.5, 6.7, 6.8 through 11
Identify at least three stages of development in using graphic art materials.	Complete Post Test 3 satisfactorily.	6.2, 6.3, 6.4, 6.10, 6.11
Describe the roles of the teacher that encourage children to use graphic art materials.	Complete Post Test 4 satisfactorily. During participation, demonstrate verbal and nonverbal support.	6.1, 6.6

Other(s).

THE GRAPHIC ARTS

Pre/Post Tests

1. Describe three properties of graphic art materials that lend themselves to the affective dimension in a child's development.

2. Describe five ways in which the graphic arts contribute to cognitive learnings in each of the following: reading, writing, social studies, and science.

3. Identify at least three stages of development in using graphic art materials.

4. Describe five roles of the teacher that encourage children to use graphic art materials.

The graphic arts provide for a diversity of experiences, including opportunities for motor activities, for the expression of feelings, and for the clarification of ideas. Since there is no one right way to use art materials, each child can work in his own way. It is important for a child to find out what he can do. It is the interaction with the materials rather than the finished product that is important. A teacher who values graphic art experiences provides enough space, materials, and time so that when a child feels like participating he can do so.

CRAYONS

Many children have experience with crayons long before they come to school. Early play experiences often involve coloring books. The coloring book, with its outlined and predetermined form, restricts a child's imagination and stifles his creativity. Because of this type of experience, children are frequently at a loss when presented with a blank piece of paper. In addition, a child is asked to stay within the lines at a time in his development when he may not have the control to do so. A coloring book implies that scribbling is no good, whereas it is actually important for children to scribble.

When given a sheet of blank paper, a young child scribbles. He does not even look at the paper as he vigorously swings his arm round and round. There is no eye-hand coordination involved. As his eye begins to follow the crayon, he makes circular enclosures without lifting the crayon. As he gains more and more control, he lifts the crayon, and he repeats lines and curves. Many times he repeats lines across the page or randomly on the page. He is consciously gaining control of the crayon, and directs it where he wants it to go. At times, he will talk about what he is drawing, and, although a picture may not be recognizable to an adult, a child may tell great stories about it. The strange configurations on paper become symbols for him.

When a child has repeated experiences with drawing symbols of familiar objects, he eventually does draw the traditional sun, house, tree, and path. It takes a longer time to perceive relationships and develop a concept of distance.

A child has to put forth great effort with crayons in order to get a deep and satisfying color. He often holds the crayon the way he would a pencil. He may discover that when a crayon is stripped of its covering and used on its side it gives an interesting texture and covers a wide area.

Thin crayons are fragile and break easily. They call for a greater coordination of small muscles than a young child is prepared to use. Thick, soft crayons are easier to handle and more satisfying to use.

Since children are likely to put crayons into their mouths, one must be sure that the crayons used are nontoxic. Children do not need many shades of the same color. Six to eight short, stubby crayons are sufficient.

Manila paper or newsprint, 9″ × 12″ or 11″ × 18″, is satisfactory for crayoning. After children have had many experiences with crayons, colored paper may be introduced from time to time.

TEMPERA PAINT

Experiences with tempera paint are very different from experiences with crayons. Color is a more dominant factor in painting. There is lightness, darkness, and the excitement of seeing colors come together on the page. A child becomes the creator of color. As he explores the world of color, he discovers infinite possibilities. There are those who feel that a child should be introduced to one color at a time in order to get the essence of the color. The blueness has more and more meaning with every stroke.

As a second color is introduced, new discoveries can be made. The yellow touches the blue, which makes green. If the introduction of a new color is not hurried, a child can savor the joy of his discovery.

Some teachers provide the primary colors for beginning experiences and depend upon children to create other colors. When they are given too wide a variety of colors, they may miss many of the discoveries and pleasures in mixing paint.

If colors are not introduced too rapidly, a child is able to concentrate on learning to manage his brush. Paint drips. A child can catch the drip with the brush or let it drip and incorporate it into his painting.

Painting is a means of self-expression. Paint should be available daily. Children of all ages use the medium in different ways. Each child can set his own standards and work at his own pace. He can express feelings that he might not dare talk about through paint. As he paints, his feelings emerge and he becomes aware of those he did not know he had. He may have strong feelings that can safely be expressed on paper.

When a child is painting, he uses many parts of the body and gains motor control. He can paint by himself, next to someone, or with a group. As he works, there are many decisions to be made—for example, where he should put the first stroke, or how he will position shapes on the paper. A child who paints near others can talk about his work and begin to develop a new vocabulary concerning the properties of paint, line, and symbols. This language skill will contribute to reading and writing. Eye-hand coordination, figure-ground, configuration, and the creation of shapes are all part of the reading experience.

Whether a child paints indoors or outdoors, he needs space to move his arms and to accommodate a large piece of paper. A child should have time to work at his own rate and be allowed to finish and paint more pictures if he wishes. Space can be set aside for many children to work at the same time. Experience shows that as more spaces are provided for painting, more painting is actually done. Therefore, if one of the values is to encourage many children to paint often, several spaces must be provided.

There are many ways for providing space. Painting may be done at an easel, at a table, or on the floor.

Easels placed side by side add a social dimension to a painting experience. When space is at a premium, easels can be hung on a wall. Although commercial easels are available, they are not necessary. Placing the paper on a table varies the painting experience. The arm and shoulder are held in a different position, and the whole body posture changes. Applying paint on a horizontal plane poses other problems. No longer are there drips, but there may be puddles. Another space for painting is on the floor. Space can be set aside for several children to work at the same time. Here, other movements and types of body control are required.

Painting should be done in a well-lighted place, near water, and out of the line of traffic. A low sink is preferable but a pail will do. Painting need not be limited because of the type of floor covering. There are many ways of protecting a floor. Newspaper or heavy brown wrapping paper will serve the purpose. Plastic runners are easily cleaned and are reusable.

Drying racks or shelves are available commercially or can be made. These provide space for many paintings to be dried at one time. When space to hang paintings is not available, children are discouraged from painting. A child should be given the opportunity to decide which paintings to take home.

Brushes of good quality withstand cleaning, while brushes of poor quality soon lose their bristles. Even though children often enjoy cleaning the brushes themselves, it is important for a teacher to thoroughly clean brushes daily. Dirty brushes disintegrate quickly. When dirty brushes are used, the true color of the paint is lost.

Short-handled brushes are easy for children to use. They may be purchased in ½-inch, ¾-inch, one-inch, and 1½-inch sizes. Paint should be thick and in vivid colors. A separate brush for each color keeps the color in each container true. A small amount of paint, enough to cover half the bristles, should be poured into each container. Too much paint may be wasteful. Colors become clouded with use.

A change of experience is provided when a palette is made available. Then children mix the paint before they apply the brush to the paper. A piece of corrugated paper or a disposable pie tin, will serve the purpose. Nontoxic tempera paint should be used. The kind of container used for paint is limited only by the ingenuity of the teacher. Some containers, such as milk cartons or juice cans, are disposable and make cleaning easy. Most easels have a tray attached so that containers are secure, thereby avoiding spillage. A lightweight box can serve the same purpose and may be used on the table or on the floor as well.

Unprinted newsprint paper (18″ × 24″) is most frequently used in classrooms. Occasionally, this can be varied by using different sizes, textures, and shapes of paper. The classified section of the newspaper makes an interesting background for painting. Brown wrapping paper can be cut into appropriate sizes. Colored paper, although costly, can stimulate new experimentation with color. Outdoor painting on the fence or side of a building requires sturdy paper. Corrugated paper and brown wrapping paper have proved to be satisfactory.

Paper is stored underneath the easel or on a shelf beside the painting area. Some teachers insert L-shaped cup hooks into the easel and hang a supply of papers on the easel. In this way, children may help themselves to additional paper, thus gaining independence. The heavy clamps often used on easels are difficult for many children to manipulate and require the aid of an adult.

In order to protect children's clothing and at the same time allow for freedom of movement, some kind of waterproof covering is necessary. Although commercial smocks and aprons are available in a wide range of styles, colors, and materials, an old shirt with a plastic piece sewn on the front is satisfactory. If a child is wearing a long-sleeved garment, it is important for an adult to roll up the sleeves.

FINGER PAINT

Finger painting is a multisensory activity. There is no instrument between the child and the medium. He uses his fingers, fingernails, knuckles, hands, and arms, and tests what he can do with these parts of his body as he gives variety to his designs. Since the designs made with finger paint can be changed and repeated, the medium lends itself to risk-taking.

Watching changes in the shapes as he moves the color around, and feeling the texture of the paint under his hands, has a soothing effect on a child.

Finger paint has a very distinct odor. The colors are bright and appealing to the eye. Children learn many concepts as they watch colors blend together. There is an element of surprise in not knowing exactly what will happen when a bit of red is added to yellow.

In the beginning, children are not at all concerned with their pictures but rather with the movement of their arms and shoulders as hands and fingers make contact with the medium. They enjoy the legitimacy of making a mess.

As they become more experienced, children experiment with different parts of their hands in order to refine shapes they create. It takes different movements to paint a tree top from those used to depict grass.

A plastic tabletop is most suitable for finger painting. If it is approximately 20 inches high, children can stand and use their bodies freely. If such a table is not available, a piece of oilcloth thumbtacked to a table will serve the purpose. Both of these surfaces can be cleaned easily by children. Sponges close at hand facilitate the job. This is a graphic medium in which paper is not necessary. However, when a child wishes to keep a picture he has painted, a teacher can make a print by pressing glossy paper over his picture.

Very fine, commercially produced finger paints are on the market in a variety of colors. However, there are many finger-paint recipes. In some schools teachers use a mixture of wallpaper paste and water with powdered tempera paint. In others, they beat together two cups of flour, two teaspoons of salt, three cups of cold water, and, when it is smooth, add two cups of hot water. This should be brought to a boil and, when clear, beaten until smooth. Nontoxic powder paint adds the color. Some people add a drop of oil of cloves. Paints made in this manner should be refrigerated.

A supply of primary colors should be on hand but very often only one color will be used.

A second color can be introduced as the need arises.

In most cases, approximately three tablespoons of finger paint are sufficient for a child. When paper is used, it should be dipped in water before paint is applied, so that it remains flat on the table and the paint spreads along the paper easily.

One of the basic rules that needs to be established is that children do not walk around a room after they have started to finger paint. It is also important for them to wear aprons or smocks.

CHALK

There are many things children can do with chalk. They can use either white or colored chalk on a chalkboard.

The movement of the hand, arm, and shoulder when children stand up to draw on a board hung on the wall at eye level is different from the movement they use when they sit.

A child can use chalk on paper and achieve different effects depending upon whether the paper is wet or dry. Sometimes white chalk on colored paper provides variety.

In dramatic play, children often act out the role of teacher as they use chalk in scribbling and writing. When primer pencils are available, children often draw with them and pretend to be writing.

OTHER MATERIALS

There are many graphic art materials on the market. Even though some of them may look appealing, most lack flexibility in the ways they can be used. While many of the colors are bright, they are static because the flow is constant, leaving no element of surprise. The marking pen is the most popular among these materials.

Sometimes teachers become intrigued with the quick end-products that can be made through using strings, squeeze bottles, and sponges, or making block prints, spatter paints, or folded blot prints. Often so much attention is placed on technique of using these products that the children are rushed through the processes.

When children work in the graphic arts, they develop specific concepts and skills. As a child places one brush in one jar, he is practicing one-to-one correspondence. As he moves a brush, pencil, or crayon across a page, he is practicing eye-hand coordination. As he looks at the shapes he has created on paper, he sees figure against ground. As he paints or draws a stripe around a paper, he is enclosing space. As he makes lines and dots, he is becoming aware that symbols can be used to represent real objects. As he combines colors, he begins to recognize likenesses and differences. As he paints or draws, he becomes aware of comparative sizes and shapes and begins to classify them as circle, square, triangle. He can progress at his own rate and have enjoyment in learning every step of the way.

ROLE OF THE TEACHER

A teacher's primary function in encouraging children in the graphic arts is to provide adequate time, space, and materials. If children are going to paint and to express themselves, they have to have something to express. A teacher tries to arrange for rich sensory experiences both in the classroom and on trips. As children touch and smell and look, he helps them verbalize the experience, and, through verbalization, they gain greater understanding of what they have done. They can recall details. As children paint, a teacher listens to what they say, respecting their thoughts and their right to have them. His very presence encourages them to be more daring with the material. His nonverbal communication can often be more effective than asking a question or making a comment.

When children begin painting, they manipulate and experiment with materials in their own ways. A teacher should accept a child's way of handling a brush and applying paint. It takes many tries and many different ways of holding a brush before a child finds the ways that are comfortable for him. He may stand back holding the brush at the tip, pressing it lightly against the paper, leaving splotches of color. He may grasp it near the base with his fist and scrub vigorously. He may hold a brush like a pencil, swishing it across the page leaving lines. As he has more experience with brushes, he begins to form patterns of dots and lines. Having created a pattern, a child will repeat the symmetry of his design.

When a child has time to go through this exploratory process, he is able to immerse himself completely in what he is doing; it then follows that he can comfortably elaborate on his design. Out of such explorations come conscious attempts to create form. After children have been scribbling and scribbling, they begin to give labels to what still appears to the adult to be scribbles.

Early intervention concerning either the content or technique short-circuits learning processes. After a great deal of exploration, many children will find out for themselves how to control the amount of paint on a brush.

If every artistic expression must be discussed a child will soon lose interest or be discouraged and lose confidence in himself. A picture is an expression of a thought or feeling and a child should not be required to talk about it. A painting should not be judged. The value is in the doing, and, if a child is having a positive experience, then whatever he is doing is worthwhile; the experience does not require either his evaluation or the teacher's. Holding a picture up for group evaluation puts emphasis on the product at a time when the process should be the important part of the experience.

Children should have opportunities to drip or spatter paint and playfully experiment with different approaches. However, a teacher should be sensitive to the difference between playful experimentation and destructiveness.

Brush painting and finger painting should be introduced into a program at a time when a teacher is available to help establish routines that will make for freedom of expression later on. The routines of putting on an apron, placing one brush in each cup, washing brushes, and knowing how to remove the paper from the easel and hang it to dry, encourage independence.

In early childhood classrooms art work is usually displayed. Some teachers feel that every child's work should be dignified by being displayed. When this is done, the walls are likely to become cluttered and none of the pictures are actually seen because figure cannot be distinguished from ground. Some children say, "I want my picture hung on the wall." When children's pictures are not judged, then the criteria for selecting them for display can be determined by space and individual needs.

Often children like to take their paintings home. Parents enjoy seeing children's work. For some children, the experience of using brush and paint is enough.

Some teachers keep folders with samples of children's work. When pictures have names and dates on the backs, the teacher has a record of a child's development over a period of time.

Part of a teacher's responsibility is to interpret for parents the values of the processes children go through in painting and the danger of setting adult standards for children's work. If parents understand this, they can enjoy each stage of their child's growth without comparing their child's work with that of other children. When parents understand the values of self-expression, they will be less inclined to use precut patterns or ask children to imitate the work of others. If an adult demonstrates how something should be painted, the demonstration inhibits the child's self-expression.

ADDITIONAL RESOURCES

Hess, Robert D., and Craft, Doreen J. *Teachers of Young Children*. Boston: Houghton Mifflin, 1972. Chapter 8, "The Versatility of the Arts in a Preschool Program," pp. 229-263.

Hildebrand, Verna. *Introduction to Early Childhood Education*. 2nd ed. New York: Macmillan, 1976. Chapter 7, "Creative Art Activities," pp. 138-168.

Jefferson, Blanche. *The Color Book Craze*. Washington, D.C.: Association for Childhood Education International, 1963. (8 pages)

Kellogg, Rhoda. *Analyzing Children's Art*. Palo Alto, Calif.: National Press Books, 1969.

Leeper, Sarah Hammond; Skipper, Dora Sikes; and Witherspoon, Ralph L. *Good Schools for Young Children*. 4th ed. New York: Macmillan, 1979. Chapter 19, "Creative Expression," pp. 418-461.

Margolin, Edythe. *Young Children*. New York: Macmillan, 1976. Chapter 8, "Art and Young Children," pp. 229-260.

Merritt, Helen. *Guiding Free Expression in Children's Art*. New York: Holt, Rinehart and Winston, 1966.

Rudolph, Marguerita. *From Hand to Head—A Handbook for Teachers of Preschool Programs*. New York: McGraw-Hill, 1973. Chapter 10, "The Child as a Multimedia Artist," pp. 80-96.

Spodek, Bernard. *Teaching in the Early Years*. Englewood Cliffs, N.J.: Prentice-Hall, 1972. Chapter 9, "Music and Arts in the Early Years," pp. 177-197.

Todd, Vivian Edmiston, and Heffernan, Helen. *The Years Before School*. 3rd ed. New York: Macmillan, 1977. Chapter 13, "Arts and Crafts for a Preschool Group," pp. 481-510.

Wills, Clarice Dechant, and Lindberg, Lucille. *Kindergarten for Today's Children*. Chicago: Follett, 1967. Chapter 15, "Art Through Form and Color," pp. 213-224.

Film (16mm). *Concept Development in the Outdoors.* New York: Campus Films, 1974.

Filmstrip and Audiotape. *Brush Painting.* Early Childhood Curriculum Series II. New York: Campus Films, 1976.

Filmstrip and Audiotape. *Drawing.* Early Childhood Curriculum Series II. New York: Campus Films, 1977.

Filmstrip and Audiotape. *Finger Painting.* Early Childhood Curriculum Series II. New York: Campus Films, 1977.

Worksheet 6.1   Curriculum Components

(This worksheet is appropriate for use when only one observation will be made in this area.)
Experiences with graphic art materials are an important part of the program for young children. The way in which these materials are set up and presented helps determine the quality of the experiences that the children will have. Observe children engaged in art activities. Note the materials, the role of the teacher, and possible learnings.

Materials	Description of teacher's role	Learnings
Include a description of arrangements, quantity, and location in the room. How many children can participate at one time?	Verbal: Nonverbal:	Mathematics Science Social Studies Language Arts Aesthetics

Worksheet 6.2   Crayons

A crayon is an art material closely related to a pencil. Pressure is required in order to make an impression on the paper. The crayon is often held the same way a pencil is held. Observe children crayoning.

Ways the crayon is held:

Use of space (size of paper):

Color(s) selected and how they are integrated on the page:

Examine several of the drawings. Identify and reproduce shapes, designs, and symbols in the drawings that are used in creating letters.

Worksheet 6.3   Painting I

There is no "right" way to paint. If permitted, each child will work in his own way to develop his own style. It is important for a child to find out what he can do with paint. It is interaction with the material rather than a finished product that is of value. Observe three children as they paint. If possible, observe a three year old, four year old, and five year old child. Describe how they perform the operations listed below.

	Child 1	Child 2	Child 3
1. Hold the brush			
2. Dip the paint			
3 Apply paint to the paper			
4. Make beginning strokes			
5. Use of space			
6. Deal with problems (e.g., drips)			

Can you draw any generalizations about the ways in which the children use materials?

Worksheet 6.4   Painting II

(To be used in classroom where provision is made for painting at an easel, on the floor, or on a table.)
Although paintbrushes and paper are used, the experience is different depending upon whether the
paper is placed on the floor, on a table, or at an easel. Observe children engaged in each experience
and note the differences in approach.

	Easel	Table	Floor
Body movement			
Hand movement			
Application of paint to paper			
Use of space			

Record conversations that occur.

Worksheet 6.5   Painting III

When children paint, they use concepts and skills that are important for them later when they learn to read and write. Observe children painting and give illustrations of any of the following skills or concepts being learned.

Concept/skill	Description of experience
One-to-one correspondence	
Figure-ground	
Eye-hand coordination	
Enclosing space	
Developing symbols	
Creation of patterns that are alike and different	
Verbalizing differences in size and shape	

Worksheet 6.6   Painting IV

Painting is an important part of a program for young children. The way in which the materials are set up and presented helps determine the quality of the experiences that a child will have. Observe children painting.

Description of materials	Description of teacher's role
Include a description of arrangements, quantity, and location in the room.	Include a description of verbal and nonverbal behavior of the teacher.

What evidences do you see that indicate the way children feel about the materials?

Worksheet 6.7   Problem Solving

Children engage in problem-solving activities in many areas of the room. With each stroke of the brush, a child poses problems for himself and finds solutions with subsequent strokes.

Duplicate each stroke you observe a child make, numbering them so that the order in which the strokes were made will be clear. Using that numbering system, choose two or three strokes and describe how the child solved the problem.

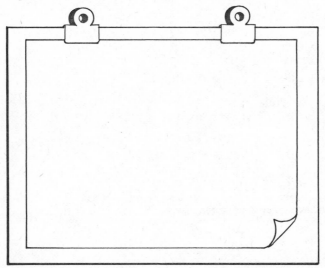

If more space is needed, use additional paper.

Worksheet 6.8   Finger Painting I

Finger painting is a medium that allows a child direct contact with a fluid material. He is able to create a pattern and change it at will. Finger painting is a multisensory activity that provides an opportunity to practice some of the skills required for reading and writing. Observe two children finger painting and describe their reactions.

| Child 1 | Child 2 |

What skills do you observe that could be related to skill in writing?

Record each time a child paints and changes his pattern in a two-minute time span.

Was the painting representational? If not, how would you describe it?

What does finger painting allow children to do that brush painting does not?

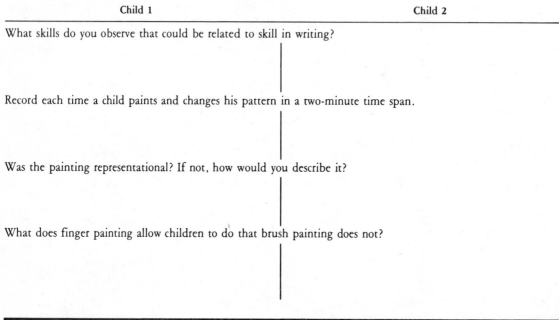

Worksheet 6.9   Finger Painting II

While a child often works on his own, finger painting is sometimes a group activity. The very fluidity of the material seems to stimulate imagination and conversation.

Sit close enough to a finger-painting activity so that you can hear and record the conversation. If more space is needed, use additional paper.

Conversation:

What concepts were revealed through the conversation? For example, what concepts are involved in this child's remark: "This is a house but it doesn't have any windows."

Were there evidences that children enjoyed using the materials?

Worksheet 6.10   Representation

Boys and girls have their own ways of representing objects. There are certain universal representations that children make of parts of their world (e.g., sun, tree, house, man, path, and dog). Watch children drawing and painting. Reproduce any representations they make of objects.

What might they have done if they were older? What might they have done if they were younger?

Worksheet 6.11   Chalk

Children use chalk on chalkboards and paper. Although chalk has some of the same qualities that crayons and pencils have, it has other properties and, therefore, children use it in different ways. Observe children using chalk. Record examples of each of the following and indicate the age of each child whose work you have recorded.

Scribble

Design

Representative drawing

Attempt at writing

Describe the different ways in which children use their bodies when sitting at a table or standing at a chalkboard.

Objectives	Behavior Indicators	Worksheets
To describe the ways in which the children make use of the properties of paste (stickiness, softness, spreadability, odor, taste).	Complete Post Test 1 satisfactorily.	7.5
To identify concepts that children can develop while working with paste and collage materials.	Complete Post Test 2 satisfactorily	7.1 through 7.4
To identify skills that children can develop while working with paste and collage materials.	Complete Post Test 3 satisfactorily.	7.1, 7.2
To describe the ways in which children behave that indicate their feelings while working with paste and collage materials.	Complete Post Test 4 satisfactorily.	7.4, 7.5
To identify the roles of the teacher in the preparation and supervision of paste and collage activities.	Complete Post Tests 5 and 6 satisfactorily. During participation, prepare a collage table and describe the rationale for the selection of each material.	7.1

Other(s).

PASTE AND COLLAGE

Pre/Post Tests

1. Describe the ways in which children make use of such properties of paste as stickiness, softness, spreadability, taste, odor.

2. List ten concepts that children can develop while working with paste and collage materials.

3. Identify six skills that children can develop while working with paste and collage materials.

4. Describe the affective components of paste and collage materials.

5. Identify the roles of the teacher in preparing these materials.

6. Identify the roles of the teacher in supervising this type of activity.

Many children have very satisfying experiences smearing paste on paper. It is a very soothing activity. Sometimes the paper becomes so heavy with paste that a child becomes aware of the weight. The paper sags or even tears as he lifts it.

In the beginning a child is simply intrigued with the properties of the material. He is fascinated by the stickiness in his fingers and will sometimes rub the paste over his hands. It is soft and squishy and can be spread easily so that a little goes over a large area. It feels different when he places his sticky hands under the faucet. The idea that one object can be made to adhere to another is also intriguing to a child.

Young children often use paste in the same way they use finger paint. As their movements become more coordinated, they become more involved in what they are pasting. They concentrate on pasting one shape on top of another without any attention to the design. With experience and time they begin to pay more attention to the shapes and their arrangement on the page.

There is no right or wrong way to use paste. If the end product is the important part of the experience, then a teacher will have particular interest in the quantity of paste used and the manner in which it is spread. When this interest is expressed too often, children miss the opportunity to discover the properties of paste for themselves.

All pastes have a distinct odor of which children are aware. Because children taste everything, all paste used must be nontoxic.

SELECTION AND ARRANGEMENT

Interesting scraps of construction paper are often precut by a teacher. Some teachers provide larger pieces of paper for children to tear or cut themselves, depending upon their abilities and desires. Bear in mind, though, that children need practice in handling scissors before they can cut with accuracy.

In some classrooms teachers combine the pasting process with experiences in shape and color; for example, a child may find dozens of blue circles available for pasting on white paper. Another time there may be the same kind of circles but in light blue, medium blue, and dark blue, or the circles may be varied in size. These activities give children opportunities to have many experiences with shape, size, and pattern. They discover similarities and differences. As children arrange shapes on a paper, they create their own configurations and learn to discriminate between large and small and light and dark. They classify according to more than one attribute, such as shape, size, and color.

A collage consists of shapes arranged on paper. As a child becomes aware of the variety of shapes on his paper, he is practicing the kind of discrimination required in the reading process.

There are many varieties and categories of materials that teachers can provide for stimulating experiences with collage. A teacher may arrange an assortment of papers of various textures, for example, sandpaper, wallpaper, and tissue paper. There may be a variety of cloths, such as burlap, velvet, and wool. Small cardboard boxes of many sizes are also used. In addition, natural objects such as leaves, sticks, shells, and sand can be used.

Children can arrange materials of a given category in a scrapbook. When a teacher knows a child's interests he can prepare a scrapbook or a chart with some of the objects, on which the child may paste additional items. He can prepare a scrapbook of dogs, cats, foods, or automobiles, for example.

After a child becomes aware of the properties of paste and has had many opportunities to explore them, he can then give attention to the artistry of his composition as he combines various materials.

Paper or other lightweight materials can be pasted on pieces of construction paper. If materials are a bit heavier, a light cardboard is needed. A wooden board can be used as a base too.

It is important to have an ample supply of paste available; although children should not waste it, they should have enough for their purposes. White paste can be obtained from commercial sources. It is also possible to make paste. A simple flour and water mixture can be used. Some teachers use cornstarch and water. However, of the homemade varieties, many teachers prefer cooked paste. One cup of sugar and one cup of flour cooked in one quart of water makes a good paste. This mixture should be boiled until thick and stirred constantly. Many teachers add one-quarter teaspoonful of oil of clove or oil of wintergreen.

Paste should be distributed to children in small paper cups or in metal- or plastic-jar lids. In the case of commercial paste, it can be spooned out on small pieces of cardboard or construction paper. In some classrooms sticks or brushes are used for spreading paste, but in the long run the finger is the most satisfying applicator, since a child can control the amount and the placement of the paste more easily. Children quickly form the habit of washing their hands after pasting.

When heavy objects that cannot be held by paste are used in a collage, it is necessary to use glue. Glue provides a more limited experience because it does not have the same versatility as white paste.

ROLE OF TEACHER

Teachers should give care to the arrangement of collage materials. The experience has greater depth if materials are laid out according to some classification scheme. If papers are arranged on a sectioned tray where pieces are organized according to size, shape, or color, children can more readily distinguish likenesses and differences. There should be enough shapes so that they can make choices. Too many may confuse them. A messy tray or table is uninviting to children.

The same materials should not be left out on a collage table for days at a time. However, a teacher is careful not to make changes too frequently, since children should have repeated experiences with the same material.

Making a collage is a satisfying way in which children can gain independence quickly, without rules or instructions from a teacher.

ADDITIONAL RESOURCES

Cohen, Dorothy H., and Rudolph, Marguerita. *Kindergarten and Early Schooling.* Englewood Cliffs, N.J.: Prentice-Hall, 1977. Chapter 10, "The Importance of Art for All Children," pp. 221–222.

Hildebrand, Verna. *Introduction to Early Childhood Education.* 2nd ed. New York: Macmillan, 1976. Chapter 7, "Creative Art Activities," pp. 164–168.

Todd, Virginia Edmiston, and Heffernan, Helen. *The Years Before School.* New York: Macmillan, 1977. Chapter 13, "Arts and Crafts for a Preschool Group," pp. 482–486.

Filmstrip and Audiotape. *Paste and Collage.* Early Childhood Curriculum Series I. New York: Campus Films, 1976.

Worksheet 7.1   Paste and Collage

(This worksheet is appropriate for use when only one observation is to be made in this area.)
When children create collages they have a multisensory experience as they feel the paste on their fingers, feel the textures of the materials used, see the shapes, sizes, and colors, and smell the paste. Of course, young children will taste the paste as well. The selection and arrangement of the materials do much to influence the learnings.

Observe children at a collage activity. Note the materials, the ways in which they are arranged, and the role of the teacher.

Materials:

Arrangement:

Did the arrangement seem to influence the children's selections?

What concepts and skills can be gained?

Role of the teacher:

Worksheet 7.2   Classification I

Depending upon the shapes, sizes, and colors of the materials, many learnings can take place when children create collages. Select either circles, squares, or triangles of three different sizes. With construction paper (using one color only), create many forms of each size. Provide background paper and paste. Watch as children paste. As a child pastes, draw and number each successive design he creates below.

What learnings might he gain from engaging in such an exercise?

Worksheet 7.3   Classification II

Paste has a unique quality and function: the tactile pleasure of smearing paste and the functional quality of adherence. There are additional learnings depending upon the selection of materials being pasted. Select two categories (e.g., dogs and red). Supply a few magazines; provide scissors and encourage children to cut out pictures to illustrate the categories chosen. Make a chart for each category. Label each picture with the appropriate category. As children cut and paste, record highlights of their conversations.

As you listened to the children, did you become aware that there were other categories you could have chosen for the charts that might have been more appropriate?

What learnings might the children have gained?

Worksheet 7.4   An Art Medium

Observe children creating their own designs with collage materials. Describe the materials and the ways in which the children use color, form, design, and texture to create collages that are pleasing to them.

Color:

Form:

Design:

Texture:

Describe the way in which the collage materials were arranged on the table.

What clues led you to believe that children's feelings were involved?

Worksheet 7.5   **Properties of Paste**

Children are intrigued with paste. In their first contacts, they like to simply handle it.
Observe children as they paste. Indicate the ways in which they explore the properties of paste (e.g., touching, smelling). Indicate ages of the children.

Stickiness:

Softness:

Spreadability:

Odor:

Taste:

Other:

Objectives	Behavior Indicators	Worksheets
To make dough for or with a class of children and store it appropriately.	Complete Post Test 1 satisfactorily.	8.11
To draw a diagram of the room showing where clay will be placed and stored in relation to other activities.	Complete Post Test 2 satisfactorily.	8.1, 8.6
To describe the values of modeling materials that are related to the affective development of the young child.	Complete Post Test 3 satisfactorily.	8.2, 8.4, 8.7, 8.8, 8.10
To list cognitive learnings that are possible for children to develop while playing with modeling materials.	Complete Post Test 4 satisfactorily.	8.1 through 8.5, 8.7, 8.8, 8.10, 8.11
To identify the parts of the body involved when children use modeling materials, and to describe the ways in which these materials can help physical development.	Complete Post Test 5 satisfactorily.	8.7, 8.9
To describe the aesthetic experiences available to children in working with modeling materials.	Complete Post Test 6 satisfactorily.	8.8, 8.10
To describe the ways in which the teacher can encourage the use of modeling materials.	Complete Post Test 7 satisfactorily. During participation, sit with a small group of children who are modeling with clay. Demonstrate two ways in which a teacher encourages the use of modeling materials.	8.1, 8.3, 8.8

MODELING MATERIALS

Pre/Post Tests

1. Write a recipe for play dough using one pound of flour.

2. Draw a diagram of the room showing where clay will be placed and stored in relation to other activities.

3. List ten values derived from play with modeling materials that are related to the affective development of young children. Give an illustration of how each value is demonstrated during play.

4. List fifteen cognitive learnings that are possible for children to develop while playing with modeling materials:

5. Identify the parts of the body involved when children use modeling materials. Give five illustrations of how any of these body parts are used.

6. Describe three aesthetic experiences available to children as they use modeling materials.

7. Describe four ways in which a teacher can provide experience with modeling materials for young children.

Children like to squeeze, press, pinch, push, pull, and shape malleable materials. There is a great variety of malleable materials. Clay, sawdust, soft wax, sand, and papier-mâché are frequently used. Of the many commercial mixes on the market, the two materials most satisfying to children and most frequently used are clay and dough.

Making mud pies is a perennial form of play. Mud, when firm, will hold its shape; when in the squishy state, it can be dribbled and poured and a child can rub his hands in it and let it run through his fingers. Children enjoy digging in moist earth as they plant bulbs or flower and vegetable seeds. They see the dirt change consistency when they add water.

In some places, children can dig their own clay. As they work the clay out of the ground with their hands and then manipulate it, they are having two different kinds of experiences. After children have had many opportunities to make objects out of clay, it will be easier for them to understand that tiles, bricks, vases, and cups are made of this material. Many tools are made of clay.

Clay is a satisfying medium. Just manipulating it is a stimulating experience for a child. It can be used for modeling into shapes that can be changed with every push, pull, pinch, or squeeze. It is pliable and yet, when dried, its shape remains. It is a three-dimensional material with which one can make objects that can be held and looked at. A child acquires a feeling of strength as he struggles with the resistance of the clay. The unusual properties of clay cannot be found in many other substances.

There is direct contact between child and material as he creates shapes, to which he may or may not give names. A child has a physically satisfying feeling as he coordinates the large and small muscles of his shoulders, arms, hands, and fingers.

As a child pats and pounds clay, he becomes aware of his own body rhythm. Later on he picks up the rhythm of other children who pound and later, with still more experience, he incorporates these rhythms into his own.

Working with clay often serves as an outlet for aggressive feelings that a child has concerning his own limitations or his frustrations with those around him. Aggressive urges can be tempered or dissipated as he bangs away at the material. As he pounds, squeezes, and pulls, he gains a feeling of control. He learns a different kind of control when he gently pats and shapes the material.

Clay is a valuable medium through which a child can clarify concepts and shapes, such as flat, cylindrical, or spherical. He can make clay shapes long and wormlike. Pieces can be added or pulled off to change shapes. Impressions can be made with his hand or other objects to change texture and shape.

As a modeling material, dough is a very realistic medium that lends itself to many forms of dramatic play. It provides great opportunities for creativity and imagination. When made properly dough does not stick to the hands. Children who hesitate to put their hands into clay will readily attack dough. It has resiliency and shapes can be formed quickly. Children enjoy squeezing, pounding, and pulling dough and cutting many kinds of strange and wonderful shapes out of it.

Playing with dough is especially conducive to social interaction. As children play with dough, they recount experiences at home related to cooking and baking.

As with clay, the consistency of dough allows the children to express both negative and positive feelings as they beat and pound.

Children are able to create figure-ground relationships as they cut out shapes in dough. Long, snakelike forms can be made into symbols as children experiment with letters, figures, roads, and houses. Sometimes they create symbols with cookie cutters.

ARRANGEMENT

Clay can be used both indoors and outdoors. Cleanup after clay or dough activities is facilitated if a place for washing hands is nearby. A table with a mica surface is recommended so that clay can be placed directly on this large area. Usually children sit when they work with clay. However, when they wish to exert pressure, they stand, using their shoulders and arms to apply greater force. If a large table top is not available, boards at least 12 inches square can be used. Sponges should be stored near the clay activity table. Children enjoy cleaning up after this activity.

A program should be arranged so that clay is available when children want to use it. Time must be allowed for children to explore the medium.

When clay is stored in a covered crockery container or a covered plastic pail, it will remain moist and reusable. When it is returned to the container, it can be rolled into balls with a thumb indentation in each ball where water can be placed so it will be ready for use the next day. A ball of clay about the size of a small grapefruit provides enough material for a child to really manipulate.

MATERIALS

There are many kinds of clay. A smooth gray clay is very satisfactory and does not discolor hands or clothing. It can be bought in a moist form, ready for use, in five-, twenty-five-, or fifty-pound bags. It is also available in powdered form. The mixture can be prepared in the bag by adding water to the bag.

At first children do not need any accessories with clay. Getting the feel of it and finding out for themselves what they can do is enough of an adventure. As children gain experience, some teachers give them cookie cutters and rolling pins, but these are not necessary for a satisfying experience.

When older children work with clay, a kiln is often available so that their products can be preserved. With children three to six years of age, there is no need for a kiln. The joy is in the doing. Occasionally, if a child wants to preserve his clay work, the teacher can place it on a shelf to dry.

Plasticene appears to be an ideal material. It retains its moisture, does not stick to surfaces, and can be used over and over again. Because it is an oily substance, dirt clings to it. It does not respond to the touch in the same way that clay does, and so does not have the same appeal. Clay is a natural material that is both satisfying and challenging for a child.

It is easy to use dough in a classroom without running water. Although commercially made dough is readily available, the homemade variety is usually better. Using two cups of flour, one cup of salt, two tablespoons of olive oil, and water to make it soft enough for manipulating and yet not sticky, one can get an economical and satisfactory product. Vegetable coloring can be added. Color may detract from a child's explorations of the properties of dough. Children are satisfied to work with dough in its natural state.

A covered plastic container may be used for storage. If dough is stored in an airtight plastic container, it will become sticky, so a teacher should have additional flour available in order to prepare it for the children's use.

Dough is made in every culture. The fact that children can see the process of making dough from the beginning and engage in its preparation is very valuable to their experience.

After children have had a chance to explore the properties of dough, they can be given rolling pins and cookie cutters. A plastic tabletop lightly sprinkled with flour is a suitable working area. A dough board at least 12″ × 12″ will serve the same purpose.

ROLE OF THE TEACHER

A teacher can encourage children to experiment with clay by allowing them opportunities to handle it in whatever ways they wish. Left on their own, children are likely to form bulky shapes and push and pull pieces from big lumps. If a teacher does not place value on products, children will be less likely to make fragile products that can frustrate them. When a teacher asks a child what he has been making, a child gets the idea that he should be making a product that should be identified and saved.

If children are reluctant to use clay, all a teacher needs to do is to sit at the table with the child, thus indicating that he values this activity. A teacher might handle the clay, but he should not make an object. This might create a standard that children would try to emulate, and so inhibit the child's creativity.

ADDITIONAL RESOURCES

Cohen, Dorothy H., and Rudolph, Marguerita. *Kindergarten and Early Schooling.* Englewood Cliffs, N.J.: Prentice-Hall, 1977. Chapter 12, "The Importance of Art for All Children," pp. 224–228.

Hildebrand, Verna. *Introduction to Early Childhood Education.* 2nd ed. New York: Macmillan, 1976. Chapter 7, "Creative Art Activities," pp. 168–172.

Rudolph, Marguerita. *From Hand to Head—A Handbook for Teachers of Preschool Programs.* New York: McGraw-Hill, 1973. Chapter 10, "The Child As a Multimedia Artist," pp. 80–96.

Filmstrip and Audiotape. *Clay.* Early Childhood Curriculum Series II. New York: Campus Films, 1977.

Filmstrip and Audiotape. *Dough.* Early Childhood Curriculum Series II. New York: Campus Films, 1977.

Worksheet 8.1   **Modeling Activities**

(This worksheet is appropriate for use when only one observation can be made in this area.)
Clay and dough are the modeling materials most frequently used. Both of them are media that
contribute to learnings in all of the disciplines. If good use is to be made of them, special arrangements
must be made for their care. Observe children as they work with these materials. Note the
arrangement, the learnings, and the role of the teacher.

Clay	**Dough**
Arrangement in room:	Arrangement in room:
How stored and cared for:	How stored and cared for:
Concepts:	*Concepts:*
Mathematics	Mathematics
Social Studies	Social Studies
Language Arts	Language Arts
Science	Science
Role of the teacher:	Role of the teacher:

Did some children merely manipulate the materials? Describe. Indicate ages of the children.

Did some children create objects which they labeled? Describe. Indicate ages of the children.

Worksheet 8.2   **Dramatic Play**

When a child works with clay, he has opportunities for talking with his peers or for engaging in dramatic play. Describe ways in which children use verbal and nonverbal communication at the clay table.

Record the conversation of one child who is using a modeling material.

Worksheet 8.3   **Role Playing**

Children often engage in role playing while they use clay or dough. Sometimes this takes place at the table where the material has been placed. They talk, laugh, and explain what they are doing. At other times, objects they have made are brought into the housekeeping area. Observe children as they work with those materials, and describe the roles they assume. Indicate the ages of the children.

Role 1

Role 2

Role 3

What accessories might you introduce that would change the roles?

Worksheet 8.4   Cognitive and Affective Components

As children work with modeling materials, they are developing concepts and skills. Being physically involved with materials that are so malleable in an informal setting facilitates awareness of internal feelings. Observe both the cognitive and affective components of activities with a modeling material.

Cognitive components	Affective components

Worksheet 8.5   Whole-Part Relationships

As children manipulate clay or dough, they develop concepts of whole-part relationships. Observe children as they play with clay or dough and describe ways in which they separate and put together their pieces of clay. Wherever possible, observe a three year old, four year old, and five year old.

	Child 1	Child 2	Child 3
Division			
Addition			
Subtraction			
Multiplication			

Worksheet 8.6   Problem Solving

As children play with modeling materials, they are faced with problems. Sometimes the material is too wet or too dry. Children often devise their own problems, for example, attempting to make two pieces of clay rope stay together. Observe children as they play with a modeling material. Describe the problems that occur and how children resolve them.

Problems	How resolved

Worksheet 8.7   Development

Children everywhere play with clay and dough, activities which provide for an integration of social, emotional, intellectual, and physical development. Observe children as they work with these materials. Record opportunities for development in the areas listed below.

	Clay	Dough
Social		
Emotional		
Intellectual		
Physical		

Worksheet 8.8   Self-Expression

Modeling materials can serve as art media. They lend themselves to many forms of self-expression. Watch children manipulate and create shapes with clay or dough. Record with words and/or pictures your observations of children using these materials as art media.

Child 1	Child 2
Observations:	Observations:
Role of the teacher:	Role of the teacher:
What might be done to extend the experience?	What might be done to extend the experience?

Worksheet 8.9   Physical Activity

As boys and girls play with modeling materials, they squeeze, push, grasp, pound, and stretch. They strengthen the muscles of the hand and develop agility with the fingers, developing control and power as they experiment. Observe children playing with a modeling material. Describe in detail the ways in which children use their hands.

Fingertips:

Finger joints:

Thumb:

Palm:

Fist:

Wrist:

Observe and describe the way other parts of the body are used.

Shoulders:

Arms:

Torso:

Other:

Worksheet 8.10   **Properties of Clay and Dough**

Because of their unusual properties, clay and dough are important media in programs for young
children. They offer many opportunities for exploration. List the properties of clay and dough that make
them such valuable media.

Clay	Dough

Worksheet 8.11   **Dough—Preparing the Material**

Preparing and manipulating dough provide children with opportunities to experience textures and
consistencies that differ from those of clay or finger paint. In the process of preparing dough, children
see materials change shape and form.

Observe dough being prepared in a classroom. Record the conversation and the possible learnings.
Draw arrows between the conversation and the learnings involved in each statement.

Conversation	Learnings involved
Child: "That's heavy."	

Objectives	Behavior Indicators	Worksheets
To list the qualities of pegs, table blocks, and beads that make them open-ended media.	Complete Post Test 1 satisfactorily.	9.1, 9.3, 9.4, 9.5
To describe the cognitive learnings that can be developed as children use pegs, beads, puzzles, etc.	Complete Post Test 2 satisfactorily.	9.2, 9.6
To identify the affect that can be developed as children use table blocks, puzzles, pegs, etc.	Complete Post Test 3 satisfactorily.	9.2, 9.3, 9.5
To describe and demonstrate the verbal and nonverbal roles that the teacher can assume in facilitating both affect and cognition as boys and girls manipulate materials.	Complete Post Test 4 satisfactorily. During participation, demonstrate verbal and nonverbal teacher behaviors that facilitate both affect and cognition.	9.7, 9.8

Other(s).

MANIPULATIVE MATERIALS

Pre/Post Tests

1. List four qualities of pegs, table blocks, and beads that make them open-ended media. List six other materials that fulfill these qualifications.

2. Describe ten cognitive learnings that can be developed as children use pegs, beads, puzzles, and other manipulative materials.

3. Identify the affect that can be developed as children use table blocks, puzzles, pegs, etc.

4. List six roles that a teacher can assume in facilitating learnings with manipulative materials.

Children learn by active participation. Through firsthand experiences, they develop and clarify concepts. From the time a child is born, he is manipulating one thing after another. He gets to know his fingers as he touches them, puts them in his mouth, and handles other things with them. He grabs his crib covers and touches and tugs at any objects within reach. Many parents provide mobiles and other crib toys so that children can have variety in shape, size, color, and sound. When a child has none of these toys, he will improvise with the bars on the crib or with other objects. Most children will drag pots and pans out of a cabinet. All of their senses are involved as they play with them.

Almost everything in a classroom is a manipulative material. Blocks are manipulated as they are removed from the shelves, as children build with them, and as they put them away. Toys in the water, and the water itself, are handled constantly, as are the shoes, pots, and hats in the housekeeping area. While manipulation of materials is often a sedentary, relatively quiet activity, children use many small muscles. There is opportunity to develop eye-hand coordination as they twist, turn, screw, thread, and fit objects into small spaces. Many of the concepts involved, such as shape, color, space, and matching, are important in children's intellectual development. Children begin to see likenesses, differences, and relationships between shapes. These concepts are directly related to reading and writing. Many of these materials lend themselves to self-imposed drill in classification, seriation, and configuration.

The term *manipulative materials* is usually reserved for materials that children manipulate using their hands and fingers and for which little physical exertion is required. Table toys such as pegs, beads, and cubes fall into this category.

A child can work by himself, next to children, or together with others, and in each case have a satisfactory experience. Or he may wish to be away from others. There are times when a child wishes to concentrate on a self-imposed task such as fitting forms into a form board or making his own pattern with the colored cubes. Sometimes he wishes to sit and be quiet after an activity that required great physical exertion. Children can play independently with pegs, beads, or cubes, and engage in conversations with others sitting nearby. Sometimes they will combine their efforts and work on a joint project.

MATERIALS AND EQUIPMENT

Good manipulative materials can either be made or purchased. Any materials used should be simple and durable. Many fine toys are made of natural wood. If they are painted, they should be rich in color and nontoxic. The toy market is inundated with manipulative materials, and too often the environment is overloaded with so much "stuff" that children do not get a chance to explore any of it in depth. Often overabundance makes the problem of choice confusing and, for some children, utterly frustrating. A small number of carefully selected materials will result in more discoveries and make it possible for children to elaborate on their creations.

Puzzles are one of the oldest and most popular of the manipulative materials. They are multipurpose, multisensory, long-lasting, and provide countless opportunities for the development of many kinds of concepts. If puzzles are carefully chosen according to a child's development, they require no instructions. A child knows that when all of the pieces are in place a puzzle is finished. It is a self-correcting material. Puzzles for young children should be made of wood so that they can hold the pieces in their hands and feel the thickness of the shapes. The configuration of wooden pieces is clearly defined, and the pieces remain more precise than do cardboard pieces because the edges do not fray or tear.

Puzzles may be found in a variety of types and complexities. Whatever the developmental level of a child, there are many appropriate puzzles for him. The form board with geometric shapes that can be lifted out and replaced is a suitable first puzzle. There are also puzzles in which the shape and not the color provides the clue for matching. Simple puzzle pieces of one category—fruits, articles of clothing, animals, for example—are placed on a board in such a way that each shape lifts out in one distinguishable piece. Puzzles that are a bit more difficult consist of one object in two pieces, such as an orange and apple, each as an individual unit, while the banana is in two pieces. Puzzles in which there is still more overlap include figures where each part of the body is a piece, for example, head, arms, legs, and torso. Here the clues may derive from color, shape, content, or a combination of these. It is only after children have had many experiences with puzzles that they can handle a jigsaw puzzle where the clues are very subtle.

Children need not be rushed into puzzles of a complex nature. When a child has mastered a simple puzzle, he will initiate self-imposed drill, repeating it sometimes dozens of times, increasing his rate of speed, and placing the pieces in the board with greater and greater precision. Not only is he developing clue awareness, he also is achieving a feeling of self-satisfaction and success. Given enough time, a child will invent new challenges with a very simple puzzle, turning the frame so he does it upside down, putting pieces together outside the frame, or even completing the puzzle backwards and outside the frame. Sometimes he will deliberately mix the pieces of two or three puzzles and race to complete them.

In working with puzzles, children match shapes, using clues of color, size, and shape. In reading, a child will seek and utilize clues. Each puzzle piece has a configuration, as does each letter or word. As a child moves to increasingly more complex puzzles, he develops his own ways of completing them.

SELECTION AND ARRANGEMENT

There is a difference of opinion about an empty table. Some teachers prefer to have materials placed on a table so that children see them. Some feel that when a table is empty children will gravitate to other areas of the room, and so a teacher arranges pieces of equipment on the table to attract the children's attention. If too many materials are placed on a table, it is difficult for a child to distinguish figure from ground.

Some teachers feel that the environment is structured too much when a teacher chooses what will be used. These teachers like to leave several carefully selected materials on a shelf so that children can get what they want and have the choice of working at a table or on the floor. Other teachers feel that children are less restricted in their movements when they work on the floor.

Sometimes puzzles are arranged on the top of a cabinet or shelf within reach of children. There are commercial racks of metal or wood available that make it possible to store several puzzles in a small amount of space.

Because there are so many manipulative materials available, teachers can be very selective. Materials that focus on one concept at a time, for example, push-button toys, do not really provide opportunities for experimenting. One criterion for selection might be that a material not dictate which concepts a child must focus his attention on. Some materials are designed in such a way that children can work with as many as four attributes (shape, size, color, or thickness). A set of 100 colored cubes may be stacked, placed in a line, arranged according to color or pattern, or fitted into a frame box, for example.

Another criterion for selection might be that the child can do the same thing again and again and still feel satisfied with the results. A child who uses a windup toy usually is intrigued with it for only a few minutes. With pegs, a child can make an infinite variety of arrangements, placing pegs in rows, organizing them by color, patterning them by color or number, or skipping spaces on a board.

Toys of fragile construction are wasteful and frustrating. Well-constructed items, which are properly stored, will withstand years of wear and require minimum care.

There are many unpainted toys as well. The quality of wood is very important. Children build the standards of a lifetime when they handle aesthetically appealing materials. A fine quality paint gives a satisfying visual experience. Toys should be painted with a high quality, nontoxic paint of a color that is easily identified.

As a child threads large or small wooden beads, which may be round or cubed, works the locks, screws, or bolts on a board, nests or stacks nesting blocks, and fits shapes into a box, he is developing both hand-hand and eye-hand coordination. Children delight in screwing and unscrewing caps on plastic bottles. They can spend long periods of time taking things apart. Dismantling an old alarm clock, telephone, or radio is a fascinating task to children.

A few old standbys are known to everyone because they are really sound pieces of equipment. There are several kinds of building sets, some consisting of blocks of various shapes and sizes, others consisting of interlocking blocks, and the Tinker Toy variety is always popular. Dominoes, large or small, found in many classrooms, are used as blocks or for matching.

ROLE OF THE TEACHER

The nonverbal support of a teacher who sits with a child working with a puzzle might stimulate the child to take chances and provide him with the confidence to complete the task. There are occasions when a teacher might ask a question to help a child use a clue, but very often this is viewed by the child as interference and tends to interrupt his own explorations. If a teacher provides suggestions and solutions too often, the child does not learn to deal with frustration. He may become dependent upon others for success, thus developing a feeling of inadequacy.

When children use manipulative materials, a teacher has an opportunity to observe their developmental levels in coordination, concept development, and problem-solving skills. When they are not being told what to do with materials, different children will use them differently. A teacher should be aware of how children use materials. Should children become disruptive and throw or step on materials, a teacher should consider that the materials are either too difficult or not challenging enough.

Care of the materials is as much a learning experience as discovering ways of using them. If a teacher makes a practice of picking up pegs off the floor, children will follow his example. A puzzle should have no missing pieces when it is made available to children. A teacher should check for missing pieces before a puzzle is put away to ensure this.

The open-ended quality of manipulative materials provides the children with many satisfying aesthetic experiences as they feel the materials and arrange them in pleasing patterns.

ADDITIONAL RESOURCES

Filmstrip and Audiotape. *Manipulative Materials.* Early Childhood Curriculum Series I. New York: Campus Films, 1976.

Filmstrip and Audiotape. *Puzzles.* Early Childhood Curriculum Series I. New York: Campus Films, 1976.

Worksheet 9.1   Manipulative Materials

(This worksheet is appropriate for use when only one observation will be made in this area.)
The term *manipulative materials* is used in different ways. For purposes of this observation, use the following categories: a) materials especially designed for manipulation (e.g., pegs) and b) materials that lend themselves to manipulation but are not primarily designed for that purpose (e.g., scissors or paintbrush).

    Describe the materials in the appropriate box and identify the learnings involved with each one.

Materials especially designed for manipulation	Materials not primarily designed for manipulation

After making a survey of the room, write your own definition of manipulative materials.

Worksheet 9.2   Cognition

Children gain concepts and skills and make use of cognitive processes as they manipulate materials. Handling materials is an important part of learning.

    Observe children using manipulative materials. Identify some concepts, skills, and processes involved in the following:

Mathematics

Language Arts

Aesthetics

Worksheet 9.3   Criteria for Selection

Some criteria for selecting manipulative materials in an early childhood classroom are:
1. Do they encourage an open-ended response (no limit to the number of ways the material can be used)?
2. Do they lend themselves to self-directed behavior (permitting the child to set his own goals and challenges)?
3. Are they safe to use (nonlead paint if colored, etc.)?

Observe ways in which children engage in open-ended and self-directed behaviors as they use manipulative materials. Give illustrations.

Using the criteria listed above, identify manipulative materials and describe the ways in which children use them.

Worksheet 9.4   Open-Ended Materials

A child can do many things with open-ended materials. Some materials can be used in only one way and some are designed to be self-correcting; for example, colored cubes are open-ended while a puzzle is self-correcting.

Using a stopwatch or a watch with a second hand, observe the amount of time that a number of children take when working with open-ended or self-correcting materials. Name the materials.

Less than 1 minute	Less than 2 minutes	Less than 5 minutes	Longer than 5 minutes

Worksheet 9.5   Individual Differences

Some materials may be used in many different ways and for tasks of various levels of complexity. At every developmental level, a child can gain many learnings as he plays with puzzles. When a child has mastered a puzzle, he invents different ways of using it. Observe three children as they play with puzzles. Where possible, observe a three year old, a four year old, and a five year old. Observe each child for three minutes and describe the ways in which he puts the puzzle(s) together. What clues did each child use? What learnings seem to be involved?

Child 1

Child 2

Child 3

Worksheet 9.6   Problem Solving

In most classrooms for young children there is a variety of manipulative materials. Usually one or two are available for the children on any given day. Observe the children as they work with manipulative materials. What problem-solving situations develop? For example, seeing how fast the pegs can be placed in a board, or putting a puzzle together upside down?

Problem Situation I

Problem Situation II

Problem Situation III

Worksheet 9.7   Arrangement

In some classrooms, manipulative materials are arranged on tables. In other classrooms teachers arrange materials on low shelves, and children have more choices. Each arrangement has advantages and disadvantages. Observe children as they select and use manipulative materials. Describe the arrangement of the materials in the classroom in which you are observing.

Advantages	Disadvantages

Describe a different arrangement of materials and list its advantages.

Worksheet 9.8   Role of the Teacher

Manipulative materials allow children opportunities to set their own challenges and to find their own ways of dealing with them. Poorly timed, inappropriate intervention closes off a child's thinking processes and makes him dependent upon outside resources. Therefore, a teacher needs to acquire supportive techniques that will not inhibit a child's activity. Describe children's activities as they play with manipulative materials. What is the role of the teacher?

Description of children's experiences with materials	Role of teacher (verbal & nonverbal)	Role of other adults
1		
2		
3		
4		

On another sheet of paper record children's language. Indicate ages of children.

Objectives	Behavior Indicators	Worksheets
To list the properties of sand that make playing with it a desirable activity for young children.	Complete Post Test 1 satisfactorily.	10-1, 10-4
To identify the learnings in mathematics, language arts, social studies, aesthetics, and science that young children gain through playing with sand.	Complete Post Test 2 satisfactorily.	10-3, 10-9
To describe the activities children engage in with sand that contribute to an enhancement of their self-concept.	Complete Post Test 3 satisfactorily.	10-2
To describe the ways in which different parts of the body are used as children play with sand.	Complete Post Test 4 satisfactorily.	10-5
To state the ways in which sand as a material contributes to the social development of young children.	Complete Post Test 5 satisfactorily.	10-6
To draw an indoor and outdoor sand area indicating the size and possible equipment for each one.	Complete Post Test 6 satisfactorily.	10-7
To describe the role of the teacher in facilitating physical, social, emotional, and intellectual development in young children.	Complete Post Test 7 satisfactorily. During participation, demonstrate one verbal and one nonverbal teaching behavior in both the affective and cognitive domains.	10-8, 10-10

Others(s).

SAND

Pre/Post Tests

1. List six properties of sand that make playing with it a desirable activity.

2. Identify the learnings in the following subject areas that young children may experience when playing with sand: mathematics, science, social studies, language arts, and aesthetics.

3. Describe three activities children engage in with sand that contribute to an enhancement of self-concept.

4. Describe the ways in which children use their head, shoulders, arms, hands, and fingers, torso, legs, and feet while playing with sand.

5. Describe four types of dramatic play that children might engage in while playing with sand.

6. Draw one indoor and one outdoor sand area. Indicate the size, placement in the classroom or playground, and the equipment involved in each area.

7. Describe the role of the teacher in the following areas of child development: physical development, emotional development, social development, and intellectual development.

One who has seen children at the beach knows how engrossed they become as they play with sand. They are completely absorbed as they invent ways to play with this textured material. A child can hold sand in his hand and feel the mass of it get smaller and smaller as it sifts between his fingers and out the sides of his closed hand. He can pour it over himself using his hands or a container until he is completely covered. In the damp sand he can leave foot prints, hand prints, or the print of his whole body. Sand can be transferred from one pail to another by pouring or spooning or dumping or sifting. A child can fill containers of many shapes and sizes. He can write in the sand with his finger or a stick. He can dig a hole and fill it with water.

Due to the versatility of sand many concepts can be learned by a child. Sand has weight and volume. A child finds that wet sand is heavier than dry sand. A set of clean plastic or aluminum measuring cups is sometimes used for measuring sand. A child has experiences with mathematical concepts as he compares shapes he has made with the wet sand.

As a child finds ways of controlling sand in order to build tunnels, bridges, or roads, he engages in scientific processes. At the same time, he has experiences in communication as he talks with other children about what he is doing or even as he stands back to admire his own work. The sophisticated and the not-so-sophisticated, the younger children and older children can play together. Highly developed cooperative play is possible with sand, as children construct highways and cities. On the other hand, a child can be comfortable while working alone and still feel he has a place in the play that others are engaging in near him as he watches them out of the corner of his eye. His vocabulary increases as he plays many roles in his sand-building activity, such as cook, baker, or engineer. He tests out different roles to clarify concepts. The medium of sand lends itself to limitless uses of imagination.

When a play area is big enough, a child can be immersed in the sand, and, as he sits down, rolls, stands up, squats, and moves about, he uses every muscle of his body.

There is no permanent product when a child works with sand. The same material can be used over and over. A child can make the same thing repeatedly or he can try something different. He sets his own challenges. The tunnel collapses. He can try to build it up or, during this effort, come up with a new idea and try that. All of these opportunities in noncompetitive activity help develop a positive self-concept.

ARRANGEMENT

Sand play can be provided for children both indoors and outdoors. The size of the area is determined by the overall available space. Wherever possible, a partially shaded area is recommended. Whether indoors or outdoors, sand should be out of the line of traffic. When outdoors, a sand area at the ground level should have a specially prepared base about one foot deep with 2 to 3 inches of gravel covering the bottom so that there will be drainage. This should allow for about 9 or 10 inches of sand. A ledge bordering the area helps keep the sand confined. Consideration must be given to where sand toys will be stored. An enclosed area near the sand is most convenient.

EQUIPMENT

When children begin to explore with sand, they are satisfied to use only their hands and feet as tools as they dig, push, scoop up, and mold shapes with damp sand. Short-handled shovels provide for a different experience. These are extensions of their hands, and they find that they can dig with more force. They also realize that they can use tools to control the environment. Wooden spoons can serve the same purpose as shovels. Some shovels are made of wood and are very satisfactory for digging. A metal shovel allows for more scooping and carrying of sand. When they are used, they must be rustproof or else they will need to be replaced often.

Sand pails come in a variety of sizes and materials; for example, plastic, metal, and wood. Durability is an important consideration when purchasing equipment. Old pots, muffin tins, plastic containers, receptacles of many sizes and shapes make it possible for children to shift sand from small containers to large ones, or pour the contents of a large container into several smaller ones.

As children proceed with their play, various materials can be added. A rolling pin, cookie cutters, strainers, funnels, and pie plates encourage dramatic play as children bake pies and bread, cook, or set up stores.

Sometimes, as children become more advanced in their dramatic play and more skilled in handling sand, toy trucks, cars, boats, or airplanes can be added. As important as these pieces of equipment are, too many materials inhibit the imaginative aspect of children's explorations. If the area is cluttered, children cannot make necessary discriminations. When materials to be used are arranged in an orderly manner near the sand, children can make meaningful selections. When equipment is brought out and left in a big basket, children are not exposed to the experience of orderliness and are more likely to make a random selection of materials than a thoughtful one.

There are commercial sand tables that can be used outdoors and indoors. They are usually about 26 inches high, hold about 7 inches of sand, and have a cover that can be used as a table top when the sand is not in use. A sand table can be constructed by parents or teachers. Either a metal or plastic covering should be used to make the table waterproof.

When the sand table is used indoors, a brush and dustpan stored nearby can be used for picking up sand that does spill.

ROLE OF THE TEACHER

It is important for a teacher to supervise the sand area. Some children do not yet understand the ground rules of sand play such as throwing sand is dangerous and sand must be confined to the sand area. Tools are to be used for the purpose intended, not as weapons. When more children wish to play with sand than the area will accommodate, a teacher should have alternative activities available and invite some children to come back later.

A teacher needs to encourage the children who are reluctant to try a new material. The teacher can sit near the sand area, thus making it an inviting place to be. He must also be supportive of children who are working on a tunnel or castle and protect their constructions.

If a teacher helps children get sand out of their shoes and shakes sand out of clothes, there is less danger of slipping and the sand is not wasted.

ADDITIONAL RESOURCES

Rudolph, Marguerita. *From Hand to Head—A Handbook for Teachers of Preschool Programs*. New York: McGraw-Hill, 1973. Chapter 11, "Water, Sand and Other Natural Materials," pp. 97–106.

Film (16mm). *Concept Development in Outdoor Play*. New York: Campus Films, 1974.

Filmstrip and Audiotape. *Sand*. Early Childhood Curriculum Series I. New York: Campus Films, 1976.

Worksheet 10.1   . **Sand**

(This worksheet is for use when there will be only one observation in this area.)
Sand is a satisfying medium that lends itself to a great variety of experiences. As you observe children playing with sand, record their behavior next to the appropriate headings below. Indicate ages of children.

Enjoyment in handling the material:

Satisfaction in trying own ideas:

Conducting explorations:

Use of the body:

Worksheet 10.2   **Self-Concept**

You can learn a great deal about how a child feels about himself and how he copes with his environment, including the persons around him, when he plays with sand. Observe a child for ten minutes. Indicate the number of children in the area and the equipment available. Include age of child.

What did the child do?

What did the child say?

What behavior helped you to sense how the child was feeling?

Worksheet 10.3   Cognition

The free-flowing quality of sand provides many possibilities for learning. A teacher can study the conversations that are a part of children's play as they pour, measure, construct tunnels and castles, and add water to change the consistency of the sand.

Select some experiences, either those listed above or others, which you observe as you watch children playing with sand, and describe in detail what the children do, and what the resulting learnings seem to be. In parentheses beside the activity, in red pencil, state the learnings.

Worksheet 10.4   Properties of Sand

Sand has specific qualities that make it very appealing to young children and that also make it a valuable medium for learning. Describe the way in which each of the following properties of sand contributes to the play.

Can be poured.

Has flexibility.

Has weight.

Has volume.

Has consistency.

Has texture.

Does not dissolve.

Other.

Worksheet 10.5   Body Movement

(For observation during outdoor sand play.)
The size of a sand area determines how much of a child's body can be involved with the medium.
When space permits, practically every muscle in the body is used. Observe children playing with sand.
Describe the ways in which the various parts of their bodies move and contribute to the play.

Head:

Shoulders:

Arms:

Hands and fingers:

Torso:

Legs:

Feet:

Worksheet 10.6   Social Roles

As children play with sand, they often engage in the dramatic play of reenacting adult roles as they
perceive them. Observe children at play with sand. Which of the roles noted below do you see them
playing?

Roles concerned with:	Description
Transportation	
Home and family living	
Engineering or construction work	
Other	

Worksheet 10.7   **Arrangement and Equipment**

There is no right or wrong size for a sand box. It is often determined by the size of the available area. However, the size of the box does determine the nature of children's play. Make plans for indoor and outdoor sand play. Draw the area and the location of the sand box. Indicate the size of the area and the equipment you would use.

Outdoors:

Equipment:

Indoors:

Equipment:

Worksheet 10.8   **Accessories**

Sometimes accessories are added to the sand area. Observe children playing with and without accessories. Describe the differences in the play.

No Accessories:

Accessories:

Description of differences in the play:

Worksheet 10.9   **Problem Solving**

As children play in sand, they try to solve many problems. They develop methods of transporting sand from one area to another. They search for ways of keeping the walls of their tunnels from caving in. Identify the problems that children create as they play with sand and indicate how they were solved.

Problem	Problem
How it was solved:	How it was solved:
Problem	Problem
How it was solved:	How it was solved:

Worksheet 10.10   **Role of the Teacher**

The importance a teacher assigns to sand play will determine the quality of the experience he provides for children. Observe sand play and describe your perception of the teacher's role in relation to areas listed below.

Physical development

Social development

Emotional development

Intellectual development

Objectives	Behavior Indicators	Worksheets
To gain knowledge of the cognitive learnings possible through water play.	Complete Post Test 1 satisfactorily	11.1, 11.2, 11.3, 11.5, 11.8
To describe the affective components of water play.	Complete Post Test 2 satisfactorily.	11.3, 11.4
To describe physical experiences possible through water play.	Complete Post Test 4 satisfactorily.	11.5
To have knowledge of the criteria for use in evaluating the location and arrangements for water play.	Complete Post Test 3 satisfactorily. During participation, arrange a water table for two children and supervise the area.	11.1, 11.7
To analyze the role of the teacher in water play.	Complete Post Test 4 satisfactorily.	11.6
Other(s).		

WATER

Pre/Post Tests

1. List learnings in the following areas which children might gain as they play with water: mathematics, science, social studies, language arts.

2. Describe the affective components of water play.

3. Draw a floor plan of an early childhood room and give rationale for the location of the water play area.

4. Describe teacher behavior in supervising water activities that offers opportunities for growth in the following areas: physical development, social development, intellectual development, emotional development.

As one watches children at the beach, in the bathtub, or simply at the sink washing hands, it is obvious that playing with water is fun. After a rain children like to wade and stomp in puddles. In climates where weather permits a wading pool, they will immerse as much of themselves as possible. They splash and make waves. Play with water is soothing. It is an acceptable way to vent feelings.

Children socialize, communicating with their splashes or language. They can engage in either solitary or group water play and can be totally absorbed. They can play together as they bathe their dolls or wash doll clothes or dishes. They can use a sponge to wipe water off a floor or clean a table. With a brush they can "paint" the wagon or outside wall with water. They become increasingly imaginative as they play with water.

Water can be used again and again. If a child enjoys what he is doing he can repeat his actions. If not, he can stop and do something else with the same water. There is no feeling of failure.

There is something about water that commands a child's attention. He becomes completely involved with it. A child enjoys hearing the splash. He watches the water pour and he blows waves in the basin. He feels the difference between dryness and wetness as he holds the dry sponge and then wets it. He digs in dry sand and then in wet sand. When washing his hands, he feels the difference between the warm and cool substance. He sees reflections. When he is thirsty he tastes the water. Water from the refrigerator and water from the faucet are different.

The amazing properties of water make many kinds of exploration possible. Water has weight. Some things will float on it, some things will sink. It flows. When pushed, it generates force. When children water plants, they must take great care so that the force of the water does not wash the soil away from the stem of the plant. Water takes the shape of the area in which it is confined whether it is a pitcher, a basin, or a puddle. On some surfaces it forms into droplets. It can change from liquid to vapor, become ice or snow. When things are mixed with water, their properties change. A material such as salt or sugar forms a solution while dirt forms a mixture. A child can explore the force of the water when he turns on the faucet. He can pour it from a large container into several smaller ones or from a small one into a larger one. Sometimes a funnel is used to direct the water. This requires coordination. As a child gets practice, he gains control and spills less as he pours. Using a small pitcher at juice time allows a child to control the pouring, which gives him a sense of achievement.

Sometimes measuring cups add another dimension to pouring activity. Children enjoy pouring liquids into various-sized containers, even though they do not understand the concepts of liters or ounces. They enjoy creating a siphon with a clear plastic tube and watching the water flow through. It is also a great experience for children to get the water from the sink to the pail using siphoning equipment.

To a child, the discovery that some objects float is remarkable. At first children test one object after another. Eventually, they observe that some objects always fall to the bottom, and others always remain on the top. After a rain, they may float objects such as leaves or sticks in a stream they create with water. If there is a slope on the playground, they can make a little river with tributaries running downhill. If water is put in a pan and left for a few days, children will learn that water evaporates. When water is boiled in a pot, children can see the steam in the air as the water disappears from the pot.

When detergent is added to water, all it takes is a drinking straw to fill the air with bubbles. The bubbles float, separate, reflect rainbows, go up in the air and disappear. When water is added to clay, dough, or paint, their textures change. Lemons and sugar added to water make lemonade.

Ice is another medium children find remarkable. Children step on thin ice over puddles and hear it break. A pan of water can be put out overnight so that children can observe the change the next day.

Snow is a form of water that is particularly exciting to children. They can catch snowflakes on their tongues, or on a piece of colored paper or plexiglass. They squeeze it, they hold it in their hands and press it against their cheeks because they enjoy the physical sensation. With shovels they dig paths and make mounds of snow and snow figures. Sometimes drops of paint in snow make beautiful snow pictures. Children delight in rolling in snow and they can tolerate the cold for long periods. They lie down and wave their arms back and forth making impressions in the snow. If children have containers of various sizes, they will fill them with snow and engage in dramatic play, making cakes, pies, and candies.

ARRANGEMENT

If children are to explore with water, they need to work in small groups away from other activities. At most indoor water play areas, two children can be comfortable; no more than four should be ac-commodated. The water activity area should be arranged in such a position that the table or container stands on a waterproof, or at least a water resistant, surface. If an area is carpeted, plastic runners can serve as protection. When a water table is arranged near the source of water, cleanup is faciliated. Provisions for water play can be made both indoors and outdoors. If a water table is placed underneath or near an overhang in the outdoor area, children can be protected from the sun.

EQUIPMENT

Water play can take place in a sink, in a pail or dishpan, or in a puddle outdoors. There are commercial plastic water tables that are usually about 22 inches high, 2 feet × 3 feet, and hold 5 to 6 inches of water.

Items such as sponges, corks, pieces of light wood, sieves, colanders, plastic tubes, funnels, siphons, sprays, sprinkling cans, squeeze bottles, rubber bulbs, transparent plastic pitchers, jars, and cups are suitable accessories that can be acquired easily. However, the number of accessories included at any given time should be limited. There must be enough space in the water for children to play. Too many objects in the area at one time detract from the play and stifle imagination. Often certain categories of materials are placed in the water; assorted corks may be used one day, and on another day, containers may be added to the water. On yet another day, a tube, a funnel, a pail, and a cup may stimulate a different kind of play. Detergent can be added. This changes the nature of the play as children blow and try to catch bubbles between their hands. A 4-inch paintbrush or a painter's long-handled brush or roller permits a child to cover large surfaces with water. In areas where the climate permits, a small portable wading pool is a valuable addition to outdoor equipment. Plastic aprons provide protection when children play with water. Either homemade or commercially produced aprons are satisfactory.

ROLE OF THE TEACHER

When a wading pool is used, it must be supervised every minute. It is safe when an adult is giving it full attention; left alone, children could be in danger.

A teacher should be prepared to help to clean up puddles while children are playing. Although wanton splashing should not be encouraged, too many restrictions inhibit experimentation.

A teacher needs to observe carefully so that as the children exhaust their own resources, he may introduce a new piece of equipment. On the other hand, a teacher must be careful not to allow too much clutter in the water play area. This prevents children from distinguishing figure from ground. If a teacher recognizes the value of water play, he will make provisions for this activity regularly.

ADDITIONAL RESOURCES

Cohen, Dorothy H., and Rudolph, Marguerita. *Kindergarten and Early Schooling*. Englewood Cliffs, N.J.: Prentice-Hall, 1977. Chapter 9, "Exploring the Environment," pp. 127–148.

Rudolph, Marguerita. *From Hand to Head—A Handbook for Teachers of Preschool Programs*. New York: McGraw-Hill, 1973. Chapter 11, "Water, Sand and Other Natural Materials," pp. 97–106.

Film (16mm). *Concept Development in the Outdoors*. New York: Campus Films, 1977.

Filmstrip and Audiotape. *Water*. Early Childhood Curriculum Series II. New York: Campus Films, 1977.

Worksheet 11.1   Properties of Water

(This worksheet is appropriate for use when only one observation will be made in this area.)
If a teacher is to make the arrangements for maximum learnings with water, he needs to keep in mind
the nature of water and what water can do. Observe children playing with water. In the appropriate
spaces, describe any experience the children have that is related to the properties of water. (Some
experiences may be listed under more than one rubric.) Include age of child.

Water

Is wet:

Is colorless:

Has weight:

Can be mixed with other ingredients:

Is a medium for a solution:

Flows:

Takes the shape of whatever container it is in:

Changes shape, freezes, melts, evaporates, and forms drops:

Has buoyancy:

Has force:

Acts as a mirror:

Other:

Draw a diagram of the classroom and indicate the location and arrangements suitable for water play.

Worksheet 11.2   Cognition

Most children are attracted to water. They like to pour, measure, siphon, strain, and feel the force of water. In addition to the pleasure of using water, there are many possibilities for learning. Observe one or more children playing with water. What possibilities for learning do you observe, and to which curriculum areas are they related?

Mathematics

Science

Social Studies

Language

Aesthetics

Worksheet 11.3   Developmental Processes

The growing child is developing socially, emotionally, intellectually, and physically. Observe children as they play with water. Record activities related to each of these areas, indicating the age of each child you describe.

Intellectual development

Social development

Emotional development

Physical development

Worksheet 11.4   Ice and Snow

Most children are fascinated by ice and snow. Observe children and discover why ice and snow seem to capture their attention. While observing, fill in the spaces below.

Ice	Snow
Properties of ice that make it interesting to children:	Properties of snow that make it interesting to children:
What did children do with it?	What did children do with it?
Children's reactions and what they said.	Children's reactions and what they said.

Worksheet 11.5   Wading

There is pure physical pleasure when children put their hands in water, and there are even greater satisfactions when other parts of the body can be immersed, too. Children can do this alone at home in the bathtub, but when they are in a wading pool with other children they can share their joys. Observe children in a wading pool. Record their language and describe their physical activity.

Language	Physical activities

How did the children's behavior enhance their self-images?

Worksheet 11.6   Use of Accessories

When accessories are added to a water table, the nature of the play changes. Observe children using accessories during water play and describe the ways in which they use them.

Accessories	How they are used

Worksheet 11.7   Problem Solving

As children play with water, they create problems that they attempt to solve. Describe the problems and the processes they use for solving them.

Nature of problem	Processes used for solving problem

Worksheet 11.8   Role of the Teacher

Water play is a medium through which children can sharpen the senses of touch, taste, sight, and hearing. The teacher can play an important role in providing the arrangement and equipment that will encourage this. Observe water play and describe what children did and how the teacher contributed to the arrangements for the experience.

What children did related to:	Teacher role	What else teacher might have done
Touch		
Taste		
Sight		
Hearing		

Objectives	Behavior Indicators	Worksheets
To list experiences in food preparation that are appropriate for young children.	Complete Post Test 1 satisfactorily. During participation, plan, prepare for, and carry out a project in which a small group of children works with food.	12.3
To list concepts in mathematics, science, social studies, language arts, and aesthetics that can be learned through experiences in food preparation.	Complete Post Test 2 satisfactorily.	12.1, 12.2, 12.3, 12.5, 12.6, 12.7, 12.8
To identify steps in problem solving that children may experience as they prepare food.	Complete Post Test 3 satisfactorily	12.4
To describe the role of the teacher in planning, preparing, and implementing an experience in food preparation.	Complete Post Test 4 satisfactorily.	12.1, 12.3, 12.5, 12.6
Other(s).		

FOOD

Pre/Post Tests

1. List ten different kinds of experiences in food preparation that are appropriate for young children.

2. List concepts that children might develop in the following areas as they engage in food preparation activities: mathematics, reading, listening, social studies, science, writing, speaking, aesthetics.

3. Describe a food-preparation experience and indicate how the steps in a problem-solving process occur.

4. Describe the role of the teacher in planning, preparing, and implementing experiences in food preparation.

Children not only like to eat food but also enjoy preparing it. In many classrooms teachers make provisions for activities with food. Churning butter, cutting celery, and making applesauce are popular. Doing these things just because they are fun is a good enough reason. However, food preparation is also a medium for learning concepts that can be applied in every area of the curriculum.

There are opportunities for sharpening the observations children make through their senses. Their taste is stimulated as they experience sweet, sour, bitter, and salty. They see shape, color, size, pattern, and change. They smell various fruits, vegetables, and spices. They touch and feel consistency—soft, smooth, wet, dry, sticky, or slick. They hear snapping, beating, grating, pouring, and popping.

There is much to talk about as children prepare food. They are excited about the discoveries they make. They do not just feel the cucumber, but describe it as light green or dark green, bumpy or smooth, wet or seedy. Beans are long and skinny, snap when broken, crunch when chewed. The cake batter gets thicker as they add flour and smoother as they stir. Each piece of equipment has a name, too. There is a grinder, a beater, and a strainer. Children gain a rich vocabulary which they will use later in their dramatic play. As they discuss plans and evaluate results they gain facility in the meaningful use of language. Sometimes the teacher keeps a record of the recipe on a chart or in a book. Pictures next to the names of the ingredients help children become aware of the relationship between abstract and representational symbols. As a child sees an egg against a mixture of flour and water, a peanut against a background of a shell, he is focusing on the figure in relation to the background.

There are many mathematical experiences involved in preparing food. Children count the number of eggs, oranges, peas in a pod, or seeds in an apple. Fractions are involved as they cut carrots, quarter bread, or as they measure one-half a cup of flour. There are other measurements such as tablespoon, teaspoon, or a pinch of salt. There is also time and temperature measurement involved when children bake bread or muffins. Children are able to see the volume of flour in a container diminish as they remove it and the quantity in a bowl become more and more as they fill it. They weigh the butter they have made and the apples they have bought.

There are opportunities for making predictions. Will there be enough applesauce? Is the cake pan big enough? How high will the bread be when it comes out of the oven? What changes will take place as ingredients are added to the mixture? What will happen to the milk, eggs, sugar, and flavoring while it is in the ice cream freezer? How many peas will I find in this pod? Does your pod have the same number of peas? Will brown eggs and white eggs look different inside? Will these tomatoes ripen by tomorrow?

Foods come in many shapes and there are likenesses and differences. Peas in the pod, string beans, cucumbers, and bananas are all long—but they are also different. Apples, oranges, and grapefruits all have roundness, but they differ in size, color, texture, and taste. Long carrots can be sliced into circles which may be thick or thin.

Experiences with food can demonstrate scientific principles. Children can observe, for example, gelatin congeal, cream become butter, and pudding thicken. Solids change to liquids as apples cook and as butter melts. Corn changes in color, texture, and consistency as it pops. Sugar completely dissolves in water and forms a solution, whereas flour and water form a mixture. Cooked spinach and raw spinach look different, feel different, and taste different.

Another kind of change takes place as foods ripen. The green banana becomes yellow and the green tomato becomes red.

The observations that children make preparing food are as basic to the problem-solving experiences in social studies as they are to those in science. Food preparation provides opportunities to go through processes from beginning to end. Through the processes children have opportunities to describe appearance, taste, and changes. After they have completed a process, they sometimes enjoy recalling the sequence of events.

Other aspects of social studies are dealt with as children become aware of the sources of foods. One can buy a cake, a mix, or the eggs, flour, and sugar needed to make a cake. The ideas of product and consumer are clarified as children go to the market to buy lemons for lemonade. They become aware of the primary source of food as they go out in the garden late in the spring to harvest radishes and lettuce for a mixed salad. They plant seeds in the ground, care for and cultivate young plants, and finally they pick the vegetables and eat them.

Sometimes children take a trip to a farm where potatoes, pumpkins, and assorted vegetables are grown. They might bring a pumpkin back to school, roast the seeds, and use the pumpkin for pie.

When children are fortunate enough to have peers from different cultural and religious backgrounds, arrangements can be made for family members to share some of the foods unique to their ways of life. Irish soda bread, Chinese rice, chili, or collard greens are interesting foods for children.

As children prepare foods, even with the simplest utensils, they must coordinate their movements. Cutting, chopping, and sprinkling all require eye-hand coordination. Grinding peanut butter takes a great deal of energy, while patting the ground beef into hamburger calls for other muscles and a different quality of movement. Peeling potatoes takes hand and finger control. Cracking an egg requires both judgment and coordination in determining just how much force will be necessary. Greasing a pan involves many parts of the body. It takes balance to carry liquid in a bowl and tremendous strength to crack a coconut. Energy is needed to break open walnuts or butternuts. Squeezing an orange with a hand squeezer requires energy and a different body position as well. As a child beats a mixture with a spoon, he sees changes taking place—but how much more rapidly he can mix the ingredients with a beater!

When planning food experiences, a teacher should take into consideration the nutritional values of the food that is served. Children become accustomed to enjoying foods that are good for them. The actual tasting and eating of food is a learning experience. Even if it is a food he does not like, a child is more likely to try it if he engaged in its preparation. Sometimes children prepare their own snacks. Bread and butter is a favorite. Children enjoy using a spreader to cover the bread with butter, and they love to eat it.

A child feels pleased with himself when he can prepare food for himself and others. There is a genuine feeling of accomplishment upon completing a worthwhile task, which helps develop a positive self-concept.

ARRANGEMENT

If a teacher incorporates a variety of experiences into her regular planning, then no one experience becomes the focus of attention for the whole classroom.

For food preparation, a table should be arranged for four or five boys and girls. Some children will stay during the whole process, and some leave after a while and make room for others. A small group permits each child to become deeply involved in what he is doing. The table should be placed against the wall near an electric outlet if a hotplate is used. This eliminates the danger of a child tripping over an electric cord or upsetting the pot. The teacher stays at the table for the entire time. Attention must be given to the cleanliness of utensils and table top. Although boys and girls participate in the cleanup, the teacher makes sure that all utensils are clean before putting them away.

Planning must be done well in advance so that materials are available and ready. Sometimes arranging materials on a large tray simplifies transporting them into the room. Classifying food and utensils on a tray provides a learning experience for the children and makes it easier to proceed with a project.

EQUIPMENT

Wooden cutting boards help protect the table top. When knives are required they should be small enough for children to handle and the right sharpness for cutting. An assortment of measuring cups (clear plastic if possible), measuring

spoons, wooden spoons, and bowls should be available. Other equipment—such as a beater, hand squeezer, corn popper, grinder, or ice cream freezer—can often be borrowed when a school has a working kitchen. For cooking, clear glass pots permit children to see the action of the water and the change in the consistency of the food as it occurs.

Although prepared mixes can be used, children do not see all the steps involved in cooking. When cream for butter is placed in small jars rather than in one large jar, several children can shake butter at the same time.

ROLE OF THE TEACHER

Cooking and cutting food requires constant supervision. Children need to be reminded to wash their hands and know why they are doing it. Simple rules of safety concerning sharp objects and hot liquids need to be discussed. A teacher's enjoyment of the food helps promote children's enjoyment.

ADDITIONAL RESOURCES

Hildebrand, Verna. *Introduction to Early Childhood Education*. 2nd ed. New York: Macmillan, 1976. Chapter 15, "Snack, Lunch, and Cooking Experiences," pp. 373–393.

Rudolph, Marguerita. *From Hand to Head—A Handbook for Teachers of Preschool Programs*. New York: McGraw-Hill, 1973. Chapter 5, "Breaking Bread: Customs and Pleasures of Eating," pp. 32–41, and Chapter 6, "Cooking: Sensory Involvement," pp. 42–53.

Audiotape. Williams, Bruce. *Food and Cooking with Young Children*. Tape of the Month. Washington, D.C.: Childhood Resources, 1972.

Film (16mm). *Jenny Is a Good Thing*. Headstart, New York University Film Library.

Filmstrip and Audiotape. *Food: A Medium for Learning*. Early Childhood Curriculum Series I. New York: Campus Films, 1976.

Worksheet 12.1   Food

(This worksheet is appropriate for use when only one observation will be made in this area.)
Working with food should be an integral part of an early childhood education program. Both the food-preparation process and the food items have important educational significance. Observe children as they work with food and record the information called for below.

Number of children	What teacher says	Children's conversation	Cognition
			Mathematics
			Science
			Social Studies
			Language
			Aesthetics

Worksheet 12.2   Change

Many types of changes take place in food substances as children work. These include changes in shape, texture, color, volume, temperature, consistency, and taste. As children prepare food, observe which of the changes noted below are involved. Also indicate the senses involved.

Change	Sense(s) involved
Shape	
Texture	
Volume	
Color	
Consistency	
Taste	

Worksheet 12.3   Planning an Experience with Food

Children need simple, one-step experiences with food. When preparation is elaborate, they are likely to lose interest. With such simple experiences as buttering bread, shelling peas, or grinding peanuts for peanut butter, they have opportunities to use all of their senses, to be aware of the changes that take place and develop habits of good nutrition.

List six cooking and six non-cooking food experiences suitable for young children and plan to implement one of them with a small group. Make certain that each item meets standards of good nutrition.

Cooking	Non-Cooking
1.	1.
2.	2.
3.	3.
4.	4.
5.	5.
6.	6.

Write a plan for recipe, equipment, and arrangement.

What opportunities were there for children's development of such concepts as size, shape, figure-ground, and seriation?

What opportunities did children have to develop skills in classification, measurement, etc.?

What were the reactions of the children to the experience? Did they seem to enjoy new and nutritious food?

Worksheet 12.4   Problem Solving

Many experiences children have with food preparation involve all the steps in problem solving.
Observe children preparing a food item and describe each step in the process as a step in problem
solving.

Statement of problem:

Planning:

Using resources:

Observation of change:

Generalizations:

Evaluation:

Worksheet 12.5   Reading and Writing

Using manuscript writing, write a recipe on a chart or in a book. If possible, write the recipe with the
help of a group of children.

Make a copy of your recipe (in manuscript writing).

What learnings might children attain as they use and refer to this recipe?

If possible, use the recipe as you work with a small group of children in preparing the food. List the learnings
below.

Worksheet 12.6   Food in Children's Books

Many children's books contain concepts about food. Select six books from children's literature and list the main concepts related to food found in each book.

	Title	Author	Publisher	Concept
1.				
2.				
3.				
4.				
5.				
6.				

Choose one of the books and read it to a group of three or four children. Was there a discussion following the story? What was the nature of the discussion?

If no discussion followed, what could have been discussed?

Worksheet 12.7   Sensory Experiences

There is probably no medium that provides as many sensory experiences as food. As children prepare foods, they touch, taste, smell, hear, and see. They have opportunities to sharpen their observation skills through their senses.

Observe children engaged in the preparation of food. Record the opportunities they have for sensory experiences and describe the relationship to later learnings.

Senses	Description of experience	Relation of experience to cognitive learnings
Smelling		
Touching		
Tasting		
Hearing		
Seeing		

Worksheet 12.8   Role of the Teacher

Observe children as they prepare food. List any aspects of problem solving that evolve and describe what the teacher did to sharpen children's awareness.

In what other ways might the processes of problem solving have been implemented and clarified?

Was the teacher's attitude toward nutritious foods reflected in the children's attitudes?

Objectives	Behavior Indicators	Worksheets
To diagram the location of a housekeeping area in a classroom and the arrangement of materials and accessories in it.	Complete Post Tests 1 and 2 satisfactorily. During participation, arrange some materials and accessories that might stimulate a specific type of play.	13.1, 13.2, 13.3
To list the criteria for selecting materials and accessories for a housekeeping area.	Complete Post Tests 1 and 2 satisfactorily.	13.2, 13.3
To describe the values of housekeeping play in the social development of young children.	Complete Post Test 3 satisfactorily.	13.4, 13.7, 13.9
To describe the values of housekeeping play in the emotional development of young children.	Complete Post Test 4 satisfactorily.	13.4, 13.5, 13.9
To describe the values of housekeeping play in helping children clarify roles.	Complete Post Test 5 satisfactorily.	13.4, 13.6
To describe the values of housekeeping play in the cognitive development of young children.	Complete Post Test 6 satisfactorily.	13.8, 13.9
To identify the roles of the teacher in supervising housekeeping play.	Complete Post Test 7 satisfactorily.	13.3, 13.4, 13.10

Other(s).

HOUSEKEEPING

Pre/Post Tests

1. Diagram a classroom and indicate the position of the housekeeping area. Give your rationale for its placement.

2. Diagram the materials and accessories in a housekeeping area. Give your rationale for the arrangement and selection of materials and accessories.

3. Describe five values of housekeeping play in the social development of young children.

4. Describe six values of housekeeping play in the emotional development of young children.

5. List eight roles that a child might have the opportunity to clarify as he plays in the housekeeping area. Describe the types of play that might be used in clarifying these roles.

6. Describe the ways in which housekeeping play contributes to cognitive development in each of the following curriculum areas: mathematics, science, social studies, and language arts?

7. Identify four roles of the teacher in supervising housekeeping play.

The housekeeping area in a classroom contains materials and equipment that are already a part of a child's life at home. Even children who hesitate to play with other materials may feel comfortable here. Both boys and girls should make use of this area, and adults should be discouraged from perpetuating sex-role stereotypes by considering house play an activity only for girls.

As a child plays, he begins to identify and clarify the roles of those around him. He can role-play members of his family—his mother, father, sister, or brother. He can become involved in community services and lead the exciting life of a fire fighter or a bus driver. He can live the life of an adult and find out how it feels to cook dinner or go to work. As he does this, concepts related to family and occupational roles are developed and clarified.

There are many opportunities to practice language skills. As children communicate, they learn new words from each other. A child who speaks Spanish and hears English spoken soon uses the English language in his speech. His English-speaking friends begin to speak Spanish words they hear frequently. A teacher may introduce new words and new parts of speech. In the kitchen, a pot is labeled a pressure cooker. As Mother prepares dinner, she shows her child how she beats, grinds, stirs, and whips foods. The hat on the dress-up shelf is a decorated hat, a stylish hat, or a fancy hat. As children become involved in these roles, they increase their facility with language.

The housekeeping area is an arena for social interaction. There is time for socializing over the breakfast table. Father talks about how busy he is at work. Mother tells of her experiences on her new job. The children report about the new teacher in the school. The baby communicates by tapping his cup on the table. The grocer takes an order on the telephone. Mother calls Father at the store. Sister talks to her friend about her new outfit, but her brother wants to use the telephone too.

The housekeeping area is conducive to developing problem-solving situations. The baby's clothes need to be washed. The children make the refrigerator into a washing machine. Now they need to find a way to put up a clothesline to dry the clothes. The family is going on a picnic. They search for something that will serve as a picnic basket.

When the area becomes a store, children are involved with money and exchange. When they set up a bakery, they assume the roles of producers and consumers. As police, fire fighters, and sanitation workers, they help in their community. When a white cap and stethoscope are placed in the area, a house becomes a hospital.

There are opportunities for learning scientific concepts as children make observations. Changes take place as they add soap to water, as water is transformed into ice or to steam.

Principles of mathematics are brought into play as children classify and arrange dishes according to shape or color or size. They organize groceries in categories according to contents, shape, and size. They measure water in plastic containers, cups, or pots.

As a child engages in imaginative play, tries out roles, and gains competence in many situations, his concept of himself improves. He experiments with many different kinds of relationships in this kind of play. As he gains confidence in various roles, his movements become more coordinated.

ARRANGEMENT

The housekeeping area should be set apart from heavy traffic in the room. Sometimes the area is arranged as one room; sometimes it is set up as two rooms or even three. When interest is high, the area can be enlarged to accommodate more children. Arrangements should be made for adequate, accessible storage space. A supply of many different kinds of materials can be stored and arranged so that a teacher can reach for them quickly as needed. This allows for a variety in play. Keeping too many materials out makes it difficult for children to maintain order, and can be overstimulating as well.

EQUIPMENT

Furniture such as a bed, table and chairs, sink, and refrigerator make it possible for children to play out the daily functions of family life. Each piece should be large enough for children to use it. For example, a child should be able to sit in a chair or sleep in a bed in the housekeeping area.

Equipment for washing and cleaning extends the opportunities for play. A cardboard box is easily transformed into a washing machine or dryer. Dolls with very simple clothes can be dressed and undressed by the children. High-heeled shoes, jackets, dresses, and jewelry serve many purposes. Hats are particularly versatile. Sturdy utensils, pots, and plastic dishes for no more than four people are usually sufficient. A mirror, a rocking chair, and a telephone are valuable pieces of equipment.

Parents or teachers can make some equipment themselves. A bed, table, sink, stove, or refrigerator can be constructed out of wood or corrugated paper. When play furniture is painted, lead-free paint must be used.

ROLE OF THE TEACHER

A teacher is often a silent observer in the housekeeping area. He listens and by his mere presence makes it possible for a shy child to enter the area. He sometimes inconspicuously provides a piece of equipment when the play seems to indicate it. A cash register on a table might convert the housekeeping area into a shoe store. He is careful not to interrupt children's thinking. When a teacher has had time to observe he is more likely to select an appropriate time to intervene with a question, comment, or material.

Before children can incorporate a piece of equipment of material into their play, they need time to become familiar with its function. It is therefore helpful if a teacher selects a few items at a time, and gradually introduces others as the need arises. Sometimes additional materials are not necessary to enhance the play. By rearranging the space the play can take on a different dimension.

It is a teacher's responsibility to be sure that clothes, dishes, and other materials are kept clean and orderly. Because children are developing habits, it is important that they have a good model.

ADDITIONAL RESOURCES

Cuffaro, Harriet K. "Dramatic Play—The Experience of Block Building." In *The Block Book,* Elisabeth S. Hirsch (ed.). Washington, D.C.: National Association for the Education of Young Children, 1974.

Curry, Nancy E. "Dramatic Play as a Curricular Tool." In *Play as a Learning Medium,* Doris Sponseller (ed.). Washington, D.C.: National Association for the Education of Young Children, 1974.

Hildebrand, Verna. *Introduction to Early Childhood Education.* 2nd ed. New York: Macmillan, 1976. Chapter 12, "Dramatic Play," pp. 300–323.

Lay, Margaret Z., and Dopyera, John E. *Becoming a Teacher of Young Children.* Lexington, Mass.: D.C. Heath, 1977. Chapter 11, "Resourcefulness with Children's Pretend Play," pp. 299–317.

Leeper, Sarah Hammond; Skipper, Dora Sikes; and Witherspoon, Ralph L. *Good Schools for Young Children.* 4th ed. New York: Macmillan, 1979. Chapter 12, "Growth Through Language Activities," pp. 269–290.

Audiotape. *Children's Dramatic Play,* Tape of the Month. Washington, D.C.: Childhood Resources, 1972.

Film (16mm). *Dramatic Play: An Integrative Process.* New York: Campus Films, 1972.

Filmstrip and Audiotape. *Houseplay.* Early Childhood Curriculum Series II. New York: Campus Films, 1977.

Worksheet 13.1   Housekeeping

(This worksheet is appropriate for use when only one observation will be made in this area.)
The selection of materials and the arrangement of equipment often influence the nature of play. Observe children in the housekeeping area. List below the materials available there. Check those materials the children used and describe how they used them:

Indicate other materials that can be added and give reasons for selecting them.

Worksheet 13.2   Space and Materials I

Draw a diagram of the housekeeping area in relation to the rest of the room.

Draw a diagram of the housekeeping area; next to the diagram, list materials in that area.

Worksheet 13.3 Space and Materials II

Draw an arrangement of the housekeeping area different from the one that you are observing. Perhaps you will wish to create different rooms typical of a home setting. Describe the materials you would use.

What were your considerations in making these changes?

Worksheet 13.4 Dramatic Play

Much dramatic play takes place in the housekeeping area. Observe the dramatic play and the role of the teacher in the housekeeping area.

Number age and description of children	Description of play	Description of teacher's role

Worksheet 13.5   Self-Concept

A child can enhance his self-concept as he interacts with children, with adults, and with materials. Before a child can accept others, he needs to have a good feeling about himself. He needs to feel his "self" alone and in relation to others. One of the areas in which he has the opportunity for the type of play that allows for these experiences is the housekeeping area.

    Observe and describe how children's interactions with peers, adults, and materials may enhance self-concepts.

With peers:

With adults:

With materials:

Worksheet 13.6   Exploring Roles

Children will engage in certain types of play if certain materials are available. Given other materials, their play would be different. Identify the materials you observe that encourage children to assume particular roles. Describe the roles. Indicate five other materials that might be added to the housekeeping area, and describe how they might change the roles children assume.

Material	Roles

Worksheet 13.7   Social Interaction

Children play alone and with others in a variety of ways. A very young child engages in *solitary play* most often, but as he develops and becomes more aware of others, he seeks out their company more often. A child begins to engage in *associative play* when he is playing with others but not working with them to accomplish a common goal. Play becomes *cooperative* as children respond to each other in their planning and in their actions. Using these definitions, describe the play you observe, indicating the age of each child.

Solitary	Parallel	Associative	Cooperative

Worksheet 13.8   Cognition

Housekeeping play provides many opportunities for cognitive development. Children measure food, they float objects in the sink, they speak over the telephone, and they engage in consumer and producer roles. Observe in the housekeeping area and record illustrations of cognitive learnings related to the curriculum areas listed below:

Mathematics

Social Studies

Science

Language Arts

Worksheet 13.9   Using Imagination

Most children are able to play whether or not they have the props needed for carrying out their roles. Some children take an available object and relabel it to suit their purposes. Others create needed objects with paper, clay, or wood. Others pretend to have what they need and are not dependent upon props of any kind. Observe children in the housekeeping area and describe their imaginative play.

Examples of relabeling materials	Examples of making objects	Examples of continuing play despite absence of needed objects

Worksheet 13.10   Management

A teacher plays an important role in the management of the housekeeping area. He stimulates the play as he adds materials, makes comments, or lends his silent support. Observe children in the housekeeping area. Describe the play and the teacher's role.

Description of play	Teacher's roles (verbal and nonverbal)

Description of the cleanup process.

Were both boys and girls involved in the play?

Objectives	Behavior Indicators	Worksheets
To describe the ways in which a child can be helped to develop an awareness of the rhythm of his own being and that of others.	Complete Post Test 1 satisfactorily. During participation in an organized or spontaneous rhythm activity, follow a child's rhythm with a drum or hand clapping.	14.1, 14.2, 14.3, 14.4
To describe the ways in which children can develop an awareness of sounds (including the sounds of their own voices) and elaborate on ways of doing this.	Complete Post Tests 2 and 3 satisfactorily. During participation, sing one familiar children's song with a small group. While children are playing, initiate an appropriate chant.	14.5, 14.6, 14.7
To describe uses of instruments in a music and movement program. To learn which instruments are suitable for use with young children.	Complete Post Test 4 satisfactorily.	14.8, 14.9
To describe the relationship between sound, movement, and self-concept.	Complete Post Test 5 satisfactorily.	14.9
To identify the cognitive learnings that might result in a program of music and movement.	Complete Post Test 6 satisfactorily.	14.10, 14.11
To describe the roles of the teacher in developing a program of creative music and movement.	Complete Post Test 2 satisfactorily.	14.1, 14.4, 14.12
Other(s).		

MUSIC AND MOVEMENT

Pre/Post Tests

1. Describe the types of rhythm that a child produces as he works at a workbench; with blocks, modeling materials, and paints; in the housekeeping area; and with manipulative materials.

2. Describe the roles the teacher plays in developing a child's awareness of his own rhythm.

3. Identify some of the sounds in a child's environment: sounds made by a child, sounds of the natural surroundings, sounds made by other people, sounds made by machines. Select two sounds from each category and explain how a child can be helped to develop an awareness of them. How can he be helped to elaborate on them?

4. List eight instruments suitable for use with young children.

5. Describe ways in which experiences with sound and movement can enhance a child's self-concept.

6. Identify six cognitive learnings in mathematics, social studies, communication arts, and science, which might result from experiences with music and movement.

Children come to school with varied backgrounds in music. All of them, however, have had some experiences with sound and movement. As children engage in spontaneous play, they create many rhythmic patterns. Each child has his own internal rhythm and before he can repeat the rhythms of someone else, he must be thoroughly imbued with the rhythms he creates himself. If a child has opportunities to enjoy his own rhythms, he becomes aware of the rhythms of others.

As a child sweeps his brush across a paper, he makes a rhythmic movement. Picking up his own rhythm, a child begins to chant, "I am painting, I am painting." A teacher picks up this rhythm, replying, "You are painting, you are painting."

As a child walks around the housekeeping area wearing high-heeled shoes, a teacher, hearing the rhythm of his steps, claps to call attention to the rhythm. As a child moves a boat back and forth in the water, making rhythmic waves, a teacher chants "Back and forth, back and forth," moving the child's arm as he does so.

A child pounds two balls of clay. A teacher seated at a table repeats the sound. The child then elaborates with a more complicated pattern, as though testing to see if the teacher will reproduce that one, too.

One child at a workbench pounds on a board. Bang, bang, bang goes the hammer. Another child sawing the wood pushes the saw to the rhythm. A child playing with pegs picks up this rhythm as he places each peg in the board.

Two children remove blocks from the shelves. One chants, "I'm taking out two at a time, I'm taking out two at a time." The other child responds with, "I'm taking out more than you, I'm taking out more than you." Each child follows the rhythm of the other as the blocks are placed on the floor. A teacher, seated nearby, repeats the chants, alternating between a high and low voice.

Children enjoy creating their own variations in tempo and rhythm. When a child is able to maintain a steady pattern of his own, then a teacher can repeat the pattern, tapping with one hand as he improvises a secondary rhythm with the other hand. Sometimes children have fun doing this themselves.

Sounds are everywhere—the drone of the jet plane, the drip from the faucet. Children respond to some sounds and tune out others. There is great flexibility in the variety of sounds that a child can make, and he takes real pleasure in the ways in which he can create interesting combinations of sounds. Control of his voice enables him to sing in different pitches, which he enjoys doing.

Children sing as they play. They have fun making up their own words; they enjoy nonsense sounds. It is easy for them to learn songs with repetitive refrains. There is likely to be more spontaneous singing and experimentation with sound in a classroom where the teacher sings spontaneously with a small group than in a classroom where all activities stop for formal singing. While a piano or other instrument is not necessary, it does add a different dimension to both singing and dancing.

When a teacher shows a child how to hop or skip, his attention is focused on the technique and he is likely to become self-conscious. Children enjoy moving their bodies in different ways. They twist, turn, jump, stretch, bend, wiggle, and leap. As they combine these movements, they create patterns, develop timing, and get acquainted with themselves in space. They discover what it feels like to hop and then to skip. A child learns how to skip or hop by himself when he has gained sufficient control of his body. When a child flies like an airplane as part of play initiated by him, then he really becomes involved in play. A child who responds to a teacher's suggestion that he fly like an airplane is not likely to become totally involved in imagining or in body movement.

When a teacher directs dance activities by playing a piano or a phonograph for children to respond to, he is providing an external framework into which they are supposed to fit. While they can learn to create patterns to these rhythms, it is a more limiting experience than when they create the rhythms themselves. When a teacher picks up a child's rhythmic pattern, with piano, drum, or hand-clapping, he encourages that child to become more aware of his own inner rhythms and thereby to create his own rhythms.

After children have had many opportunities to create their own rhythms and body movements, simple dances may be introduced. To reverse this order—to teach dancing first—denies children an opportunity for self-expression and inhibits their own creativity.

A child wearing dress-up clothes or a flowing scarf delights in twirling and moving in space, freely experimenting with movement. Although the many popular circle games, such as Looby Loo and Hokey Pokey, provide physical activity for a group, they cannot be classified as dancing.

As children become aware of their own rhythms, they can add to their experiences by using instruments. Drums are a favorite. A child can feel, and sometimes even see, the vibrations.

He can hear that drums of varied sizes make different sounds, and learn that the sound he makes when striking the edge of the drum head differs from that made when he strikes it near the center. He can play loudly, softly, rapidly, or slowly, and he can move to the rhythm too.

If cymbals, tambourines, rhythm sticks, and bells are made available, children are encouraged to experiment with rhythmic activities. Instruments should always be available so that children can use them in their play as the need arises. However, it is important to establish certain rules so that children gain respect for the instruments.

Large cans can be made into drums. Sandpaper on a rectangular piece of wood can make sand blocks. Some homemade instruments such as rhythm sticks or drums have a satisfactory tone. The quality of the sound should be the deciding factor in determining whether instruments should be made or bought.

When a child sings or dances, he learns with his whole body. He develops language skills such as pronunciation and articulation. He gains facility with language as he becomes conscious of patterns and rhythms. His vocabulary improves with repetition. He counts and develops sequences. His listening and hearing abilities are sharpened.

ARRANGEMENT AND EQUIPMENT

Children need space in order to move freely, whether indoors or outdoors. In a classroom with limited space, furniture should be moved when children are involved with music or dancing.

Movement and music outdoors is a different kind of experience. The spatiousness of the outdoors influences the nature of a musical experience. The interests that children have are reflected in their music and movement experiences.

In some classrooms, a guitar or an autoharp serves as a stimulus for music activities. These instruments need to be treated with care. A record player is often part of the equipment in a classroom, and a small collection of good records provides children with opportunities to hear music of quality. The collection should include the music and dance of other cultures.

Playing music while many other activities are going on makes it difficult for children to attend to the music, and often deters children from attending to what they are doing. Filling the air with sounds does not foster good listening habits.

Playing records to accompany rhythmic activities inhibits rather than stimulates creative movement and singing. The activity for a child becomes an exercise in matching his rhythm to that on the record.

ROLE OF THE TEACHER

Many teachers feel that because they do not play the piano or think of themselves as musicians, they cannot provide musical experiences for children. If a teacher can play an instrument he can make at times a fine contribution to a program. However, if playing an instrument requires a teacher's concentrated attention he may miss opportunities to observe children, and observation is an important part of a teacher's role in a music program. When a teacher is an observer he knows when to add a song, to repeat children's rhythms, to elaborate on rhythmic patterns, or to match a sound a child makes on the piano or autoharp. Many times a teacher will observe children sing and dance during their dramatic play without intervening.

At times a teacher may sit with a small group of children, a song book in his lap, and sing song after song. Boys and girls join in on their favorite songs and quickly pick up new ones. Line-by-line teaching is often a deterrent. Unless a child asks a question about a song, there is no need to explain the content. The pleasure comes in the sounds and the rhythm.

A teacher shows an interest in what a child is doing when he repeats the child's rhythm. This does not mean that every time children engage in rhythmic activities the teacher must participate. Children like to have someone listen to the sounds they make. A good listener serves as a model for a child, and a teacher should arrange for time to do this. The teacher's attitude toward music and movement in the program will determine the quality of the experiences and will influence the way children value music and movement.

ADDITIONAL RESOURCES

Gerhardt, Lydia A. *Moving and Knowing*. Englewood Cliffs, N.J.: Prentice-Hall, 1973.

Hildebrand, Verna. *Introduction to Early Childhood Education*. New York: Macmillan, 1971. Chapter 13, "Creative Music Activities," pp. 324–356.

Leeper, Sarah Hammond; Skipper, Dora Sikes; and Witherspoon, Ralph L. *Good Schools for Young Children*. 4th ed. New York: Macmillan, 1979. Chapter 19, "Creative Expression," pp. 419–461.

Margolin, Edythe. *Young Children*. New York: Macmillan, 1976. Chapter 9, "A World of Music for Young Children," pp. 261–281.

Myerson, Edith S. *Ideas That Work with Children*. Katherine Read Baker (ed.). Washington, D.C.: National Association for the Education of Young Children, 1972. "Listen to What I Made! From Musical Theory to Usable Instrument," pp. 109–111.

Rudolph, Marguerita. *From Hand to Head—A Handbook for Teachers of Preschool Programs*. New York: McGraw-Hill, 1973. Chapter 10, "The Child as a Multimedia Artist," pp. 80–96.

Sheehy, Emma D. *Children Discover Music and Dance*. New York: Teachers College Press, 1968.

Spodek, Bernard. *Teaching in the Early Years*. Englewood Cliffs, N.J.: Prentice-Hall, 1972. Chapter 9, "Music and Art in the Early Years," pp. 177–197.

Stetcher, Miriam. *Ideas That Work with Children*. Washington, D.C.: National Association for the Education of Young Children, 1972. "Concept Learning Through Movement Improvisation," pp. 112–122.

Todd, Vivian Edmiston, and Heffernan, Helen. *The Years Before School*. 3rd ed. New York: Macmillan, 1977. Chapter 14, "Enjoying Musical Sounds," pp. 511–538.

Wills, Clarice Dechand, and Lindberg, Lucile. *Kindergarten for Today's Children*. Chicago: Follett, 1967. Chapter 16, "Music, Music Everywhere," pp. 225–239; Chapter 17, "Creative Dramatics—Making Believe," pp. 241–255.

Worksheet 14.1   Music and Movement

(This worksheet is appropriate for use when only one observation can be made in this area.)
Many classrooms provide few experiences with music and movement. Often teachers hesitate to sing or use the simplest instrument because they feel self-conscious and inadequate. Music, however, should be part of the daily program. Observe a small group of children in music and/or movement activities and describe their activities and the teacher's roles.

Description of activity	Number of children	Description of teacher role	Additional comments

Worksheet 14.2   Rhythm I

Each child has his own internal rhythm, and this rhythm is reflected in all of the activities in which a child engages. When a teacher draws a child's attention to his own rhythm, the child develops an awareness of his creation.

Listen and look in various parts of the room for rhythms that children create. Describe the activity. Illustrate the rhythm with dots and dashes and leave spaces to indicate the pauses. (Example:
— · · · — — · · · —)

Description of activity	Description of rhythm

In any given activity two or more children may create different rhythms. Indicate these above.

Worksheet 14.3   Rhythm II

Each child has his own rhythm. This rhythm is in evidence no matter what he does. For example, a child walking down the hall creates his own rhythmic patterns. Observe the activities in a classroom. Indicate rhythms you observe.

Area of room	Describe the rhythmic patterns you see or hear	How does the teacher pick up rhythmic patterns (if at all)?

What opportunities for reinforcing a child's rhythmic pattern were not picked up? How might these patterns have been reinforced?

Worksheet 14.4   Rhythm III

Some teachers encourage children to create more intricate patterns of movement as they repeat a child's rhythmic pattern by beating a drum, clapping hands, or using other musical instruments. Observe a teacher as he engages a small group of children in a rhythmic activity accompanying their movement.

How does the teacher reinforce movements?

How does the teacher encourage elaboration and experimentation with more movement?

As a child becomes more aware of his own body movements, he is able to use his body in space in different ways. He gains greater and greater control and becomes more precise in his movements. Describe the ways children use parts of their bodies while moving in space, with or without the teacher's accompaniment.

Worksheet 14.5   Singing and Chanting I

Children enjoy playing with sounds. At any given time, an observer may hear them chanting or singing while engaged in some activity. Find as many places in the room as you can where a child is chanting or singing and record the sounds or words and rhythms he makes.

Area of room	Description of sounds and words

If possible, try to imitate some of the children's sounds you have described above.

Worksheet 14.6   Singing and Chanting II

Some of the most important opportunities for singing occur informally. Every area of the room may serve as a setting for singing and chanting. Sometimes a teacher may make up a song on the spot; at other times he may introduce a familiar song. List all the areas of the room where there might be opportunity for a teacher to sing or chant with children. Select two areas of the room. Choose a familiar song or chant and compose a song or chant for each area.

Description of area	Suitable song or chant	Original song or chant
1.	1.	1.
2.	2.	2.

Worksheet 14.7   Singing and Chanting III

A careful look around a classroom will reveal that singing or chanting activities are always going on. For example, while pounding a piece of clay, a child might chant, "boom-boom-boom." Listen for such sounds. Indicate the way in which an adult might help a child become more aware of the chant he has created and thus encourage him to play with these sounds.

Singing can take place on an informal basis in any part of the room during any activity. Where do you observe the opportunity to introduce a song? What song would you introduce? (This may be a familiar song or one created on the spot for the occasion.)

Worksheet 14.8   Body Movement

As children grow, they develop more control in the use of their bodies and greater awareness of this control. A teacher has opportunities to strengthen a child's awareness of the movements of his body in space by making simple suggestions. Observe a teacher with a small group, and describe the movements that the children create.

Which of the above are in response to the external rhythm of hand clapping or an instrument, and which are in response to the children's own internal rhythm? Code *E* for external and *I* for internal.

Worksheet 14.9   Instruments

As children play with rhythm instruments, we find them patterning, repeating, and comparing sounds. Observe children as they try different patterns and sounds. Record these patterns using dots and dashes (. . __ . . __), listening for the accents children place as they shift the volume. Indicate the accents with a slash mark (__/__ . . .)

Episode I

Episode II

What indications were there (if any) that the child had a good feeling about himself in each case above?

Worksheet 14.10   Curriculum Concepts

As boys and girls sing and engage in body movements, there are many opportunities for developing and reinforcing concepts related to other curriculum areas. From your observations, identify the cognitive learnings that might result from these experiences.

Mathematics

Social Studies

Science

Communication Arts

Worksheet 14.11   Music Appreciation

Very young children develop preferences for certain sounds and rhythms. Observe children in a classroom. What evidence do you see that they are enjoying sounds or rhythms?

Child 1

Child 2

Child 3

What evidence did you observe that children were not enjoying particular sounds or rhythms?

Worksheet 14.12   Role of the Teacher

A teacher encourages musical activities by the provisions he makes for them and by his general attitude. Observe music and movement activities in the classroom. Describe each one and indicate whether it was structured by the teacher or developed spontaneously by the children.

Activity	Description of teacher role	Comment
Singing		____ spontaneous
		____ structured
Dancing		____ spontaneous
		____ structured
Using instruments		____ spontaneous
		____ structured
Other		____ spontaneous
		____ structured

In this setting, what other music or movement experiences could you provide?

Objectives	Behavior Indicators	Worksheets
To identify ways in which children control and strengthen their bodies through physical activity.	Complete Post Test 1 satisfactorily.	15.1, 15.2, 15.3, 15.8
To describe activities that help a child control his direction and movement in space.	Complete Post Test 2 satisfactorily.	15.3, 15.8
To identify the cognitive learnings involved in physical activities.	Complete Post Tests 3 and 4 satisfactorily.	15.1, 15.5, 15.6
To describe the ways in which physical activities can contribute to a positive self-concept.	Complete Post Test 5 satisfactorily.	15.1, 15.7, 15.9
To describe the roles of the teacher in providing for space, safety, and equipment.	Complete Post Test 6 satisfactorily. During participation, demonstrate two kinds of teacher support intended to encourage a child to complete a task or solve a problem on his own.	15.1, 15.4, 15.8, 15.10

Other(s).

PHYSICAL ACTIVITIES

Pre/Post Tests

1. Identify ways in which children control and strengthen their bodies through physical activities.

2. Describe activities that help a child control his direction and movement in space.

3. Describe the relationship between cognitive learnings and physical activities.

4. Identify cognitive learnings that can be developed as children engage in physical activities in mathematics, communication arts, social studies, science.

5. Describe six ways in which physical activities can contribute to a positive self-concept.

6. Describe the roles of a teacher in providing for physical activities.

Provisions for physical activities can be made both indoors and outdoors. A good program of physical activities is noncompetitive. As a child gains control of his own movement and his own balance, he pits his skill and his strength against outside forces. Jumping over a log, balancing on a thin board, climbing up a rope, or pushing a heavy packing box are self-chosen activities. Children with different levels of ability can use this same equipment with satisfaction. Sometimes special arrangements have to be made for children with handicaps. Often this requires a very slight modification. A ramp instead of a step can make it easier for a handicapped child to enter a play area.

A child finds different ways of using his body, setting his own challenge as he decides how high he can climb. He puts every ounce of energy he can muster into his pushing and pulling as he interacts with materials. He creeps over a board, then jumps over it, and then rolls across it, using both large and small muscles. As his coordination improves, he can balance in different ways. He develops his strength as he exerts himself just a bit more and a bit more.

SELF-CONCEPT

When a child has the freedom to explore his own potentialities he begins to develop an awareness of what he can do. He gains a new respect for himself. He has a sense of accomplishment when he has finally reached the top of the climbing apparatus. He has a feeling of joy as he surveys the scene below. As he reaches the top again and again he begins to develop feelings of confidence. He is then ready for new achievements, expressing his satisfaction with triumphant remarks such as "See me, I can stand up without holding." He tests his strength as he tries to push the log, and he feels a sense of power as he gives one more big push and it moves. He begins to judge his strength and attempt tasks that are possible for him to achieve.

Physical activity provides for emotional release. A child establishes equilibrium as he generates energy and uses it. When children are engaged in demanding but noncompetitive activities they have opportunities to interact and show consideration for others. In a classroom where children are allowed to make choices they usually alternate between subdued and vigorous activities.

Physical activity is much more than just providing for a daily release of energy. Movement is basic to every aspect of learning. Children communicate with each other verbally and nonverbally. They engage in conversation as they combine their efforts to roll a large cable spool. Jumping, climbing, and running often lead to very interesting types of dramatic play. As imaginations soar, speech becomes more fluent. When these activities are self-initiated language is accelerated. As children interact in adventuresome play, vocabularies are extended to meet the situation.

Children learn about space by fitting themselves into it. They also learn about space by fitting boxes into each other or putting blocks into a wagon. They become aware of height as they stretch, reach, and climb. They arrange the graduated barrels in order according to size.

They develop their powers of observation as they collect leaves, seeds, and rocks, and see changing cloud formations. They test the force of the wind as they run back and forth with a piece of paper attached to a string (their own version of a kite). They enjoy the feel of the soil as they dig in the garden and are fascinated by the movements of worms and bugs.

Not every school has a garden or a patch of grass, but this in no way hinders a child's observation. Watching an ant crawl across the pavement can hold a child's attention for a long period of time.

ARRANGEMENT

Ideally, children have access to an outdoor play area. They have freedom of movement from indoors to outdoors when weather permits. The outdoors is an extension of the classroom. There is both shade and sun. There are different kinds of surfaces, grassy areas for running and rolling, a rubberized area under the climbing equipment, and asphalt for wheel toys. A large sand area and water facilities are available. Elevations in the ground, besides being aesthetically pleasing, provide for different kinds of exercise. Children can run up and down little slopes and roll down grassy hills. A garden area permits digging, planting, and raking. Storage space with easy access to materials is available.

Programs must be planned according to the facilities. In some urban areas there is no outdoor space other than a roof or a public park. Gardening is arranged for in a box or in flower pots. Whatever the situation, the area should be kept in good condition, cleared of debris. The surface must be free of potholes, which are extremely dangerous when active children are moving about.

EQUIPMENT

Some types of commercially made equipment are permanent, stationary, sturdy, and provide for many types of physical activity. These serve an important function where there is little or no adult supervision. In a school for young children movable pieces of equipment are desirable. Boards, saw horses, barrels, cable spools, logs, ropes, and ladders lend themselves to innovative play. Heavy wooden packing boxes and huge cardboard cartons add excitement to play. Sometimes a teacher and sometimes the children arrange these materials, adding to the design as they seek more challenges.

There are many kinds of wheel toys for young children. A wagon provides children with physical activity as they load and unload it and use it in their dramatic play. Unless there is an ample amount of space, tricycles and scooters can be dangerous pieces of equipment. They may interfere with the play of others.

Perhaps the most dangerous piece of outdoor equipment is the swing. There is really no place for the traditional wooden swing in a playground for young children. Children are unable to comprehend that when the swing zooms forward it will inevitably also come back, and they are unable to judge the distance or force with which it moves. Children do enjoy the swinging motion, and it has value for them in learning how to move in space. A rubber tire attached to a rope on a solid, stationary, specially constructed pole or a tree serves as a satisfactory swing. There's an opportunity to get different kinds of perspective as a child goes back and forth.

When children want the experience of a seesaw, a saw horse and board, movable pieces of equipment, can be arranged to provide for it. A slide can be made with the same equipment. There are specially constructed balance boards with narrow and wide bases. A log provides a slightly different experience.

Large hollow blocks, which often take up too much space to be used indoors, have many values. They can be stacked, jumped over, and carried. Children incorporate them into their dramatic play because rather imposing constructions can be made quickly with them.

A rope net for climbing makes it possible for a child to use every muscle in his body. It is strong and durable, and he can depend on it to hold his weight; yet its shakiness provides a certain kind of risk that children find very invigorating.

In recent years architects have taken an interest in developing new designs for children's playgrounds using a variety of materials. There is also great interest in adventure playgrounds. Old cars, boats, and buses provide a setting for physical activity and dramatic play. Care must be taken to prevent rust in such equipment and to keep it in good condition.

Balls are favorite pieces of equipment. A school should have balls of many sizes, small ones that can be grasped in a child's hand and larger ones that require two hands and extra force to control. The difference in texture provides an added experience.

When shovels are used, they need to be child size, rustproof, and sturdy because they get hard use in dirt, sand, or snow.

ROLE OF THE TEACHER

If a teacher feels that physical activity is important to a child's growth and development and considers the outdoors an extension of the classroom, careful planning is necessary. Planning requires observation. He must think about the needs of children before determining which pieces of equipment to introduce and which parts of the playground to use. As much teacher involvement is required in the outdoor program as in the indoor program. It is not a place for teachers to rest or catch up on gossip. A teacher is responsible for childen's safety on the playground, including checking the way in which the equipment is assembled and the way children use it. Children need the close supervision of a supportive adult. They do not want help, but they do want a teacher to see what they are doing.

Dressing for outdoors is as important for a child's physical development and self-concept as any activity he might engage in when he is outdoors. Time should be provided for a child to manage his own zipping, button his own coat, and put his fingers into his glove—valuable physical activities. A teacher can provide help when it is needed and encourage independence as well.

Too often children do not have opportunities to experience weather changes. This is part of the learning experience. Teachers should plan for outdoor physical activities in snowy, misty, sunny, windy, cloudy, hot, and cold days. If a teacher is going to enjoy the weather conditions, he himself must be dressed appropriately.

ADDITIONAL RESOURCES

Baker, Katherine Read. *Let's Play Outdoors*. Washington, D.C.: National Association for the Education of Young Children, 1966.

Cohen, Dorothy H., and Rudolph, Marguerita. *Kindergarten and Early Schooling*. Englewood Cliffs, N.J.: Prentice-Hall, 1977. Chapter 13, "Problems and Pleasures of Outdoor Play," pp. 323–339.

Engstrom, Georgianna, ed. *The Significance of the Young Child's Motor Development*. Washington, D.C.: National Association for the Education of Young Children, 1971.

Gerhardt, Lydia A. *Moving and Knowing*. Englewood Cliffs, N.J.: Prentice-Hall, 1973.

Hildebrand, Verna. *Introduction to Early Childhood Education*. 2nd ed. New York: Macmillan, 1976. Chapter 6, "Learning Activities in the Outdoors," pp. 107–137.

Leeper, Sarah Hammond; Skipper, Dora Sikes; and Witherspoon, Ralph L. *Good Schools for Young Children*. New York: Macmillan, 1979. Chapter 22, "Physical Facilities, Equipment, and Materials," pp. 499–516.

Rudolph, Marguerita. *From Hand to Head—A Handbook for Teachers of Preschool Programs*. New York: McGraw-Hill, 1973. Chapter 9, "Safety: Awareness in Action," pp. 70–79.

Sponseller, Doris, ed. *Play as a Learning Medium*. Washington, D.C.: National Association for the Education of Young Children, 1974.

Todd, Vivian Edmiston, and Heffernan, Helen. *The Years Before School*. 3rd ed. New York: Macmillan, 1970. Chapter 7, "Furthering Physical Development," pp. 240–262.

Wills, Clarice Dechand, and Lindberg, Lucile. *Kindergarten for Today's Children*. Chicago: Follett, 1967. Chapter 19, "Physical Fitness at Five," pp. 267–278.

Film (16 mm). *Concept Development in Outdoor Play*. New York: Campus Films, 1974.

Film (16 mm). *Dramatic Play: An Integrative Process*. New York: Campus Films, 1972.

Film (16 mm). *Outdoor Play: A Motivating Force for Learning*. New York: Campus Films, 1973.

Filmstrip and Audiotape. *Outdoor Play*. Early Childhood Curriculum Series II. New York: Campus Films, 1977.

Worksheet 15.1   Physical Activities

(This worksheet is appropriate for use when there will be only one observation in this area.)
Physical activities provide children with opportunities for body development. They also stimulate problem-solving tasks and social interaction. Choose one activity to observe, and record the following:

Materials	Number, age and sex grouping	How used	Conversation

Worksheet 15.2   Physical Development

As a child engages in physical activities, he uses every part of his body. Describe how and under what circumstances a child uses the following parts of his body:

Head: Hand:

Neck: Fingers:

Shoulder: Trunk:

Arm: Legs:

Wrist: Feet:

Worksheet 15.3   Body Movement

Young children are always engaged in physical activities. When a child paints, he has to raise his arm and change the position of his body. While playing with blocks, a child moves about in many ways. Follow one child for thirty minutes, describing with words and stick figures as many movements of his body as you can capture. Try to divide the record of the activities into five-minute segments. Indicate age of child.

Time	Movement

Worksheet 15.4   Outdoor Play

A playground should be considered an extension of the classroom. While space and equipment may differ, interactions and learnings are the same. The activities outdoors play as important a part in learning as activities that take place indoors. Observe a child outdoors to see how he plays. Indicate age of child.

Description of child:

Description of activity, including equipment and talk (if any):

Description of activities that help children develop figure-ground perceptions, laterality, and directionality.

Description of involvement with other children and with teachers:

Worksheet 15.5   Problem Solving

Physical activities lend themselves to many challenging problem-solving experiences. Select a location where a child will encounter some kind of problem, for example, on the climbing equipment. Watch a child try to get to the top and relate his activity to problem-solving processes.

1. Identification of problem:

2. Approach to solution of problem (trial and error, on-the-spot planning, etc.):

3. Assessing progress:

4. Evaluating results:

5. Elaborating on his or her success:

Select one of the pieces of equipment on the playground and describe how it can be related to problem-solving processes with three-, four-, and five-year-old children.

Three year olds	Four year olds	Five year olds

Worksheet 15.6 — Curriculum Components

It is important to be aware of the learning opportunities in every part of a child's environment. Wherever he is playing, a child is learning. Observe children outdoors and describe activities that might lead to learnings in the curriculum areas listed below.

Curriculum area	Description of activities that might lead to learnings
Mathematics	
Science	
Social Studies	
Language Arts	
Aesthetics	

Worksheet 15.7 — Self-Concept

Before a child can conceptualize the world beyond him, he needs to develop an awareness of himself in his immediate environment. Through physical activities, a child can test where he is in space and his relationship to the larger space. Follow a child and describe how his activities contribute to his developing self-concept.

Description of activity	Possible contribution to development of self-concept

Worksheet 15.8   The Physically Handicapped Child I

Children with physical handicaps must find their own ways of using equipment.
Observe a child with a physical handicap for ten minutes. Describe the way he plays.

Description of child	Description of equipment	Description of play

Worksheet 15.9   The Physically Handicapped Child II

When children with handicaps are placed in regular classes, all of the children learn ways of developing relationships. Observe a physically handicapped child in a mainstream program to see the ways in which a child with a handicap interacts with other children and the ways in which they interact with him.

Behaviors of handicapped child	Behaviors of other children

Was any reference to the handicap made by the other children?

Worksheet 15.10   Roles of the Teacher

Whether children's physical activities take place indoors or outdoors, a teacher must provide a safe environment in which children can play together and encounter challenges that they can meet with success. Observe an indoor or outdoor play area. Describe the roles of the teacher in each of the areas designated below.

Providing for safety

Providing equipment and arrangement of space

Extending learnings in cognitive areas

Encouraging creativity

Providing for the development of positive self-concept

Providing for social interaction

Objectives	Behavior Indicators	Worksheets
To list a set of criteria for use in selecting a story to tell to young children.	Complete Post Test 1 satisfactorily.	16.2
To list a set of criteria for use in selecting a story to be read to young childen.	Complete Post Test 2 satisfactorily.	16.1, 16.3
To list a set of criteria for telling a story to young children.	Complete Post Test 3 satisfactorily. During participation, tell a story to a small group of children.	16.2
To list a set of criteria for reading a story to young children.	Complete Post Test 4 satisfactorily. During participation, read a story to a small group of children.	16.1, 16.3
To describe teacher behavior that can contribute to children's appreciation of good literature.	Complete Post Test 5 satisfactorily. During participation, take dictation and make a book for a child.	16.1, 16.2, 16.4, 16.5, 16.8
To make arrangements appropriate for storytelling or reading of stories.	Complete Post Test 6 satisfactorily.	16.1, 16.6
To distinguish between hearing, listening, and auding.	Complete Post Test 7 satisfactorily.	16.7
Other(s).		

BOOKS AND STORIES

Pre/Post Tests

1. List six criteria for use in selecting a story to tell to young children.

2. List six criteria for use in selecting a story to read to young children.

3. List six criteria to keep in mind when telling a story.

4. List six criteria for reading a story.

5. Describe three ways in which a teacher can help children develop an appreciation for good literature.

6. Draw a classroom and place an "X" in the spots you consider to be appropriate places for telling or reading stories. Indicate the number of children involved.

7. Define: hearing, listening, auding.

The first books that a child is exposed to and the ways in which they are introduced may determine his literary tastes for a lifetime. When adults put emphasis on the mechanics of reading before children have an understanding of the value of books, children are likely to resist books. When a teacher is excited about books and stories, children become enthusiastic and look forward to hearing stories and looking at books.

If a teacher frequently reads books to small groups during the day, and children are free to come and go, stories become an integral part of a child's life.

Children enjoy poetry. They will listen carefully when a teacher reads it or quotes it from memory, and they will become aware of the cadence and sounds. If children hear the same stories and poems again and again they cannot resist chiming in. At first, they join in on the repetitive parts. Later, as they become more familiar with the words, they can repeat almost the whole story from memory, using picture clues. Sometimes a child will role-play a teacher reading a story. He models the turning of the pages, the expression, and the words after the teacher. Sometimes in dramatic play, a child will role-play an adult or older sibling by reading a story to a baby in the family.

STORYTELLING

Storytelling provides a different experience from story reading. Through the ages storytellers have had important roles in society. There is no book between the storyteller and the listener. A feeling of intimacy evolves as a story unwinds. It is possible to maintain eye contact when telling a story. As a teacher sees looks of pleasure or recognition in a child's expression, he can enlarge explanations or make adaptations in the story. When there is no book a child is able to use his own imagination in creating the images of the characters in the story. Because he is not looking at pictures, he is free to hear the words and gain a sense of the value of speech.

Sometimes children make up their own stories and sometimes they tell stories about pictures. As children become more and more excited about books, they may wish to make their own. As the teacher sits at a table with pencil and pad, children can dictate stories about themselves, their families, their pets, their friends, or the things they do. Some adults take notes and rewrite the story in manuscript at a later time. It is important that a teacher's manuscript writing be neat and legible because it serves as a model for children. Some teachers use a primer typewriter. However, these are expensive and therefore not available in many schools.

A child's story written in a carefully made book becomes a valuable possession. A child will wish to have it read many times, by teacher, by mother and father, and by grandmother and grandfather. Blank books can be given to children who are able to write or copy their own stories. A teacher can prepare a book that has special meaning for a child, perhaps about his birthday, his dog, or the new baby.

There are many ways of making books. A piece of cardboard covered with construction paper or cloth with pages neatly sewn in will last through many readings. Heavy wrapping paper may be substituted for a quicker version of a sturdy book. If a teacher takes the time to carefully prepare a supply of blank books for children's own stories, he is telling them that what they have to say is important. It is helpful for a teacher to prepare many books in advance so that they will be available when needed. Some teachers enlist the aid of parents in such projects.

ARRANGEMENT

Storybooks should be placed in a well-lighted area of the room. A carpet makes the area inviting. If there are some large, durable pillows, children and teacher will have a comfortable, intimate arrangement for reading. In warm weather, a shady spot in the grass outside can serve as a reading area. A library table and chairs are not essential.

Some shelf space at the children's level should house a small number of books, carefully selected and displayed. When there are a few books available for children to look at many times, children will learn to read the books. Children do not tire of good books. A large collection of books is needed, but most should be stored so they do not clutter the area. Books on the shelf should be rotated with books in storage periodically.

Children enjoy taking favorite books home. They feel very important when they sign out a book or ask an adult to sign out one for them. A sign-out sheet on a bulletin board will give a teacher a record of the books that are most popular.

SELECTION OF BOOKS AND MATERIALS

So many good children's books are rolling off the presses, that careful consideration must be given to making selections. Since there are just so many hours in a day for reading stories, books should be attractive and of high quality. Some excellent books are really more suitable for six- or seven-year-old children than for younger children. Stories that are long and involved do not lend themselves to the constant repetition that is so important to younger children.

Although books may be about children in other cultures, all children can identify with actions in the story. *Jeanne Marie Counts Her Sheep* is a story of a little girl who behaves like any little girl, but in this particular story the girl happens to be French.

Poetry, information, and picture books are available on a variety of subjects. Children like stories about their own growth, changes, pets, family life, and playmates. When characters are described vividly, children do not forget them. There are many different types of illustrations. Books for young children should have pictures they can identify easily, pictures that are clearly discernible against the background.

While it is not always possible for every book in the classroom to be bound in a hardcover, some books should have hardcovers and vivid illustrations. Good paperback versions of many children's books can be obtained when the budget does not permit extensive book purchases.

If the story is the important thing and a teacher reads or tells the story well, puppets, flannel boards, and story records are not necessary. Children do enjoy some of these supplementary aids occasionally, but a teacher should know precisely why he is using them.

ROLE OF THE TEACHER

A teacher should be responsible for keeping books in good repair. Children soon learn that books are to be respected and handled with care. If a page tears, it should be repaired.

If a teacher reads to a small group, the children can sit beside him and pages can be turned naturally. When a teacher reads to a large group, then he must sit on a chair and turn the book so that all the children can see the pictures. A teacher should not read a story that he has not practiced. Familiarity with the story allows a teacher to have more contact with children. A teacher should have a repertoire of stories that he can tell; when children know that he does, they will ask for them many times. Every story does not have to be followed by a discussion, nor interrupted for questions.

If an adult is available to read books, children will not tire of being read to.

ADDITIONAL RESOURCES

Cohen, Dorothy H., and Rudolph, Marguerita. *Kindergarten and Early Schooling*. Englewood Cliffs, N.J.: Prentice-Hall, 1977. Chapter 4, "Exposure to Literature," pp. 249–291.

Hildebrand, Verna. *Introduction to Early Childhood Education*. 2nd ed. New York: Macmillan, 1976. Chapter 11, "Children's Literature," pp. 262–299.

Leeper, Sarah Hammond; Skipper, Dora; and Witherspoon, Ralph. *Good Schools for Young Children*. 4th ed. New York: Macmillan, 1979. Chapter 12, "Growth Through Language Activities," pp. 269–290.

Todd, Vivian Edmiston, and Heffernan, Helen. *The Years Before School*. New York: Macmillan, 1970. Chapter 12, "Stories for Preschool Children," pp. 420–450.

Wills, Clarice Dechand, and Lindberg, Lucille. *Kindergarten for Today's Children*. Chicago: Follett, 1967. Chapter 13, "The World of Books and Stories," pp. 188–199.

Film (16mm). *Foundations of Reading and Writing*. New York: Campus Films, 1977.

Filmstrip and Audiotape. *Books and Stories*. Early Childhood Curriculum Series II. New York: Campus Films, 1977.

Worksheet 16.1   Literature with Children

(This worksheet is appropriate for use when only one observation will be made in this area.)
Teachers have the responsibility of selecting books and stories for young children that incorporate high standards in content, design, and art work. Observe in a classroom and select a story that you consider appropriate to read to a small group of children.

Name of book:
Author:
Illustrator:
Publisher:

List the criteria for selecting the story. Indicate age of child.

What emotional reactions did the children show?

What concepts do you feel might have been strengthened through the reading of this story?

What social interactions in the story were of special interest to the children?

What indications did the children show that they identified with the actions in the story?

Worksheet 16.2   Storytelling

Storytelling and story reading are two very different experiences for children. Observe a teacher telling a story and note the evidences of children's interest or lack of interest. Indicate age of child. Indicate the values of this experience.

Name of story:
Time story began:
Time story ended:

Number of children in the group:

Describe evidences of children's interest or lack of interest in the story:

What kind of a relationship developed between teacher and child?

What are the values of this relationship?

What did the teacher do to establish the relationship?

Select a story and practice telling it so that you can tell it to the children on your next visit.

Worksheet 16.3   Reading a Story

Since the habits and tastes of a lifetime develop in the early years, it is important that books selected for boys and girls be chosen with care. The length of the story, the quality of the language, the shape of the book, its subject matter, and the illustrations are some of the criteria to be considered. Select a book and read it to a child or a small group of children. Indicate age(s).

Name of book:
Author:
Illustrator:
Publisher:

Criteria used in selection:

Guidelines used in reading the story:

Response of children to the book:

Worksheet 16.4   Making a Book for a Child

Books are often statements about people in a child's environment. If a child has had an opportunity to own a book about himself, he gains firsthand knowledge of the function and importance of books. Observe a child for ten minutes. Indicate age of child. Record what he says and does. Transcribe the story you have just written into a book. Read it to the child.

Content of book (write out story):

Reasons for selecting content:

Child's reaction to story:

Worksheet 16.5   Writing a Book with a Child

When a child is engaging in the process of writing a book, he is in a position to see what it means to be an author. He learns that books are written about people and the things and experiences they value. Take a child's dictation. Copy his story in the space below.

Describe the child's reactions to seeing his own words printed in a book and hearing his story read.

Worksheet 16.6   Developing an Appreciation of Literature

It is important to create a climate in which boys and girls can develop an appreciation of literature. The arrangement of the books and the arrangement of space for reading or storytelling are important factors to be considered in setting up a room. Observe in a classroom and draw a diagram of the room. Indicate the location of the book area. Mark other areas in the room where a teacher might read a story to a small group.

Room diagram: Draw the arrangement of books in the book area and, where possible, name the books.

What other arrangements are possible?

Worksheet 16.7   Listening

It cannot be assumed that because a child is quiet that he is paying attention. There are degrees of attention. A child may hear sound and yet not recognize its source. He may be listening passively, merely selecting details that are familiar to him without getting the main ideas. He may be actually auding, listening closely and forming associations as he does so. Find examples of situations and/or locations where children are hearing, listening, and auding. In each instance indicate age of child.

Hearing:

Listening:

Auding:

Worksheet 16.8   Illustrations

Select four children's books that you consider to have superior illustrations. Sit with a small group of children and look at the pictures in as many of these books as you can. Describe the children's reactions.

Book	Children's reactions
Name of book: Author: Illustrator: Publisher:	
Name of book: Author: Illustrator: Publisher:	
Name of book: Author: Illustrator: Publisher:	
Name of book: Author: Illustrator: Publisher:	

What criteria did you use in selecting the books?

Worksheet 16.9   Volunteers

Teachers often recruit volunteers to read or tell stories to children. Volunteers may be older
children, parents, grandparents, or other people from the community.
Observe a volunteer reading or telling a story. What instructions, if any, did the teacher give the
volunteer?

Number of children	Name and author of book or story	Role of volunteer

Objectives	Behavior Indicators	Worksheets
To list the goals of a social studies program for young children.	Complete Post Test 1 satisfactorily.	17.1
To identify ways in which an early childhood program can contribute to the child's concept of himself in time and space.	Complete Post Test 2 and 3 satisfactorily.	17.2, 17.3, 17.4, 17.5, 17.6
To select areas of the room and identify the ways in which activities in these areas can contribute to a child's opportunities for interaction with other children.	Complete Post Test 4 satisfactorily.	17.7
To write a plan for a trip with a small group of four- and five-year-olds. List the learnings in the following areas: 1. Producer-Consumer 2. Exchange 3. Transportation 4. Communication	Complete Post Tests 5, 6, 7, and 8 satisfactorily.	17.8, 17.9, 17.10, 17.11
To list provisions that can be made in a classroom to help young children develop an awareness of their dependence on the larger community.	Complete Post Test 9 satisfactorily.	17.12, 17.13, 17.14, 17.15, 17.16, 17.20
To describe celebrations which could be planned that are related to a child's experience and that are in keeping with his concept of time and space relationships.	Complete Post Test 10 satisfactorily. During participation, plan and carry out a celebration suitable for young children.	17.17, 17.18
To state a problem suitable for young children to solve. List the steps you would include in helping them plan for its solution.	Complete Post Test 11 satisfactorily.	17.19
To list the roles that a teacher might take in helping children live together democratically.	Complete Post Test 12 satisfactorily.	17.2, 17.3, 17.4, 17.7, 17.8, 17.9, 17.10, 17.11, 17.14, 17.15, 17.16, 17.18, 17.21
Other(s).		

THE SOCIAL STUDIES

Pre/Post Tests

1. List eight goals of a social studies program for young children.

2. Identify five ways in which an early childhood program can contribute to a child's concept of himself in time.

3. Identify five ways in which an early childhood program can contribute to the child's concept of himself in space.

4. Identify ways in which each of the following activities can contribute to a child's opportunities for interaction with other children: housekeeping, block building, painting, manipulative materials, clay, woodworking, books.

5. List four ways in which learnings about the producer-consumer relationship can be developed.

6. List four ways in which learnings in exchange concepts can be developed.

7. List four ways in which learnings in transportation concepts can be developed.

8. List four ways in which learnings in communication concepts can be developed.

9. List five provisions to make in a classroom that will help young children develop an awareness of their dependence on the larger community.

10. Describe three celebrations that are related to a child's experience and that are in keeping with his concept of time and space relationships.

11. Describe one problem that might be solved by young children. List the steps you would help the children use as they attempt to solve it.

12. Describe four ways in which a teacher can develop in-depth comprehension of social studies with three- to five-year-old children.

Social studies is the study of human beings and their relationships to the environment. The ways in which humans use their resources and the ways in which they relate to other human beings determine the quality of their living.

In their early years, children are acquiring an orientation of themselves in relation to time and space. A child's universe really begins with himself and very soon extends to his family, to the community outside the family, and eventually to the world.

Every child develops a self-concept, the quality of which is determined by many of a child's earliest experiences in time and space. A child needs to feel there is a place for him and there will always be a place for him in the universe. As he has opportunities to feel himself in many relationships with many materials, he becomes more sure of his own life space. As an infant, he cries and gurgles and he receives food and comfort from his environment. A child at school runs. He feels the air against his face. He rolls in the grass and feels himself in relation to the earth. He puts his hands into the sand and feels himself changing it. He wields a hammer or uses a paintbrush and gains a sense of his own internal power.

Gradually he learns that he can control many parts of the environment. And yet there are many aspects of his world over which he has no control. A child who has had many successful experiences can accept his own limitations. If he feels he can receive from others, he can then sense the good feeling that comes from giving and is likely to be able to give to others.

Often adults try to introduce the concept of sharing to children before they have any real comprehension of what give-and-take is. A child is not necessarily being selfish when he is not willing to share everything because he has not yet developed an understanding of ownership. In order to understand the feelings of another person, one must have a clear sense of oneself as a person. The quality of interaction with others is dependent upon the extent to which a child knows who he is.

A child plays alone at a clay table, rolling his ball of clay into a long snakelike shape. Another child nearby plays with clay by himself, also making a long shape. As the ropes of clay become longer, they touch each other. The children silently and mutually agree to attach their clay, making an even longer snake. This is the beginning of a relationship.

Interacting with others can be pleasurable and profitable. A child has two choices: he can play independently or dependently. However, if he is going to play with others, he has to make adjustments. Others have needs and feelings too. As they approach him, he will be expected to modify his behavior. As he interacts with others, they will be changing their behavior as well. They may demand his blocks, his piece of clay, or his place at the easel.

As a child receives both friendly and hostile reactions from others, he tests different reactions of his own. If he is too dominating in his behavior, he meets resistance. If he is too submissive, he soon loses his freedom. There is a need in his life to both lead and follow. He takes turns and he shares as he works cooperatively with others. In doing so, he discovers his own abilities and the abilities of others. When he is not ready to give up his place at the workbench, he will resist. He will soon find out when it is appropriate to conform and when to resist.

In some situations, there are children who know more than he does and others who know less. He begins to discover individual differences. When there is interage grouping, there are more opportunities to experience different levels of interaction.

TIME-SPACE CONCEPTS

A sense of time develops gradually. A child may speak very blithely about "one hour from now," but this does not mean that he knows what an hour is. If a child dictates a chart entitled *Today is Tuesday,* this does not mean he knows what Tuesday is. He only repeats words he has heard. When a teacher states, "We will do that after lunch," a child understands. When a teacher states, "The blankets go home today because it is Friday," Friday takes on meaning. When the children bake a cake and put it in the oven and the cook says, "Come back in forty minutes," they do not understand what forty minutes is, but they understand that time must pass before the cake is done. When they see the crocus coming up through the snow, they have the idea that warmer weather is coming and they are on their way toward the understanding that spring follows winter. When they plant a seed they must wait for the plant to come up. Each day they can put a mark on a chart that indicates how long they have to wait, another opportunity to develop an understanding of the passage of time.

A teacher can help a child to see that the things he does are part of a chronological sequence. Photographs of how the avocado plant grew show a continuum. "Your birthday is Thursday. Today we have banana for dessert.

Tomorrow we have raisins and nuts, and the next day we have your birthday cake." This is history in the making. Then comes, "Yesterday was your birthday. We had your cake." This is now history of an event related to the child's future, present, and past.

A child does not know what a mile is, but he can become familiar with the route to the nurse's office and, by turning the corners, he can go all the way around the block without crossing the street. As he runs in the playground, he can make a short run or a long one. It is all relative, but he is acquiring a concept of distance.

The teacher supplements these learnings with words such as farther, far away, longer, shortest, and nearer. When children hear new words in proper relationships they tend to increase their vocabularies.

COMMUNICATION

A child improves his communication as he interacts with those around him. He begins to be aware that there are many ways of communicating. He sees and hears his mother talking on the telephone. He picks up the telephone in the housekeeping area and calls the store. His friend, dressed in cap and badge, delivers a make-believe letter to which he quickly scribbles a response. He pretends to repair the television set in the block area. He tears up pieces of paper and declares that they are train tickets.

A child has many opportunities to become acquainted with and use the conventional forms of communication. He sees a picture in the newspaper showing the shopping center that is being built around the corner. He delivers a written note to the office. He presents the storekeeper with a grocery list. He telephones his friend to invite him to his house. As children continue to play using various forms of communication, concepts of communication are clarified. They can communicate with someone far away either orally or in writing. A typewriter can be used to learn about written communication, and a tape recorder can be used for oral communication.

TRANSPORTATION

Very early in life children begin to have many experiences with transportation. This part of their experience becomes very apparent in their play. Children are fascinated by moving objects and are equally fascinated by moving themselves from place to place and shortening the time it takes to do this. In their play children like to use things that move; wagons and doll carriages see good service on a playground, and sleds are popular when it snows. Children also are happy when they are pretending that a block structure is a car or a train. A piece of wood at the workbench becomes a boat. In today's world children have experiences with a variety of transportation facilities, which adds a new dimension to their lives, their play, and their interactions with others.

Children soon discover that there are different ways to get from place to place. They can go farther if they use a means of locomotion other than walking. With the availability of machines, they can move out into the larger world to secure goods and services. Taking two long blocks and stacking shorter blocks on top creates a truck that transports blocks. As children simulate various modes of transportation, they become familiar with such words as barges, signals, viaducts, and terminals.

PRODUCER-CONSUMER CONCEPTS

Small blocks may become food, cars, or furniture that are then incorporated into producer-consumer dramatic play. As children engage in buying and selling commodities, they are enacting some of the basic concepts that make up the study of economics. In a classroom where children have opportunities to create a shoe store, a grocery store, or a repair shop, they often engage in buying and selling. With clay or dough, they can create fruits and vegetables to sell at a table that serves as a store.

COMMUNITY RESOURCES

These kinds of dramatic play explorations provide a place for reenacting a variety of specialized roles, for example, the pharmacist preparing a prescription, the newspaper distributor delivering papers, or the dealer selling a car. The purchaser must pay for the prescription, the newspaper, or the car, thus simulating monetary exchange. Sometimes money is not incorporated into the play and a child exchanges three red cubes for the green ones he needs.

In addition to those who provide goods, there are those who provide services in a child's life. The school nurse bandages his cut and tests his eyes, the custodian keeps the halls clean, the doctor examines his sore throat, and the dentist cleans his teeth. In order to clarify the concept of interdependence of persons, children should be encouraged to act out the roles of persons from whom they have received services.

BASIC PROCESSES

In some schools the very nature of the registration gives opportunities for children to learn to live with people of varied backgrounds. A teacher should be aware of children's reactions to people of different experiences and backgrounds. She might invite to the classroom members of the community of different races and backgrounds who could enrich and broaden the children's experiences. These persons can serve an important teaching function. One may prepare a Chinese dish, another may do some African dances, and still another may play the violin. The school secretary may be called in to repair the typewriter and the children can be intrigued as she shows them how she takes dictation.

People are dependent upon natural resources for food, clothing, and shelter, and children show great interest in these things. Churning butter, making bread or jelly, baking pumpkin seeds, and grinding peanuts into peanut butter are basic processes that are within a child's comprehension. There are natural resources that vary from place to place. In some areas families breed their own chickens, in others they grow their own vegetables. Children whose parents work in coal mines can dramatize the descent into a tunnel and the bringing out of the coal.

ECOLOGY

By the time children enter nursery school, some of them are able to contribute to the orderliness of their environment and others are not. Giving children opportunities to pour juice by themselves provides them with responsibility and with experience in measuring and pouring juice. They gather toys from the sandbox when they have finished playing, thereby contributing to preserving a worthy ecological goal. They are developing an appreciation for materials and natural resources while developing an awareness of and a respect for others.

CELEBRATIONS

It is important to build a foundation that will help young children acquire a feeling for celebrations and go beyond thinking of them merely as a time for candy or costumes. A celebration is a time for rejoicing over something that has happened either in the present or the past.

If celebrations are confined to such events as Columbus Day or Washington's Birthday, they may eventually lose their meaning. Young children's concepts of time and past events are not clearly developed; therefore, acknowledging events that are part of the here and now makes it possible for them to value such occasions. An experience becomes special when a child is helped to become consciously aware of his feelings about it. Adding a song or story can sharpen the significance of an event even more. Children take great joy in many things, and this joy can be enhanced through celebration, for example, celebrating a beautiful flower, a brightly colored leaf, the first vegetables from the garden, an icicle, the arrival of the new baby, newly mown grass, the first snowflakes, or finally succeeding at a task such as driving a nail in straight or reaching the top of a climbing apparatus.

In one such experience, after gathering the vegetables they had planted from the garden, children washed and cut them, admiring the shape and size of each one. Later they gathered around the salad bowl, first to admire their handiwork, and then to taste it. A teacher's enthusiasm, and the children's wonder, turned this occasion into an informal ceremony. "You like it?" asked the teacher. "We love it!" replied one child. "We picked them!" added another. "And we planted them too!" "I like it because it's red and green," a special red and green for this child. The children were not likely to forget this salad and the important part they played in its preparation. They felt good about it because they understood it. These children engaged in a process that can bring greater depth to other kinds of celebrations in the future.

A birthday is an important kind of celebration for a child and should include more than a birthday cake or party hats. This is a time when a particular child is the central figure and one should focus on the growth and changes that have taken place from year to year, and should appreciate the uniqueness and the very quality of humannness that make such growth possible. Sometimes a teacher does this with photographs. The mother of the child may be able to bring in pictures of her child when he was one, two, three, and four years of age. When a Polaroid camera is available, it is possible to take a photograph on the spot. When this is not possible, a teacher can take a picture in advance so as to have it ready for this celebration.

STUDY TRIPS

A teacher, while observing children in dramatic play about a bus trip, becomes aware of developing concepts and misconceptions about roles. One way of clarifying these concepts is to plan a trip with the children. If a teacher discovers that children do not understand what a bus driver does, he can plan a bus trip. The children can observe the role of the bus driver as he picks up passengers along the route. If they ride to the end of the line they may have time to talk to him and examine the bus more closely. For children who have a special interest in this activity, the trip has great meaning.

The size of the group directly affects the goals that are set up. One cannot expect to accomplish the same goals with a large group of children as with a small group. When a large group of young children travels together, they often have to wait for some of the group to reassemble. If there is something in particular to see or handle, it is hard for everyone to see or touch it without having long waits. Children are not all interested in the same things and so some of them may become distracted easily and create disturbances that could interfere with the learnings of others.

A trip outside the school exposes children to much more than is included in the specific plan for the trip. For example, if a group of three or four children are taken on a trip to the laundromat to wash painting smocks, they may encounter a policeman on the corner, a fire truck off to a fire, or a mail carrier down the street. They see many people doing things for others, and this gives them a firsthand opportunity to extend their learnings about the interrelationships of people in the community.

Children also extend their awareness of nature as they observe the mist on their faces, hear the sound of the wind, smell the odors from a bakery, and see budding leaves on trees lining the street. Sometimes attention is so focused on seeing that the other senses are neglected, particularly the sense of smell. Children often turn away from any strange smell and thus restrict their life experiences. Horses have a distinct odor, and children who have never been close to horses may be repelled or disgusted by it. Children who have been near horses do not find this odor objectionable at all. There should be as much excitement for children in experiencing new odors as there is in seeing new things.

Small group trips that give children opportunities to use their senses broaden their experiences. A teacher will have fewer problems concerning safety when he travels with a small group of children.

When a teacher plans trips, he is interested in spatial relationships, including the concept of distance. As children walk along they see many signs that indicate what something is, where something is, or what to do. One sign says "Stop." This is a busy street and cars need to stop so we can get across. Another sign says "Walnut Street." The pet shop is on this street, and so we make a right turn. A big sign at the filling station says "Gas." They could stop here if they were in a car. Down the street is a "pizza" sign.

Even people who live in the same community live in different ways. Visits to children's homes for snacks provide opportunities to see that some children live in high-rise apartment buildings, others in houses with yards, and others in row houses. While a snack should be simple, it will differ from house to house, so some children may be introduced to new foods. Before children can begin to comprehend that there are people who live far away and that their houses and foods vary according to the region and climate, they need to experience different life styles within their own immediate environment.

After children have been on a trip they incorporate into their play the ways in which they have seen various roles performed. Their play is thereby enriched and some of their ideas are clarified. As a teacher observes, he sees where the children are in their thinking and this provides him with ideas for decisions about future trips.

BOOKS AND CHARTS

A reference book pertaining to an experience may be brought into the room. Some commercial picture sets may add to a child's knowledge.

When children dictate stories to a teacher, they often incorporate what has taken place on a recent trip into their factual or imaginative stories. An experience chart is sometimes called for. However, when every experience ends with such a culminating activity, it becomes burdensome and boring.

DEMOCRATIC PROCESSES

A democratic way of life is dependent on the understanding and use of democratic processes. Children can learn to make decisions using these processes. If a young child is going to learn to become actively involved, he must have oppor-

tunities to make legitimate choices concerning matters that make a difference to him. This does not mean that children will be asked to assume responsibilities for planning their programs, but a classroom should be open enough so that reasonable choices are available. In such a classroom there is a choice as to which area a child will move into and what he will do. Too many choices can be confusing.

When a child is able to put his thoughts into words, he can plan with other children. They communicate their ideas and listen to each other's points of view. A group of children may plan to build the World Trade Center. Making room for the road and determining where to make space for the buildings require real decisions. Perhaps they will try out a space and, having concluded that it will not work, begin their deliberations again.

As children work together they often create tentative rules that change as situations change. In one classroom some children built a boat and established a shoreline around their structure. No one was permitted to walk into the ocean. As they landed the boat, they restructured the space and redefined the rules.

Children develop value systems at an early age. They initially reflect the values of the adults around them. Since values are developed, the ways in which children work in a classroom become very important. They learn what democratic processes are if these are the priority in the classroom. However, if the adults with whom children come in contact use authoritarian processes, these will be adopted by the children.

ROLE OF THE TEACHER

A teacher provides a setting for social studies when materials are chosen and arranged in such a way that a child has the space and time in which to use them. If a teacher is aware of the kinds of concepts that a child is struggling with, he will be tuned in on the occasions when the child has made a discovery or is busily searching for meanings.

Whether or not children will go beyond trial and error in making their decisions depends in part upon the importance a teacher places on processes of decision making. This does not mean that he needs to fill the environment with his words, nor does it mean that he must constantly bombard a child with questions. It does mean that if a teacher observes carefully what children do and sees this in relation to what they did on previous occasions, he can know when the child's progress might be promoted by a well-placed comment or question.

If a teacher respects what children are doing in their play, they gain respect for it themselves. They learn to value work and see themselves as workers. When a teacher attempts to verbalize concepts that a child is not ready to receive, there is real danger of diverting him from processes of inquiry and the pleasure he receives in making discoveries on his own.

In planning, it is important to consider what a unit of work is in a child's thinking. The concept of autumn is beyond his comprehension but raking leaves, planting a bulb, and enjoying a pumpkin are a series of individual units, each of short duration, that may eventually contribute to an understanding of the overall concept of autumn.

ADDITIONAL RESOURCES

Brody, Charlotte. "Social Studies and Self-Awareness." In *The Black Book,* Elisabeth S. Hirsch (ed.) Washington, D.C.: National Association for the Education of Young Children, 1974.

Buschhoff, Lotte. "Going on a Trip." In *Ideas That Work with Young Children,* Katherine Read Baker (ed.) Washington, D.C.: National Association for the Education of Young Children, 1972.

Hess, Robert D., and Croft, Doreen J. *Teachers of Young Children.* 2nd ed. Boston: Houghton Mifflin, 1972. Chapter 7, "Social Concepts and Behavior," pp. 200–228.

Hildebrand, Verna. *Introduction to Early Childhood Education.* 2nd ed. New York: Macmillan, 1976. Chapter 14, "Field Trips and Special Visitors," pp. 357–372.

Leeper, Sarah Hammond; Skipper, Dora; and Witherspoon, Ralph. *Good Schools for Young Children.* 4th ed. New York: Macmillan, 1978. Chapter 14, "The Social Studies," pp. 312–336, and Chapter 15, "Children and Values," pp. 337–358.

Margolin, Edythe. *Young Children.* New York: Macmillan, 1977. Chapter 5, "The Child, His Family, and Society: Social Studies for Young Children," pp. 145–175.

Rudolph, Marguerita. *From Hand to Head: A Handbook for Teachers of Preschool Programs.* New York: McGraw-Hill, 1973. Chapter 3, "The Child's Family and Home," pp. 12–18; Chapter 4, "Animals In and Out of the Classroom," pp. 19–31; Chapter 5, "Breaking Bread: Customs and Pleasures of Eating," pp. 32–41; Chapter 8, "Transportation: Everything Goes," pp. 61–69; Chapter 12, "Holidays, Celebrations, and Other Occasions," pp. 107–120; Chapter 14, "Places to Go and People to Know," pp. 132–140; and Chapter 15, "Striving for Concepts in Preschool Education," pp. 141–148.

Spodek, Bernard. *Teaching in the Early Years.* Englewood Cliffs, N.J.: Prentice-Hall, 1972. Chapter 8, "Social Studies for Young Children," pp. 155–175.

Wills, Clarice Dechand, and Lindberg, Lucile. *Kindergarten for Today's Children.* Chicago: Follett, 1967. Chapter 10, "Learning About People," pp. 149–159, and Chapter 14, "Developing Creativity," pp. 203–212.

Film (16mm). *Dramatic Play: An Integrative Process.* New York: Campus Films, 1972.

Worksheet 17.1   Components

(This worksheet is appropriate for use when only one observation will be made in this area.)
Below you will find listed some of the components of social studies. In a program for young children, there should be many opportunities for experience in these and other aspects of social studies. Find illustrations in the classroom.

Time:

Space:

Interrelationships of people in the physical and human environments:

Basic processes:

Other:

Worksheet 17.2   Self-Concept

Before a child can understand himself in relation to others, he needs to have an understanding of himself. A child who feels good about himself is able to give and receive. The experiences in the classroom can either help him to develop a positive self-concept, or they can tear down his feelings of worth. As a child works independently, having the opportunity to make decisions, he may reinforce and develop his self-image while painting a picture or building a block structure. As he is accepted by other children and adults, he becomes a respected member of a group and develops positive feelings about himself.

    Observe in a classroom. In the left column, record activities in which a child is working independently, indicating evidence that the child is a decision maker in the process. In the right column, describe inputs from others that help him develop a further sense of worth.

Independent activity	Input from others

Worksheet 17.3   Time I

A child's awareness of time develops gradually. The language a child uses often indicates his concept of time. As he hears the teacher use the language of time, his awareness is often heightened and further developed. As you observe the activities in a classroom, note the time-related language used by children and teachers. Number each of the recorded statements.

Who	What was said

Using the numbers you have indicated above, record each statement under the appropriate rubric below. Some statements may be applied to more than one category.

A. Estimating:

B. Predicting:

C. Planning:

D. Recalling:

E. Misconceptions:

Worksheet 17.4   Time II

(These particular concepts might not be observable in any given period of time. Therefore, it is recommended that this worksheet be used in conjunction with another one.)

One of the ways in which children's awareness of time is developed is through the sequencing of events. In the classroom there are many opportunities for such sequencing. For example: When snack is finished we go outside. It is time to clean up. It is spring and flowers are growing. Today is Friday; we won't be coming to school tomorrow. Describe events in a classroom. After each event, indicate whether it seems to contribute to a child's concept of past, present, or future.

Description of event	Concept: past, present, or future

Worksheet 17.5   Space I

Before a child can develop concepts concerning space, he needs many experiences in relating his home to his school, in recognizing differences in distance and the relationship of one area to another in space. The terms listed below are used to describe relationship in space. Describe the situations in which you hear any such terms used. Indicate age of child. Place a check mark beside those terms that children used that indicate a misconception concerning space.

Situation 1	Situation 2
Right	Right
Left	Left
Near	Near
Far	Far
Close	Close
Inside	Inside
Outside	Outside
Next to	Next to
Behind	Behind
In front of	In front of
Below	Below
Above	Above
High	High
Low	Low
Forward	Forward
Backward	Backward
Through	Through

What other terms do you hear, on the part of a teacher or child, that indicate awareness of or misconception about space?

Worksheet 17.6   Space II

Children engage in various activities in the classroom that help them develop concepts of space. Some of these concepts are three-dimensional, and others are two-dimensional. Observe children as they experiment with different ways of using space and creating enclosures. Describe with words or drawings where you see evidence of this in the areas listed below.

Painting:

Blocks:

Other:

Worksheet 17.7   Interrelationships

A teacher's values are reflected in the way a room is set up, in the kinds of activities planned, and in the roles that he takes in his relationships with children. The teacher also selects materials, arranges equipment, provides for routines, and encourages interaction.

Describe what has been done to help a group of children learn to establish relationships (e.g., when a child left the table, he put out a cup and napkin for the next child, or everyone in the class helped with cleanup).

Description of activity	Provisions made by teacher before, during, and/or after the activity

Worksheet 17.8   The Concept of Exchange in Society

As children reenact what they see about them daily, they develop an awareness of the relationship between buyer and seller, between producer of services and consumer of services. Observe children at play. If you see indications of the concept of exchange, describe them below.

Exchange of goods and services	Producer of services/ consumer of services

Given this classroom setting, what additional provisions could be made to foster these concepts?

Worksheet 17.9   Communication

As a child interacts with other persons and moves toward the world outside the home and the classroom, the need for methods of communication other than face-to-face talk becomes apparent. As children take on roles in their dramatic play, they frequently incorporate different means of communication, such as the telephone, letters, newspaper, radio, and television. There are also times when there is a need for using these media in the ongoing activities of the classroom; e.g., telephoning to get the weather forecast before a trip or looking at the menu to see what will be served for lunch. While children play, they often invent their own communications systems. Identify communication(s) system(s) in dramatic play:

Role played:

Describe what appear to be conceptions and misconceptions of the above communication(s) system(s).

Select one of the communication systems you observed being used. Describe one way in which a teacher might bring the function of this system to a child's awareness.

Worksheet 17.10   Transportation

When children come to school they have already experienced many modes of transportation. They ride a bicycle, ride in a bus or car, and sometimes ride in a train, boat, or plane. In a world where people are dependent upon commodities that are produced far away and where people must move themselves great distances for both work or pleasure, transportation is important.

Observe a classroom and record indications that children are aware of transportation facilities and their functions; for example, nailing two boards together to make a plane to fly somewhere, putting four chairs in a row to make a bus to go shopping, or building a spaceship with blocks to go to the moon.

Type of transportation	Construction materials, etc.	Conception or mis-conception of function

List two questions a teacher might ask in order to identify a child's conception or misconception about one of the above modes of transportation.

1.

2.

Worksheet 17.11   Trips

Trips have a great educational value for young children. They can broaden their concepts concerning many areas of social studies curriculum (e.g., communication, producer-consumer relationship, public services, exchange of goods and services, transportation).

Look at three different activities in the room. Describe each one and indicate a type of trip (preferably in the building or on school grounds) that might enhance the experience.

1.

2.

3.

Select one place you could visit in the building. Describe the landmarks you might use to help the children route their return to the classroom. If possible, take the trip with three or four children.

What values are there in taking trips with young children?

1.

2.

3.

Worksheet 17.12   Use of Resource Persons

Children are surrounded by those who provide goods and services. These people can perform an important teaching function. When a child can actually see them at work he can gain a greater understanding of the concept of interdependence of people. Observe in a classroom and look for places where a resource person might help to further learnings (e.g., children might make-believe they are baking bread with parents).

Resource person	Area in which he might serve	Ways in which he might add to the learning
Custodian		
Nurse		
Secretary		
Cook		
Father		
Mother		
Other		

Worksheet 17.13   Basic Processes

There are certain basic processes that people all over the world use in providing themselves with food, clothing, and shelter. We sometimes lose touch of this fact in a society where so much is done outside the home. Knowledge of these basic processes helps children gain greater depth in their comprehension of what is involved in living and a greater appreciation of the products and services they use.

Observe in the classroom any activities that involve the basic processes used in providing food, clothing, and shelter; for example, growing radishes, churning butter, cleaning the hamster cage, watching a silkworm. Select one (food, clothing, or shelter). Describe the activity and identify the possible knowledges and appreciations children may be acquiring.

Activity related to food, clothing, or shelter	Possible knowledge gained	Possible appreciation developed

Worksheet 17.14   Use of Natural Resources

Survival depends upon the availability of natural resources that provide people with food, clothing, and shelter. Many of the concepts involved in the change of a natural resource into a usable commodity are too complex for young children to understand. However, some fundamental concepts are comprehensible (e.g., a tree produces pecans and apples, or may be cut into pieces for the fireplace, the sun provides warmth and light, and hens produce eggs).

Observe in a classroom and playground and list any materials that can be classified as natural resources. Identify those which you feel could have meaning for young children. Describe how you would use them in a classroom to help the children develop an awareness of the place of natural resources in our living.

Natural resources

Description of use

What other suitable materials could be introduced in this classroom?

Worksheet 17.15   Ecology

Children of three and four are not too young to acquire some concepts of caring for their environment. They see the street cleaner and the garbage collector. They themselves can participate; they can throw paper wrappers in the garbage, they can rake leaves, they can conserve paper goods.
Observe children in a classroom or playground. Describe behaviors that indicate an awareness of contributing to the quality of their environment.

Children's behavior that indicates thoughtfulness concerning the environment:

What children see adults doing to improve the environment (custodian emptying waste baskets, teacher conserving paper towels):

Suggest ways of helping children to become consciously aware of caring about their environment.

Worksheet 17.16   Safety

When children are in a safe environment, they have opportunities to test their own abilities in risk-taking activities (e.g., building high with their blocks). There are many challenges to children in a well-planned classroom. In the spaces below, describe such opportunities.

Evidences of arrangements made by adults to ensure safety as children work and play:

Indoors

Outdoors

Evidence of children having internalized judgment in risk-taking actions:

Worksheet 17.17   Celebrations I

(This worksheet should be used in circumstances where there is opportunity for students to observe celebrations.)
Celebrations have been part of all cultures through the ages. They take on many forms. Celebrations may or may not carry symbols with them. A celebration may be personal or universal. It is an elaboration of an experience present or past. In celebrating, we intensify our feelings and become more consciously aware of them. Events closely related to a child's life have more meaning for him and are easier for him to identify with. For example, before a child can celebrate Washington's Birthday, he needs to have experiences with more relevant events such as the first snowfall. Some of the components of celebration are rejoicing in, intensifying, adding meaning to, and giving special attention to an experience or event, past or present.
    Observe a celebration in the classroom. Describe what evidence you see of the components of a celebration mentioned above.

Worksheet 17.18   Celebrations II

Sometimes food preparation enhances a celebration. Some foods are associated traditionally with special holidays; for example, cranberries, birthday cakes, and special holiday cookies. There are foods that in themselves call for a celebration because the children have either planted and/or harvested them. When ripe apples are in season and a child cuts them and makes apple sauce, he can develop a feeling of becoming a part of the whole universe. This is true when a pumpkin is baked or its seeds are roasted. Salad takes on a new dimension when children pick the radishes and carrots from their own garden. In a heavily populated urban area, a garden may grow in a coffee can or other available container.

Observe a food experience and describe where you see children acquiring new meanings. Include conversations that indicate the feelings of celebration. What was the role of the teacher?

Describe other possibilities for deepening and broadening meanings and intensifying feelings.

Worksheet 17.19   Developing Skills in Decision Making

The quality of democratic life depends upon skills in decision making. With very young children, there are always some decisions that must be made by adults. However, at a very early age, it is important that children engage in discovery, inquiry, and evaluation that lead to independent thinking. Children who have opportunities to engage in problem-solving activities are in a position to gain the skills required for decision making. There are many such opportunities in a classroom.

Describe any of the following activities that you observe. It is not expected that you will be able to find all of them during any one observation.

Stating a problem:

Locating and using resources:

Making tentative hypotheses:

Evaluating processes and/or solutions:

Worksheet 17.20   **Children's Books**

Many children's story and picture books incorporate the content of the social studies curriculum. Concepts of the many aspects of living are dealt with in a context that has meaning for children. Select *two* picture or story books that you consider to be good quality literature for each of the following categories:

Food

Shelter

Clothing

Transportation

Communication

Interrelationships

Celebrations

Life cycle

Producer-consumer

Democratic processes

Ethnic identification

Other

From the above list select two books that you will read to a child or to a small group of children. Tape the conversation you have with the children following the reading. Listen to the tape and list the social studies concepts that were discussed.

Worksheet 17.21

Role of the Teacher

Social studies for young children is not usually thought of in terms of separate disciplines. By the way in which a teacher arranges the room, he can make certain that the basic foundations of each discipline are being developed. Look around the room. What evidence is there that the teacher has made provisions for the following social studies areas?

Geography

History

Anthropology

Sociology

Geology

Political Science

Economics

Other

Objectives	Behavior Indicators	Worksheets
To list reasons for planning language arts experiences for young children.	Complete Post Test 1 satisfactorily.	18.1
To list objectives and plan two experiences intended to improve the quality of communication.	Complete Post Tests 2 and 7 satisfactorily.	18.2, 18.4, 18.5, 18.32
To identify situations and materials usually found in an early childhood classroom that can help in developing auditory discrimination.	Complete Post Test 3 satisfactorily.	18.6, 18.7, 18.8, 18.10, 18.14, 18.17, 18.24
To identify experiences that lead to the development of oral language skills.	Complete Post Test 4 satisfactorily.	18.2, 18.4, 18.10 to 18.12, 18.14 to 18.17, 18.24, 18.35
To identify materials usually found in an early childhood classroom that can help in developing visual discrimination.	Complete Post Test 3 satisfactorily.	18.4, 18.18 to 18.23, 18.25, 18.28, 18.31, 18.34
To describe two experiences intended to help children record information, feelings, or events. To cite at least two values of recording information, feelings, or events.	Complete Post Test 5 satisfactorily. Complete the chart.	18.26, 18.27, 18.32, 18.33, 18.35
To list the ways in which communication skills can enhance self-concept.	Complete Post Test 7 satisfactorily.	18.9, 18.13, 18.26, 18.27, 18.34
To describe the ways in which language arts can become a socializing agent.	Complete Post Tests 6 and 7 satisfactorily.	18.3, 18.13
To identify the behaviors in a classroom that would indicate appreciations of and positive attitudes toward reading.	Complete Post Test 7 satisfactorily.	18.29, 18.36
To describe the roles of the teacher in extending children's reading, writing, listening, and speaking skills.	Complete Post Test 8 satisfactorily.	18.16, 18.36
Other(s).		

THE COMMUNICATION ARTS

Pre/Post Tests

1. List eight values to keep in mind when planning language arts experiences for young children.

2. List two illustrations for the ways in which each of the following can be developed in an early childhood classroom: listening, reading, speaking, and writing.

3 . List some situations that can serve to help children develop auditory and visual discrimination (five of each).

4. List five activities that can encourage oral language skills, and describe the role of the teacher in each.

5. Write a chart appropriate for five-year-old children about a planting experience. Use manuscript writing. List three values of this experience.

6. Describe three examples of nonverbal communication. Beside each example, indicate the unspoken message.

7. Write a plan for a communication arts activity. What opportunities are provided for social interaction? What appreciation of communication might be intensified through this experience? What positive attitudes in reading and writing might be developed? In what ways might this experience enhance self-concept?

8. As a group bakes a cake, list some specific behaviors that would illustrate the following teacher roles during this activity: provides materials, asks questions, observes, and gives support.

A child begins communicating at birth. From the very beginning a child engages in two-way communication by giving and receiving both verbal and nonverbal messages. A cry calls attention to an immediate need. The waving of hands and kicking of feet bring forth a different kind of response. While children can communicate without words, they can make their ideas and feelings known more precisely as skills in language develop. When a child says, "More juice!" he is giving a clearer indication of what he wants than when he waves his cup or cries. A child soon learns the value of communicating with words.

By the time a child comes to school, he has many skills in communication. Children, however, do not acquire these skills at the same rate. The experiences that a child has had and his level of maturity determine the types and quality of both verbal and nonverbal communications. Because of their experiences, some children are very aware of communication and it is very important to them, while others have not yet realized its significance.

Whatever a child does in school, or for that matter in any aspect of his life, will require communication. Much of the time spent in school will be devoted to the refinement of skills in communication. In some schools these skills are included in the *communication arts,* and in other schools, they are known as *language arts.* In this book both terms will be used interchangeably.

Language arts form an important part of the curriculum. There are assignments to be written, teachers and peers to be listened to, books to be read, and words to be spoken. The ways in which a child performs these operations determine how rich his experiences will be. The school, then, should provide opportunities for a child to practice the skills he has, to acquire more skills, and to understand and value what language can do for him. These opportunities exist everywhere in the school environment. This is especially true in a classroom organized for self-selecting of activities. Whatever a child's level of development, he will grow and develop in such an environment. When children do what they are really interested in doing, they tend to use language more purposefully than when they are placed in prearranged, structured activities. When a communication arts program is planned to meet individual needs and time is provided to listen, explore, repeat, correct, and evaluate experiences, there are built-in opportunities for extended language experiences. At a clay table, one child is punching the clay and chanting, "It's getting bigger and bigger and bigger and bigger." Another child has made a long snake and now discovers he can use the thin clay—"I'm gonna make my name," and seeing an error says, "No, that's not it, I'll do it again." The third child, rolling his clay, is silent but apparently listening to the others.

As children have experiences that require any of the skills in the language arts, the quality of their communications improves. A teacher who takes down a story that a child dictates is providing a reason for precise speech. A child listens with interest as a teacher reads back what was written, and he hears what has been dictated. The importance of the printed word becomes evident as a teacher refers to a recipe on a chart in order to prepare for making play dough. A reference book provides information on the care of baby gerbils. A teacher writes a child's name on a cubby, and later the child incorporates his own name into his picture.

Books and other printed materials are important. However, even more fundamental to the development of skills in communication are the experiences that provide opportunities to use them. The workbench or the easel, the blocks or housekeeping areas, clay, crayons, and dough, or pegs, puzzles, beads, and other manipulative materials provide the means for total involvement with language learning.

AUDITORY DISCRIMINATION

In an early childhood classroom, all activities and materials lend themselves to formal or informal exercises in auditory discrimination. Before children can grasp the idea that patterns of sounds convey meaning, they must be able to sort out or discriminate sounds. If children are to decode sounds, they must be able to differentiate them and hear blends and combinations of sounds. If a child is aware of pitch, volume, and tone, he can gain greater meaning of what is said to him and, in turn, give more meaning to what he says in response.

A child himself can produce high and low sounds as he plays a piano or an autoharp. Sometimes a child experiments with pitch by playing up and down a scale key by key. He becomes more skilled in discriminating sounds as he repeatedly produces his own variations either with instruments or his own voice. He can play with the dynamics of sound (softness or loudness) while at a workbench or while pounding clay. He creates his own patterns and reproduces the patterns of others. A tone may be hollow, full, or rich. Children will sometimes test this attribute

of sound by tapping a hammer against pieces of wood or pressing one piano key over and over again.

Children enjoy playing with words and other kinds of sounds. They create their own phonics drills and, with a bit of encouragement, those drills can become more complex than exercises recommended in teachers' guides for reading. There are sounds all around children, such as wind whistling, rain falling against a window, an icicle snapping. There are machine-made sounds like water pouring from a faucet, an electric fan whirring in a room, a bus stopping at the corner, a jet plane flying overhead.

Children love to use their voices as they rhyme words. Some children delight in making unusual or silly sounds and will engage in this exercise for long periods of time; for example, they will invent sounds like "mingle, pingle," or "ooop, ooop, dooop." As they rhyme sounds, they sharpen their awareness of the endings of words, such as *ing, ink, ed, it.* Sometimes children play with initial consonants such as *m*an, *m*ad, *m*at, or *s*ing, *s*ung, *s*at, *s*it. A teacher who notices what a child is saying can stimulate children to experiment further and create new words. Children are equally satisfied with nonsense sounds and real words.

Children are often involved with their whole bodies as they pick up rhythmic patterns in repeating or chanting sounds. Many action songs such as "If You're Happy and You Know It" or "Put Your Finger in the Air" give children opportunities to combine body and voice in rhythmic patterns. Making up new lines to familiar songs is fun for many children. "The wheels of the bus go round and round" becomes, "The shoes on my feet go tap, tap, tap." Guessing games provide exercises in discriminating sound. One such game requires a child to cover his eyes and identify a selected object by the sound it makes. Another game calls for one child to hide and call, "Who am I? Where am I?"

Poetry offers further experience with pattern and rhythm. When a poem is read again and again, children become familiar with what can be done with sounds.

The environment is often cluttered with sounds, and children need to sort out and select those to which they will give their attention.

Where there are speakers, children need to learn to be listeners. A quiet child is not necessarily a listening child; real listening (*auding*) requires involvement. It involves giving meaning to what is said and interpreting this meaning in light of one's own experience. The experiences of a child contribute to his facility with language and in turn language contributes to his experiences.

ORAL COMMUNICATION

Before children can develop facility with the printed word (reading and writing), they must have many experiences with aural language (hearing words), as well as many opportunities with oral communication (the spoken word).

A child's first oral sound is a cry. The ways in which children develop their vocabularies are fantastic when one considers the difference between that first cry and the number of words that most children know by the time they enter school.

There are very great differences in the facility that children have in expressing themselves. While it is important for children to speak clearly and distinctly and to develop habits of correct usage, adults should be cautioned about correcting children because it interrupts their flow of language and interferes with the ideas they are trying to communicate.

As children develop skills in using language, they imitate many models. Parents, siblings, and other relatives, people in the school and the community, all influence the quality, diction, vocabulary, and fluency of language that children will develop. There are a few children who do not talk much, but for the most part children like to talk, and it is important that classrooms be arranged so that there are opportunities for them to do so. If a child has to wait too long for a turn to speak, many learning possibilities are lost. Children enjoy talking about their impressions and will quickly tell you what they like or do not like or what is big or not so big. They share their feelings. It is not hard to know whom they like, whom they do not like, and when they are frightened. They relate such fascinating facts as what they ate for breakfast, how much the baby cries, and what daddy did when the dog was lost. They like to talk about what they are doing. They will go into detail about the building they are creating in the block area, or the load of sand they can carry, or the restaurant they are running in the housekeeping area.

As they work and play together, they assign roles ("You'll be the brother and I'll be the father"). As children talk about these roles, they are clarifying ideas, reinforcing what they already know, and seeking new meanings and deeper understandings. Children role-playing the launching of a spaceship begin with the countdown. As one child shouts, "Blast off!" they shoot out of their chairs simulating the ship. The teacher asks, "Has your ship reached the stratosphere?" One child asks, "How high is the stratosphere?" "It's 1½ miles," is one answer. Another says, "No, it's infinity." "What's that?" asks another. "That's five miles." A teacher, recognizing the misconception, yet knowing children cannot comprehend the concept of infinity, says, "Infinity is on and on and on."

While most children do know many words, their vocabularies consist largely of nouns, pronouns, and verbs. There are times when a teacher can extend a child's vocabulary by elaborating on what the child says, by adding adjectives, adverbs, and prepositions. A child saying, "More" might elicit a teacher reply such as "You want more of this orange juice." A teacher hearing "See my coat!" could respond, "You have a new, red coat."

Children sometimes go around a room labeling things—"This is a door," "This is a chair," "This is a book." When a child has discovered that things have names, he enjoys this self-initiated oral exercise.

It is important for a teacher to be aware of children who seldom speak. There are many reasons why a child may not talk, and a teacher is in no position to analyze the causes. He will probably gain more if he does not insist that the child speak. Rather than risking a resistance to speech, a teacher's nearness and naturalness serve as a model and suggest speaking is a desirable and valuable behavior. A teacher will make it a point to be near a child and talk to him even though he does not respond verbally. On those rare occasions when a teacher has concern about a child's speech, outside guidance from a specialist in the field should be sought.

Opportunities for talking and listening arise throughout a school day. Snack time is often a time when a teacher engages in conversation with children. After a teacher has read a story to a small group of children, the children may continue to look at the book, talking through the sequence of events as they look at the pictures again. Often a child will make-believe that he is reading a book to a friend. Sometimes he will tell his own story, which may be either a very fanciful tale or a recounting of familiar events.

When children engage in an activity, they like to talk about it. As they do so, their vocabularies increase. The use of a tape recorder makes it possible to preserve the words so that the children can hear them repeatedly. Children can record and hear chants, conversations, songs, and original stories. Puppets often stimulate creativity in stories and conversations.

Language flows as children sing, and any self-consciousness or halting speech disappears as a child becomes involved in music. On occasion, simple choral speaking may serve such a purpose, although a teacher must be careful not to formalize this activity or set the kind of standards that might be expected in primary grades.

When a group returns from a trip, a teacher will sometimes write an experience chart with the children. However, if a teacher listens to the children in their dramatic play, she will hear what they have recalled from the trip and have firsthand knowledge of what aspects of the experience had real meaning for them.

Standard English, for the most part, is the accepted form of language in schools. There is a difference of opinion as to the place of dialect in the classroom. For some children, English is a second language. Many educators encourage teachers, if they are capable, to speak and conduct discussions with children in both languages.

As children learn language, they construct their own word forms and sentence structures. ''I dood it,'' or ''Him took it,'' or ''She shutted the door'' can often be heard from young children. Those children are using language to convey meaning, even though the structure may be incorrect. It is important to permit children to express their ideas freely, no matter how imperfect their grammar is. A teacher, careful to enunciate clearly and use appropriate construction, serves as a model and, with practice, children ultimately learn standard forms.

VISUAL DISCRIMINATION

If children are to read, it is necessary to develop their skills in visual discrimination. In order to be able to read, a child must be able to differentiate shapes and sizes, decode these patterns, and translate them into meanings.

Reading requires the ability to recognize similarities and differences in the shapes and arrangements of letters. Children become increasingly aware of similarities and differences as they match and sort buttons, nails, screws, spools, shells, and seeds. Lotto games of various sorts, either made commercially or by a teacher, utilize different categories. There are color matching and picture matching according to categories such as animals, fruits, and flowers. Sometimes the sorting is done with more than one attribute, such as *toys* with *wheels,* or all the *red clothing.* Some games use color or other-than-word symbols, such as dots. Any box divided into sections can be used for sorting a variety of objects according to one or more attributes, such as size, or size and color, or size, color, and shape. Children become intrigued with classification of objects and are very inventive in the ways they categorize them.

As children play with puzzles, they learn about the concept of figure-ground. They need to distinguish the figure of the puzzle from the background of the board. Simple puzzles, in which each object is separated on a board from other objects, provide a good beginning because all a child has to do is match the shape of an object with the outline of the empty space. At first, this may be a trial-and-error process but, later, he will look for clues and become aware of the configuration of the object.

Precut letters are made of various materials, including wood, cardboard, metal, plastic, felt, or sandpaper. Not only do children have an opportunity to feel the shapes of the letters, but they see them against the background of the table, magnetic board, or felt board, and they can arrange them in a variety of configurations. As they place the letters together to form words, the parts become a whole.

Play dough provides children with opportunities to create their own configurations, changing, correcting, and rebuilding them. As children cut out shapes in dough, they can see not only the figure-ground relationship but, when the shape is removed from the larger piece of dough, they can see the empty space as well. Dough, like clay, provides an opportunity for children to see the configurations.

Clay has many of the same attributes as dough. Children delight in creating shapes, destroying them, and re-creating them. When they make shapes that dissatisfy them, they can start over and, in doing so, they put the pieces back into the whole lump, providing experience after experience in part-whole relationships.

All of reading and writing is based on symbols put together in patterns. Children get experiences in patterning as they string wooden beads, creating their own arrangements—two orange, two green, two red, etc. Paper strips, another medium for patterning, can be pasted together to form chains. Pegs may be placed on a board in many different arrangements—horizontally, vertically, and corner to corner. As a child plays with blocks, he experiments with making his own patterns. After he has many of these experiences, he will be ready to discern patterns in written language.

In order for a child to learn to read, he needs to move from concrete (three-dimensional) objects to pictorial (two-dimensional) representations, and then to two-dimensional symbols. While children come to school having had experiences with many three-dimensional objects, continued handling of such objects helps them see the relationship between the word and the object. While it is true that children move from one stage of readiness to another, they do not proceed along an established continuum, ending one stage before beginning the next. Their development might be described as a "jagged front" approach, from concrete to representative to concrete to symbolic, etc.

As children see objects they have handled illustrated on a printed page or see a photograph of themselves or of a structure they have built, they begin to associate pictures with ideas. This is what reading is all about. Looking at pictures and discussing content provide experience in handling books. There is movement from left to right, top to bottom, and front to back as children turn pages. Often pictures provide clues for printed words before a child can decode the symbols and translate them into meanings.

From the time children can see, they are exposed to symbols. They have many opportunities to associate symbols with objects as labels are placed on their clothing, on their cubbies, and on food packages they use in their play. On trips there are street signs, traffic signs, and store signs to read.

Children's books serve an important function in their introduction to reading. When a child dictates his own story and sees a teacher translate his words into symbols and place them in a book, he is participating in a reading experience. He sees that his words can be preserved in a way that others can understand. He learns that another person looking at these symbols can repeat his exact words and can refer to them at any time.

When children work with materials, they have firsthand experiences with such concepts as configuration, part-whole, patterns, and sequence. Although there are workbooks that provide exercises intended to help children learn these concepts, they probably lead only to rote learning. When children handle materials and make their own discoveries, experiencing concepts over and over again, concepts of configuration, part-whole, patterns, and sequence are more likely to be internalized.

Writing is often thought of as a grown-up activity but children's paintings or drawings incorporate the elements of writing. From these beginning experiences with writing, children gain comprehension of the relationship between a symbol and its meaning. Their paintings move from scribbles to representations of sun, house, tree, and path.

Because there is no right or wrong way to hold a brush, a child can try out different ways until he finds one that is comfortable for him. When a child uses a brush, he is gaining the skills he will need in using a pencil. The same thing is true when he uses a crayon or chalk. There is no need for eye-hand coordination as a child scribbles, but as he develops his coordination he can refine his drawings or paintings. Hammering, catching a ball, and fitting a peg into a hole help him to acquire eye-hand coordination and develop dexterity in arm and finger movements. These activities are more relevant to a child's development than exercises in copying letters. However, when children become aware that they can create letters, they often make up their own drills, copying letters, words, or whole sentences from books, charts, or signs. Even before a child copies the letters of the alphabet, he writes his own symbols.

Straight lines and curves that children incorporate into their painting and drawing are the basic shapes they will use later in their manuscript writing. Teachers of young children should practice until they are skilled in making manuscript letters quickly and correctly. Children experiment with spatial relationships and configurations as they position shapes on paper.

Manuscript writing, rather than cursive, is usually taught in schools because a child needs to learn only the circle, curve, and straight line, and it closely resembles the print in the books he is using. Although the primer typewriter is not a standard piece of equipment in every classroom, when available it provides another experience with the printed word. As children print, they copy the letters in precise order. This prepares them for spelling.

The teaching of reading and writing are closely related. There are those who believe that children learn to read through the teaching of writing; therefore, they begin their language arts teaching with writing. Some begin by teaching the sounds of the letters (phonics) and then introduce writing. Others begin with the whole word approach. There is no one correct way of teaching skills in communication but, given appropriate experiences with concrete and representational materials, children will be ready to learn reading and writing.

SELF-CONCEPT

When a child speaks so that others can understand him, and when his words are written down for others to read, he begins to feel a sense of worth. Positive feelings accompany successful communication. The ability to communicate with others is a social tool. Social development is fostered when children acquire language skills, and language skills encourage social contacts. A child moves from a solitary person to a cooperative one as he learns to make himself understood. Children with the most advanced language skills make the most social contacts and are then able to lead others into cooperative play.

The more experience a child has, the more he has to talk about, and the more he can understand what others talk about.

ARRANGEMENT

An informal, relaxed atmosphere encourages talk between adult and child, child and child, child and children. If children are simply rushed from one activity to another, they miss valuable opportunities for initiating conversations. There are those who sit for long periods of time and talk, and those who cannot attend to conversation for very long. Provisions should be made for these individual differences. When materials are within reach and available, and when children are provided with choices, they will engage in activities requiring communication.

MATERIALS AND EQUIPMENT

There is hardly an activity or material in an open early childhood setting that does not contribute to communication arts. Play in a housekeeping or block area encourages communication and the refinement of the skills of communication. Crayons, pencils with soft lead, and unlined newsprint (before lined paper is introduced) are among the basic materials but clay, paint, hammer, paste, dough, and of course, books, books, and more books are equally valuable.

A communication arts program is enhanced when a tape recorder, primer typewriter, piano, autoharp, xylophone, and camera are available. Some teachers have found that headphones attached to record players provide ideal opportunities for listening without disturbing others.

ROLE OF THE TEACHER

A teacher is contributing to the communication arts program in almost everything he says and does. When he pays close attention to what a child is saying he is demonstrating to that child that what he says has value (thus enhancing the child's self-concept), and at the same time is also helping him to learn that when people speak, others listen. One-to-one interaction encourages both speaking and listening. When there is more than one adult in the room, there can be even more opportunities for communication. Teachers should be aware of children who are usually quiet and should observe before determining the types of intervention that might encourage talk. Through quality of voice, a teacher sets an example, and his speaking serves as a model of enunciation and pronunciation; yet, he should appreciate that each child has his own way of speaking, which may or may not be standard English.

It is recommended that teachers not talk a great deal when working with children. However, an appropriate, well-timed question may stimulate discussion, clarify ideas, or clear up mistaken concepts. The timing and appropriateness of comments or questions make the difference between interference and enrichment.

ADDITIONAL RESOURCES

Cohen, Dorothy H., and Rudolph, Marguerita. *Kindergarten and Early Schooling.* Englewood Cliffs, N.J.: Prentice-Hall, 1977. Chapter 5, "Scope and Variety in Language Learning and Use," pp. 59–76.

Hess, Robert D., and Croft, Doreen J. *Teachers of Young Children.* 2nd ed. Boston: Houghton Mifflin, 1972. Chapter 6, "Growth of Language and Cognitive Abilities," pp. 172–199.

Hildebrand, Verna. *Introduction to Early Childhood Education.* 2nd ed. New York: Macmillan, 1976. Chapter 10, "Language Arts," pp. 239–261.

Leeper, Sarah Hammond; Skipper, Dora, and Witherspoon, Ralph. *Good Schools for Young Children.* 4th ed. New York: Macmillan, 1978. Chapter 11, "The Language Arts," pp. 226–268.

Margolin, Edythe. *Young Children.* New York: Macmillan, 1976. Chapter 4, "Children Need to Communicate," pp. 93–144.

McAfee, Oralie. "The Right Words." In *Ideas That Work with Young Children,* Katherine Read Baker (ed.). Washington, D.C.: National Association for the Education of Young Children, 1972.

Moffitt, Mary W., and Swedlow, Rita. "Dynamics of Play for Learning." In *Play: Children's Business*. Washington, D.C.: Association for Childhood Education International, 1974.

Rudolph, Marguerita. *From Hand to Head—A Handbook for Teachers of Preschool Programs*. New York: McGraw-Hill, 1973. Chapter 13, "The Threshold of Literacy," pp. 121–131, and Chapter 15, "Striving for Concepts in Preschool Education," pp. 141–148.

Smith, Nila Banton. *Shall We Teach Formal Reading in the Kindergarten?* Washington, D.C.: Association for Childhood Education International, 1963. Eight pages.

Spodek, Bernard. *Teaching in the Early Years*. Englewood Cliffs, N.J.: Prentice-Hall, 1972. "Language Learning in Early Childhood Education." pp. 59–83.

Todd, Vivian Edmiston and Heffernan, Helen. *The Years Before School*. 3rd ed. New York: Macmillan, 1977. Chapter 11, "Developing Communication Skills," pp. 409–444.

Wills, Clarice Dechant, and Lindberg, Lucile. *Kindergarten for Today's Children*. Chicago: Follett, 1967. Chapter 11, "Communication Through Oral Language," pp. 160–171, and Chapter 12, "Real Experiences with the Three R's," pp. 172–187.

Yamamoto, Kaoru. *The Child and His Image*. Boston: Houghton Mifflin, 1972. Chapter 11, "The Developing Self: World of Communication," pp. 26–35.

Audiotape. *The Language of Children*, Tape of the Month. Washington, D.C.: Childhood Resources, 1972.

Audiotape. *Reading and the Child Under Six*, Tape of the Month. Washington, D.C.: Childhood Resources, 1972.

Film (16 mm). *Foundations of Reading and Writing*. New York: Campus Films, 1974.

Filmstrip and Audiotape. *Books and Stories*. Early Childhood Curriculum Series II. New York: Campus Films, 1977.

Worksheet 18.1   Components of the Communication Arts

(This worksheet is appropriate for use when only one observation will be made in this area.)
Listening, speaking, reading, and writing are components of the language arts. These skills will be
essential all the days of a child's life. Developing facility with communication skills will help a child to
understand the people, things, and processes in his world. In an early childhood education program,
children should have opportunities to develop all of these skills. As you observe in a classroom, look for
and list activities that illustrate each of the components listed below.

Listening

Speaking

Reading

Writing

Worksheet 18.2   Communication Skills

The quality of life is very dependent upon the quality of communication. An early childhood classroom
provides a setting for developing communications skills. Observe in three areas of a classroom for
experiences that can give children opportunities to develop communication skills and list them below.

1.   4.

2.   5.

3.   6.

Select two of the above. In the spaces below, plan two ways in which the teacher might extend the communications.

              PLAN 1   PLAN 2

Worksheet 18.3   Social Interaction

Facility with language helps foster social interaction, and social interaction in turn facilitates language development. A classroom provides many opportunities for this development.
While observing in a classroom, locate the areas where there seem to be the most child-child conversation. Describe how this conversation serves as a socializing force.

Area of the room	Description of communication that leads to interaction	
	Verbal	Nonverbal

Worksheet 18.4   Concepts and Skills

There are many concepts and skills necessary for reading and writing. The experiences that children have with paint, clay, blocks, and other materials help develop those concepts and skills. Eye-hand coordination, holding a pencil or pencil-like object, left-to-right progression, configuration, figure-ground, part-whole, matching and sorting, classification, patterning and creating symbols—these are some of the concepts and skills that serve as foundations for reading and writing.

Observe a three-year-old, a four-year-old, and a five-year-old, and record their behaviors that are directly related to concepts and skills required in reading and writing.

Three-year-old

Four-year-old

Five-year-old

Worksheet 18.5   Nonverbal Communication

Communication can be verbal or nonverbal. There are different kinds of nonverbal communication. Different kinds of messages are transmitted without words through body movements. Observe children's nonverbal communications. Indicate age of child.

Description of child's nonverbal behavior	Messages that seemed to be transmitted	Feelings that seemed to underlie the communication

Worksheet 18.6   Listening

While listening is only one of the language arts, it is an important facet of communication. Children hear many sounds to which they are not actively listening. The ability to hear does not guarantee listening. Listening involves recognizing familiar sounds, giving them meaning from one's own experience, reacting to or interpreting them, and integrating them with one's knowledge. It is a major means of learning. Record ways in which provisions have been made in a classroom to encourage children's listening.

Description of situation and materials	Behaviors of those involved in listening situation

Worksheet 18.7   Auditory Discrimination I

The sounds all around us vary in pitch, volume, and tone. These are important attributes of speech. When children are aware of the nuances of sound, they hear more fully what is being said. These nuances add richness to both their speech and the comprehension of others' speech. Listen for and describe the quality of sound in the classroom according to the categories listed below.

Pitch (direction upward or downward):

Dynamics (loudness-softness):

Tone quality (richness-hollowness):

Worksheet 18.8   Auditory Discrimination II

Children are surrounded by sounds that are environmental, machine-made, and vocal. It is important for a teacher to be aware of the multitude of sounds to which a child is exposed. Listen in a classroom. Identify the sounds in the categories below and indicate whether or not children were aware of them.

Kinds of sounds	Indication of children's awareness of the sounds
Environmental	
Machine-made	
Vocal	

Worksheet 18.9   Self-Concept

Children's feelings about themselves are often revealed as they speak. Listen to what children say.
Indicate what feelings about themselves seem to underlie their conversations.

Conversation— what child(ren) said	Feelings that seemed to underlie the conversation

Worksheet 18.10   Rhyming Words

Children enjoy playing with words. As they do so, they extend their vocabularies and become aware of
ways in which words are built. Children themselves will rhyme words and make up rhyming sounds for
sheer pleasure. This is a kind of exercise in auditory discrimination that is helpful in language
development. Observe in a classroom and record the ways in which children play with words.

Worksheet 18.11   Extending Vocabulary I

A child extends his vocabulary as he uses materials and equipment around the room such as a stop sign, nurse's hat, or magnifying glass. Locate some of these materials in a classroom and indicate how they are used.

Material	Description of how used	Vocabulary used by children	Suggestions for additional ways to extend vocabulary

Worksheet 18.12   Extending Vocabulary II

There are various ways in which children extend their vocabularies as they talk to themselves and others. Observe a child in a classroom. Make a running record of everything he says. Indicate age of child. Code each segment as follows: a) talked to himself; b) talked to children; and c) talked to adult.

Setting	Record of language (coded)

Worksheet 18.13   Oral Communication

As children work and play in a classroom they often talk with other children or an adult about what they are doing; for example, while painting at an easel one child calls to the teacher, "Look at this color I made!" Or, "My car went through the tunnel. Let's do it to yours." In a classroom observe children talking about what they are doing. Record their conversations.

Conversations with other child(ren):

Conversations with adult:

List three values that such conversations contribute to language development:

1.

2.

3.

Worksheet 18.14   Group Chants

As a child becomes more aware of sounds, he recognizes that language can be structured. Chanting is one way of playing with sounds. When children are at play, there will be some who will chant spontaneously; for example, "Chug, Chug, Chug," or "My car is rolling down the hill, my car is rolling down the hill," or "Whoops, whoops, whoopity whoops." Listen in a classroom as children play with language. What language patterns do you find them developing? Copy them below.

Create and record chants that you might use if you were playing with children.

Worksheet 18.15   Grammar

Children tend to employ their own grammatical constructions and sentence formations (e.g., "He sitted down," "I falled," "I taked it," "Give it me." Sometimes adults tend to correct children's grammar only to find the child repeating it in his own way. Listen to the conversations of children in a classroom. Record any constructions or word forms that appear to be unique to the way children use language.

Child	Language

Worksheet 18.16   Elaboration

Children often use a minimum of words because they have not acquired a large vocabulary or learned to combine adjectives, nouns, adverbs, verbs, and other parts of speech. Sometimes a teacher will elaborate upon what a child said, not for the purpose of correction but rather to enhance vocabulary. This may or may not be noticed by a child. For example, "See my truck!" "Yes, I see that big red truck." Or, in response to a child's comment, "My car is going down the hill," the teacher adds, "Yes, your car is going down the ramp rapidly."

    Observe as many children as you can and record children's statements and teachers' elaborations. In instances where the teacher does not elaborate, indicate your own elaborations of the child's statements. (Check those that are your own.)

Child's statement	Teacher's elaboration of statement
1.	
2.	
3.	

Worksheet 18.17   Tape Recorder

When a child has an opportunity to speak into a tape recorder, hear his own voice and words repeated, and realize that others can hear and understand these words, he becomes enthusiastic about what language can do.

Introduce a child to a tape recorder. Turn it on and engage in conversation with him. Rewind it, and play back. Record the conversation and describe verbal and nonverbal reactions of the child.

Conversation	Child's verbal and nonverbal reactions

What learnings might be developed through the use of a tape recorder?

Worksheet 18.18   Figure-Ground

Reading requires that a child be able to see the printed word against the background of the paper. Look for places in a room where children have opportunities for discriminating figure from ground. List the places in the area below.

Select one area in the room where you see an activity requiring figure-ground discrimination. Using words and drawings, describe in detail what takes place in a five-minute interval.

Worksheet 18.19　　　　　　　　　　　　Configuration

Before a child understands that shapes can be formed into symbols and that symbols can be read, he can profit from concrete experiences with the objects that these shapes symbolize. In a classroom there are many opportunities for creating shapes. Through these experiences a child becomes aware of what shapes are. Observe in a classroom and note the shapes a child creates.

Location in room	Describe way in which child creates shapes (use words and/or drawings)

As you look around the room, what other materials and equipment do you see that could be used in creating symbols?

Worksheet 18.20　　　　　　　　　　　　Matching and Sorting

Matching and sorting activities give children opportunities for developing categories and classifying objects. Seeing similarities and differences in letters is important in reading. Observe in a classroom and describe activities in matching and sorting.

Child-initiated activities	Teacher-initiated activities

What other possibilities could be included?

Worksheet 18.21   Classification

Classifying objects by such categories as shape, size, and color can serve as a prelude to seeing differences among p's, b's, and d's. Describe with words and drawings the provisions that have been made for classification experiences in the block area.

Describe possibilities for experiences in classification in the housekeeping area.

Leaf through magazines and catalogs. What do you find that could be used for classification as children prepare scrapbooks?

During your participation, sit with a child or a small group of children and look through magazines for pictures that are of interest to them. Select one category of pictures to put in a scrapbook (to be completed at a later date).

Worksheet 18.22   Classification Skills through Games

When children reach a certain stage of readiness, they can practice a skill through the use of games. Lotto-type games are popular in many classrooms. Examine the games used in the room to see if there are any Lotto-type games. List them below.

Make a list of other categories that would be suitable for Lotto games, such as dogs, things that fly, etc.

Using cutout illustrations or your own, make a Lotto game for two, three, or four children to use in the classroom.

Make a checklist for evaluating the game. Using this checklist, observe children as they play the game.

Worksheet 18.23   Precut Letters

As children handle three-dimensional letters (made of metal, cardboard, wood, sandpaper, etc.), they are able not only to see the shapes but to feel them as well. The sense of touch gives an added dimension to the experience. Children will play with letters in many ways. Some children will group them by shape, some will make the sounds of the letters, and others will identify them by their names. Sometimes children will group letters without relation to words, while others will make words.

Observe children at a table where there are precut letters. Describe ways in which they use the letters.

Ways children play with letters:

Words children make with letters:

What question, if any, might you raise that would extend the play?

Worksheet 18.24   Phonics

Children enjoy playing with sounds. If a teacher has a keen awareness of the nature of the sounds that constitute phonics, then children's play becomes the basis for a phonics program. Whenever children have freedom to make sounds, they have an opportunity to transform sounds into patterns. A teacher can encourage rhyming final sounds, such as *sing, ding, ling, ping*. A teacher can also help children develop an awareness of initial sounds, such as *stop, step, sting*.

Observe in a classroom and identify ways in which children play with voice sounds. Check those that were teacher-initiated.

Initial sounds

Final sounds

Describe situations in which a teacher might initiate play with language.

Worksheet 18.25   **Stages of Readiness**

Children gradually develop readiness for reading. Before a child can read a symbol with meaning, he needs experiences with concrete objects, three-dimensional representations, and two-dimensional representations.

   List the places in a classroom where you see children with concrete objects, three-dimensional representations, two-dimensional representations, and symbols.

1. Concrete object

2. Three-dimensional representation of object

3. Two-dimensional representation of object

4. Symbol

Identify one object for which you are able to find examples in the other three stages.

Worksheet 18.26   **Teacher-Made Books**

A child becomes increasingly impressed with the power of his own language when he sees his own words written down. Often a teacher adds dignity to a story or incident a child relates when he puts the story into a specially prepared book.

   Prepare a bound book. Take a child's dictation using a lined pad. Transfer the dictation to the bound volume, leaving room for pictures. You may use cutout pictures, draw your own, or use photographs to illustrate the book. If a child indicates a desire to draw his own pictures, permit him to do so. Read the book to the child. What values do you feel this experience had for the child?

Worksheet 18.27   **Experience Charts**

An experience chart that recalls past events provides a medium through which children can see their own words written down. They see their own words put into sentences with punctuation marks. They see the teacher record the letters by moving her hand from left to right. In a classroom, observe activities that you consider suitable for an experience chart. List them.

Select one of the above activities and using 18″ × 24″ lined paper (where available) and a heavy marking pen, record the events. Copy the chart in the space below.

What evidence was there that the event chosen really met the needs and interests of the children?

Worksheet 18.28   **Typewriter**

Reading requires specific concepts and skills. Consider the concepts and skills that may be developed as a child explores with the typewriter. List concepts and skills required for reading. Observe a child at a typewriter. Indicate age of child. Make a record of exactly what he does (e.g., which keys he presses, how often, and other explorations he makes with the machine).

Identify the concepts and skills that may be strengthened in this process.

Worksheet 18.29   Appreciation for Books I

The kinds of experiences with books that children have in a classroom can help develop an appreciation and positive attitude for reading. If reading provides pleasure and information for a child, he will be eager to repeat the experience.

Observe children with books. Describe children's behaviors that indicate appreciation for books.

1.

2.

3.

4.

5.

6.

Worksheet 18.30   Appreciation for Books II

Children like to handle and look at books. They enjoy having stories read to them. Observe in a classroom to see what use is made of the library area. Describe:

Examples of children looking at books alone	Examples of children looking at books with another child(ren)	Examples of children looking at books with teacher

Worksheet 18.31   Eye-Hand Coordination

Writing requires eye-hand coordination. Look for places in a classroom where children have opportunities to develop eye-hand coordination. List the places in the area below.

Select one area in the room where you saw an activity requiring eye-hand coordination. Describe in detail what took place in a five-minute interval, using words and drawings.

Worksheet 18.32   Written Communication

Before children write, they scribble, draw, and then copy letters or whole words. Observe children in a classroom. Describe four examples of children engaged in scribbling, drawing, or copying. Indicate age of child.

1.

2.

3

4

Worksheet 18.33　　　　　　　　Keeping Records

When children see information recorded and these records referred to, they become aware of some of the values of record keeping and eventually keep records of their own. Sometimes teachers initiate this activity, and other times children initiate their own record keeping. Observe in a classroom for both types of situations mentioned above and describe them.

Situations that teacher has structured for recording information (e.g., child dictations to teacher, attendance chart, or sign-out sheet for books).

Situations where child(ren) initiate their own records (e.g., itemizing grocery list in dramatic play, or copying a recipe).

List additional teacher-structured activities you've observed that contribute to children's experience with record keeping:

List additional child-initiated instances of record keeping:

1.

2.

3.

4.

Worksheet 18.34　　　　　　　　Manuscript Writing I

When a teacher communicates messages in manuscript form, children often ask to have them read. When a message is of special interest to a child, such as "Happy Birthday, John," a child may choose to copy it. As children develop motor skills used for writing, they like to practice and sometimes copy the same words or sentences again and again. This is particularly true after a child has learned to identify his name.

　　　　Observe in a classroom. Indicate what words or sentences are displayed that children might seek to copy.

Area of room	Words or sentences that can be copied

Worksheet 18.35   Manuscript Writing II

Since a teacher's writing serves as a model, it is important for a teacher to write correctly at all times. Manuscript writing is the accepted form in most schools. Below is a sample of upper and lowercase letters. Practice these as many times as needed to acquire the skill necessary for speed and accuracy in writing. Use additional paper if necessary.

Uppercase:

A B C D E F G
H I J K L M N
O P Q R S T
U V W X Y Z

Lowercase:

a b c d e f g h i
j k l m n o p q r
s t u v w x y z

Write your name and one sentence in manuscript form.

Worksheet 18.36   Role of the Teacher

The teacher is one of the key figures in the development of language competencies. The arrangement of the room, the selection of materials, and teacher interaction with the children all influence the language arts program. Describe these factors and their relationship to the four aspects of language.

Reading

Writing

Listening

Speaking

Objectives	Behavior Indicators	Worksheets
To identify the components of the the scientific process.	Complete Post Test 1 satisfactorily.	Read this chapter on Science.
To develop an awareness of the ways in which children gain skills in observation.	Complete Post Test 1 satisfactorily. In participation, student provides experiences for observation.	19.1, 19.2, 19.3, 19.4, 19.23
To recognize the types of problems children raise and the ways in which they identify them.	Complete Post Test 1 satisfactorily.	19.4, 19.5
To identify hypotheses that children formulate.	Complete Post Test 1 satisfactorily.	19.6
To describe the ways in which children test hypotheses.	Complete Post 1 satisfactorily.	19.7
To describe the methods of measurement that children devise.	Complete Post Test 1 satisfactorily.	19.8
To list ways in which children's experiments can be recorded.	Complete Post Test 1 satisfactorily.	19.9, 19.20
To identify evidences that children draw conclusions and make generalizations.	Complete Post Test 1 satisfactorily.	19.11, 19.20
To identify ways in which children evaluate their own behaviors as they proceed with a scientific method.	Complete Post Test 1 satisfactorily.	19.10
To identify the roles of the teacher in fostering scientific inquiry and problem-solving techniques.	Complete Post Test 2 satisfactorily.	19.12, 19.14, 19.15, 19.16, 19.17, 19.21, 19.22, 19.24
To describe ways in which children can be helped to develop attitudes toward and appreciation of scientific processes.	Complete Post Test 3 satisfactorily.	19.12
To identify which scientific concepts are suitable for young children to learn.	Complete Post Tests 4 and 5 satisfactorily. During participation, engage a small group of children in an experience that deals with a scientific concept.	19.13, 19.14, 19.15, 19.18, 19.19

Other(s).

SCIENCE 19

Pre/Post Tests

1. Name four kinds of problem-solving experiences boys and girls encounter as they interact with materials and with each other. Indicate the components of scientific processes involved.

2. Identify roles of the teacher in fostering scientific inquiry and problem-solving techniques.

3. Describe ways in which children can be helped to develop positive attitudes toward and appreciation of scientific processes.

4. Identify the scientific concepts that are suitable for young children.

5. List five materials usually found in a classroom for young children and describe how scientific concepts can be developed as these materials are used.

Very often a science program for young children centers around a table that contains plants, rocks, shells, or magnets. At best, this approach to the study of science leads to talking about the objects, handling them, describing them, drawing comparisons, performing simple experiments, and making charts. Children are already curious, and when a teacher also has enthusiasm, important learnings can result. However, science is much more than a study of natural and physical phenomena and laboratory experiments. It deals with processes through which predictions are made, tested, and applied. It is a way of thinking.

A good science program includes all the materials that children use and is incorporated in every part of a school program. A teacher who sees the broader aspects of science makes use of the whole environment. Even at an early age, children learn to make use of scientific processes in every part of their living as they engage in problem-solving activities.

If children are constantly told what to do and how to do it without having the opportunity to make discoveries, learning is rote and does not lead to further inquiry. A child who has experiences that allow him to make discoveries develops the skills he will need for independent thinking, and with independent thinking, he can make use of scientific processes of problem solving.

There are many opportunities in an early childhood program for children to gain experience in all of the components of scientific processes. They can identify problems, formulate and test hypotheses, devise methods for measurement, record their results, draw conclusions, and make generalizations based on these conclusions.

Life consists of facing problems and solving them, and there are times when everyone uses trial and error in finding solutions. Children, too, begin with trial and error but can move on to the use of scientific procedures in solving problems within their own comprehension. In the classroom there are problems in abundance for the child, such as finding a way to climb to the top of the hanging rope; balancing himself as he walks across the log; rolling the clay into a ball; choosing a bowl that will accommodate the ingredients for a birthday cake; finding an easier way to put the blocks away or selecting a nail long enough to go through two boards.

IDENTIFYING PROBLEMS

Young children identify problems in different ways. When working with sand, a child may say,

"I'm trying to keep the tunnel from falling in."
Another child, while playing at a water table,
may say, "I don't want my boat to sink." While
dressing up in the housekeeping area, a child trying to complete his outfit asks, "What can I wear
so I'll look like a policeman?" These problems
have been stated verbally. Although many
children do not express their problems with
words, when observing their behavior it is possible to see that they are busy solving them; for example, when the dough is too hard, a child adds
some water to it; a child walks around the room
trying to find objects that a magnet will attract; a
child tries to fit a piece of puzzle into its frame;
or a child tries to jump across the sand pit.

FORMULATING HYPOTHESES

In an early childhood classroom children have
many opportunities to formulate hypotheses.
Given a bit of encouragement, they will take
great pleasure in doing so. Some of these
hypotheses are verbalized. While working with
clay a child may say to another, "If you put water
on your clay it will get softer and be easier to
use." As the paint drips down the paper a child
may say, "If I don't put the whole brush in the
paint maybe it won't drip." Finding some beans
that a teacher had in a container, one child says,
"If we plant them they'll grow."

Children do not always verbalize hypotheses. If a teacher sees a child initiate the
feeding of a turtle, or put paste on a colored
shape, he cannot know for certain what his
hypotheses are but he can surmise that he is formulating the hypothesis that "If I feed the turtle
he will grow" or, "If I put paste on the shape it
will stick to my paper." A teacher, seeing a child
about to place a quadruple block on top of a high
stack of unit blocks, may raise the question,
"What do you think will happen if you put that
block there?"

TESTING HYPOTHESES

Children often plan to test their own hypotheses.
Sometimes this process is self-initiated and
sometimes it is initiated by a teacher. Three
children are constructing a tall building in the
block area. They have a problem. Can they add
another story to the building? They hypothesize
that they can, but how? Then they make alternative suggestions. "We could call Alan, he's
tall. Maybe he could reach it." "Call the
teacher." "Get a chair and maybe I can reach
it." Now, the big decision. Which shall they try
first?

In another instance children want to get
water so that they can bathe the baby. The problem is how to get the water to the basin in the
housekeeping area without spilling it. They look
helpless. They don't know quite what to do. The
teacher says, "How could we do it?" They begin
to look around the room. Somebody suggests
that the teacher carry the water but others reject
the idea because they want to do it themselves.
One child spies a can on the shelf. Then he sees a
pitcher. "Which would work better?" They
decide on the pitcher and proceed to put their
plan into action.

One child is working on a puzzle of a boy
with red trousers. He hypothesizes that the long
red pieces must be the legs. He tests his
hypothesis and proves it. Another child picks up
a handful of pegs and decides that he has enough
red pegs to make a border around the frame. His
hypothesis is disproved and he decides to finish
with a different color.

DEVELOPING METHODS
OF MEASUREMENT

As a child tests, he develops his own units of
measurement. Sometimes he uses parts of his
body, for instance, when he measures the span of
the sandpit as he places one foot in front of the
other. Sometimes a child matches one object
against another, for instance, when he selects
pages that will fit the bound cover for his book.
At snack time two children measure their celery
to see who has the longer piece.

RECORDING

Sometimes a teacher records children's heights. A
strip of masking tape attached to the wall will
keep the record. Children mark the height of
radish sprouts on a tongue depresser. One child
makes an interesting pattern while stringing
wooden beads. He records it by copying the pattern on paper with crayons. In one classroom a
small group of children returned from the
bakery. A few days later they recorded their experience by reproducing the bakery with blocks,
recollecting what they had seen. Another child,
at the easel, recorded his interpretation of the
bakery with paint.

MAKING GENERALIZATIONS

As children devise simple experiments they draw conclusions. However, it is important, especially in the beginning stages of experimentation, to be aware that children do overgeneralize. Children learn that plants must be watered regularly if they are to grow, but they often keep watering plants and soon discover that they have died. They have overgeneralized about plants needing water. Or, the children have devised a means for transporting the blocks back to the storage shelves and manage to do so successfully—"It works." The next time they load many more blocks onto their contraption. They can move it but the pile falls. They have learned that this was a good way to move blocks only under special circumstances.

EVALUATING PROCESSES

Evaluation is important in any scientific process if one is to improve upon predictions or devise better ways of doing things. There must be a careful examination of the processes that have been used and of the end product. This often involves a recapitulation of all the steps in a process. A child has created a color at the easel. The teacher asks, "How did you get that color?" At a clay table a child says, "I like it. Do you know how I did it? I'll show you. I'll do it again." "How can we get this building down without a crash?" Observing a design on a peg board, the teacher says, "What an interesting design. What made you think of that? What were you trying to do?" A child has produced several patterns with one-inch colored cubes. The teacher remarks, "Which one do you like best? What do you like about it?" The children have built a structure between two buildings. "How did you build that?"

Children don't always use every step of a scientific process but sometimes they do use all of them. "I'm going to build a garage for my cars," says Jerry (stating the problem). "I can make it with the blocks" (identifying the hypothesis). "I can make it with these little blocks. We'll put in doors and make a high roof" (making plans for testing the hypothesis). Hillary joins him. They build the foundation; then they try to push the car through the door (testing the hypothesis). The car won't go in. Jerry has not yet achieved his goal. The two children tear the structure down and start all over again. This time the car goes in (retesting the hypothesis). They decide to make the roof out of long blocks but the blocks are not long enough (testing the hypothesis). They give

up in disgust. At this point the teacher asks, "What were you trying to do?" "We're trying to put a roof on this garage." The teacher asks, "What have you tried?" "This isn't long enough" (conclusion). "What else could you try?" (seeking alternatives). As they explore in the room they find a piece of oak tag, a board in the wood box, and a blanket (assessing resources). The teacher asks, "Which do you think might work best?" The child responds, "The blanket is too soft. The car couldn't go under it. The board isn't wide enough. I think I'll try this paper" (devising measurement in the process of planning and predicting results). They try the oak tag. "It works! It works! Look!" (evaluation). "I found a roof and it's not even blocks! A lot of things can make a roof" (drawing conclusions and making generalizations). The child dictates a story of how he made his garage with a roof (record of experiment).

DEVELOPING SKILLS OF OBSERVATION

Skills of observation provide the means for collecting data and, therefore, it is necessary to observe accurately. Not only must one be able to see, hear, smell, taste, and touch, but one must be able to describe these observations precisely. The more fully a child becomes involved in this process, the richer the experience. When observations are detailed and accurate, then relationships, comparisons, likenesses and differences, causes and effects, changes and trends, become clearer. An important part of observation is developing the ability to identify characteristic features of objects such as shape, size, color, and weight.

It is important for children to become aware of the network of interactions in the natural world around them. In order to understand the concept of interdependence, they must learn to see the relationships that exist in nature: A seed is planted and grows; a guinea pig eats this food to live.

While children are engaged in these processes of inquiry, they accumulate a great storehouse of information. It is impossible to engage in scientific processes without drawing upon many resources. A child brings facts and concepts with him from previous experiences. The reliability and validity of these facts and concepts must be checked. How does he know? How did he find out? There are also facts and concepts that must be sought and determined before decisions are made. Relationships must be drawn between information newly acquired and information already assimilated.

A good science program does not deal with isolated facts. When children are active participants, information that they gather has meaning because it arises from real need. When a child has had experiences with water, he becomes familar with some of its properties and uses it in different ways. Because a child has played with water using funnels and tubes, he knows what some of the possibilities are for transferring water from one container to another. He applies and uses previously acquired information as he builds new information.

Three-, four-, and five-year-old children acquire a temendous amount of information through firsthand experience. They accumulate knowledge about gravity, centrifugal force, machines (involving levers, wheels, and fulcrums), conservation, reproduction, air, stars and moon, sound, light, weather, the habits of living things, the care of plants, and transformation of matter (botany, geology, zoology, chemistry, astronomy, physics, and geography). Making these associations is a basic part of observation. When a child sees a leaf that looks like a hand, he is relating this observation to many previous experiences.

DEVELOPING SKILLS OF CLASSIFICATION

Children extend their vocabularies as they learn to describe what they see in precise terminology. Collecting rocks is an exciting activity for boys and girls. Interest in geology is expressed as they compare size, weight, shape, and texture of the rocks. A rock may be shaped like an egg, a banana, a head, or a ball. It may be rough or smooth.

On a playground, children hunt for leaves. "Look at this one. It's more pointy." "Mine is round." "This one is green." "So is this but it's a different shape."

As children observe, they find their own ways of grouping and ordering materials they collect. When they are encouraged to find their own categories, they try many ways of matching and grouping. Each child takes pride in his own ways of organizing. He develops his own systems for sets and subsets. He arranges and rearranges materials, designing his own patterns. Sometimes the child arranges objects in a series according to size (seriation).

As children put blocks away, they sort according to dimensions of size and shape and thereby learn to classify. As they compare the shapes of blocks, they become aware of the relationship of one block to another and eventually recognize that there is an order to this relationship, sometimes referred to as a system. Creative thinking leads to new forms of classification, and this in turn leads to new information. The discipline of biochemistry was developed when new relationships in matter were discovered and categorized.

STUDY TRIPS

The outdoors is an extension of the classroom. As a matter of fact, the classroom extends into the community. Many observations are made as children explore the environment in and around school. When trips are planned, groups should be limited to three or four children whenever possible, and certainly no more than six or seven. When a whole class goes on a trip, it is unrealistic to expect that every child will have an equal interest in or the same orientation toward the intended goals.

A large group requires additional supervision. When a large group goes on a study trip, the objectives must be different from what they would be if a few interested children were gathering information or making observatons.

As children make short excursions, either to look for something specific such as seeds, leaves, or insects, or to search for signs of changes taking place in nature, they may collect items that they observe carefully, identify, label, and classify. They become aware of seasonal changes, changes over the course of time, chemical changes, and changes in the weather. They watch the leaves grow on the apple tree and then watch the blossoms form, first in bud and then in full flower. Water outdoors has become ice by the next morning. Snow on boots melts when a child walks into the building.

Because there is so much to explore near at hand, there is seldom any reason for young children to go very far on their trips. In most cases, written consent of the parents is required if children leave the school.

DEVELOPING SELF–CONCEPT

Children take pride in knowing. They discover that knowledge is worth having, and there is great self-satisfaction in being able to apply what one knows in meeting new needs. Knowledge helps a child gain control over his immediate environment, both natural and human. A child who is in the habit of using his knowledge in scientific ways is not likely to retain the fears and superstitions of childhood. He develops added strength as he uses scientific systems, and he gains respect for knowledge as he learns how useful it is.

As children use scientific processes, they develop a sense of wonder. A child begins an appreciation of the order of the universe. This leads to valuing people in the universe with their likenesses and differences, and to appreciating nature and respecting materials. A child begins to feel comfortable despite the immensity of the universe. The stars may appear tiny and far away. Although he cannot understand the distances involved, he can accept these faraway stars as part of his world. He is also developing an awareness of himself in relation to the rest of the world.

Self-concept becomes more positive as a child sees himself in a mirror or studies himself in a photograph. He is proud when the sleeves of his coat become too short—four is very much older than three.

EQUIPMENT AND MATERIALS

There is a widespread misconception that a good science program requires a great quantity of expensive equipment. While magnets, magnifying glasses, incubators, dry-cell batteries, thermometers, and other such items can lead to valuable explorations, there are many equally valuable learnings to be gained as boys and girls work with other materials around the room.

When it is possible to have materials such as those mentioned above, they should be of high quality so that they perform the functions for which they are intended. If magnets do not have sufficient pull, the experience is frustrating and may lead to inaccurate conclusions. Since a hand lens is intended to magnify objects that are being observed, it needs to be strong and in good condition. If there are scratches on it, children may come to false conclusions about what they are observing. An incubator must satisfactorily control temperature, humidity, and insulation if eggs are to hatch. A dry cell must have enough voltage to make a bell ring or a light go on. It is frustrating and confusing to wire a circuit and have nothing happen. If a thermometer is not accurate, it should not be used. Temperatures should be clearly marked on a thermometer so that children can read them easily. When these

materials are carefully stored and handled with care, they last longer and children are more likely to develop respect for them.

Planting can be done in a garden. It can also be done in window boxes, flowerpots of various sizes, or cans. Seeds that sprout quickly such as carrots, radishes, lettuce, and grass are most desirable because children can see results in a short period of time. Children enjoy watching pumpkin seeds, birdseed, and beans sprout when they are planted on a wet sponge or wet cotton. An avocado seed, sweet potato, or carrot top provides an attractive plant for a classroom. When narcissus bulbs are placed in glass jars, children can observe growth from both the roots and tops. These plants must be located so that they will receive the proper light, heat, and air, and yet be visible for children to look at and enjoy. Outdoors, children will take an interest in seeds that are blown through the air.

When animals such as guinea pigs, gerbils, or hamsters are kept in a classroom, they require appropriate housing. They must have proper heat and light and be out of the line of traffic. Cages should be constructed in such a way that they can be cleaned easily. A sliding tray to catch droppings is usually satisfactory. A mesh wire cage permits visibility, and a removable top allows for easy feeding. In many classrooms, arrangements are made to have animals on a short-term basis. Some teachers feel that children's interests are thereby heightened and the animals are not taken for granted. There is great excitement as children study the eating and drinking habits of animals and take care of them in their temporary habitats. In some schools children play with the animals, while in others they are not permitted to handle them. There is something to be said for each point of view, particularly in instances where close supervision is not possible.

Many classrooms contain a terrarium and an aquarium. Where these exist, great care must be given to keeping them functioning and attractive. Negative learnings are likely to ensue if equipment is not cared for properly. Actually, there is a difference of opinion concerning the value of either a terrarium or an aquarium for very young children. The possible learnings can be gained from other experiences, and these pieces of equipment take up table, shelf, or floor space.

Anthills may be observed outdoors. Sometimes specially prepared ant farms are kept indoors. A spider web in a classroom provides an opportunity for observation and learning.

Of course, there is the ever-present air both inside and outside the room. Children have a good time as they play with pinwheels and kites. They blow bubbles and even blow up balloons. They can feel the wind on their faces as they run, and they either gain momentum or experience resistance, depending upon whether they are running with the wind or against it. However, young children do not understand what air is.

Children's books are excellent resource materials. Picture books can be consulted in order to gain a specific bit of information or simply to stimulate the imagination and curiosity. Some stories that incorporate scientific concepts in beautiful and artistic ways are *Play with Me* by Marie Hall Ets and *The Snowy Day* by Ezra Keats.

ROLE OF THE TEACHER

A teacher plays an important role in encouraging a child's love of learning. His attitude is an important factor in determining children's attitudes. If a teacher really believes that discovery is important and the processes of inquiry are basic, then he will provide sufficient time for children to explore the materials thoroughly so that they can become familiar with their properties.

Water changes shape and form at different temperatures. Rocks are hard and heavy. Corn kernels pop in intense heat. A teacher needs to be alert to the opportunities for experimentation in a classroom. He may ask a child a question such as "How can you find out?" He may make a suggestion such as "Let's try it." He may add a piece of equipment such as a flashlight, or rearrange materials already in the room by placing shells on top of a table where they can be handled.

If a teacher is an observer, a questioner, and an experimenter, and values these processes, then he is likely to help children use them as a way of gathering information. He helps children say exactly what they want to find out (stating the problem) and encourages them to find ways of doing it (designing the experiment). A teacher may sometimes stimulate children's curiosity by raising probing questions. "How did you do that?" Teachers' questions and statements should be kept at a minimum, giving children opportunities to formulate their own. While all children will not use correct terminology, if teachers use it, then they are more likely to do so. If a teacher is a good listener, children are likely to verbalize their wonderings.

A teacher should have the steps of scientific processes clearly in mind, yet he should not expect children to follow all of them in each exploration. He can sometimes help call attention to a possible procedure by such comments as, "What are you trying to do?" "What do you think you'll find out?" "How can we find out?" "How long should it take?" "Will it work this way if you do it again?" A teacher can also call attention to a process after a child has gone through it. "How did you do it?" "Did you expect that to happen?" Children often take pleasure in recapitulating an experience, and this intensifies the meaning.

Experiments that children undertake will usually be of short duration. Concept formation is gradual for children, who need time to internalize experiences. Often children appear knowledgeable because they repeat the right words when, in actuality, they do not yet comprehend the concept. "That star is in infinity." "How long would it take to get there?" "One hour."

If we introduce too many materials, ideas, or activities at any given time, children may be overstimulated and not be able to concentrate on anything. They are not able to separate the figure from the ground.

A teacher who respects materials serves as a model to children to learn to appreciate and care for tools, equipment, and living things. He places a magnet back in the tray after using it, measures a quantity of food for the guinea pig, and carefully waters the plants.

An alert teacher will capitalize on events of the day: noting the birth of a sibling (reproduction), experimenting with the stability and equilibrium of a block structure (physics), mixing powder paint with water (chemistry), making an animal cage more livable (ecology), testing the friction of a sandblock against wood (physics), building a river in the sand (geography).

Occasionally, an animal or fish in the room, or a person known to children, dies. It is important for a teacher to face this event squarely and understand that because children do not fully comprehend the implications of death, they accept it differently. Children should not be shielded from this very normal part of the life cycle nor should teachers dwell on the subject.

The needs of each child must be considered as equipment is arranged in a room in such a manner that ongoing experiences may be elaborated upon and intensified.

The teacher knows the school, the community, and the resources available, such as the custodian's room, the nurse's office, and the bakery down the street. The custodian, the nurse, and the baker all become teachers when called on to demonstrate or answer questions in their fields. The teacher helps children become discriminating about sources of authority when he asks, "How would he know?" "Is this the best person to ask?"

Given a resourceful and knowledgeable teacher, a dynamic science program can be developed in any classroom.

ADDITIONAL RESOURCES

Cohen, Dorothy H., and Rudolph, Marguerita. *Kindergarten and Early Schooling*. Englewood Cliffs, N.J.: Prentice-Hall, 1977. Chapter 11, "Science Experiences for Children and Teachers," pp. 180–209.

Hildebrand, Verna. *Introduction to Early Childhood Education*. 2nd ed. New York: Macmillan, 1976. Chapter 8, "Fostering Mental Growth Through the Sciences," pp. 176–217.

Isaacs, Nathan. *Children's Ways of Knowing*. New York: Teachers College Press, 1974. "Children's 'Why' Questions," pp. 13–64, and "Early Scientific Trends in Children," pp. 81–97.

Lay, Margaret Z., and Dopyera, John E. *Becoming a Teacher of Young Children*. Lexington, Mass.: D.C. Heath, 1977. Chapter 9, "Resourcefulness with Animals," pp. 245–272.

Leeper, Sarah Hammond; Skipper, Dora; and Witherspoon, Ralph. *Good Schools for Young Children*. 4th ed. New York: Macmillan, 1978. Chapter 16, "Science," pp. 359–375.

Moffitt, Mary W. "Children Learn About Science Through Block Building." In *The Block Book*, Elisabeth S. Hersch (ed.). Washington, D.C.: National Association for the Education of Young Children, 1974.

Moffitt, Mary W., and Swedlow, Rita. "Dynamics of Play for Learning." In *Play: Children's Business*. Washington, D.C.: Association for Childhood Education International, 1974.

Neuman, Donald. "Sciencing for Young Children." In *Ideas That Work with Young Children*, Katherine Read Baker (ed.). Washington, D.C.: National Association for the Education of Young Children, 1972.

Rudolph, Marguerita. *From Hand to Head—A Handbook for Teachers of Preschool Programs*. New York: McGraw-Hill, 1973. Chapter 4, "Animals In and Out of the Classroom," pp. 19–31; Chapter 7, "Seeds and Plants; Flowers and Fruits," pp. 54–60; Chapter 8, "Transportation: Everything Goes," pp. 61–69, and Chapter 15, "Striving for Concepts in Preschool Education," pp. 141–148.

Spodek, Bernard. *Teaching in the Early Years*. Englewood Cliffs, N.J.: Prentice-Hall, 1972. Chapter 6, "Science in the Early Years," pp. 113–135.

Todd, Vivian Edmiston, and Heffernan, Helen. *The Years Before School*. 3rd ed. New York: Macmillan, 1970. Chapter 9, "Building Science Concepts," pp. 322–373.

Wills, Clarice Dechant, and Lindberg, Lucile. *Kindergarten for Today's Children*. Chicago: Follett, 1967. Chapter 9, "Science for Children under Six," pp. 131–148.

Film (16 mm). *Concept Development in Outdoor Play*. New York: Campus Films, 1974.

Film (16 mm). *Foundations of Science*. New York: Campus Films, 1977.

Worksheet 19.1   Observation Skills

(This worksheet is appropriate for use when only one observation is being made in this area.)
In many classrooms, observation skills are encouraged through a teacher's responses to children and by the selection and arrangement of materials. For example, a teacher may show interest in response to a child's observation, or raise a question about the observation, or encourage accurate reporting using correct terminology. Observe all areas of a classroom for ways in which a child's interest and ability to observe are encouraged by materials, arrangement, and teacher role.

Illustration I

Illustration II

Illustration III

Worksheet 19.2   Observing Growing Things

(In order to complete this worksheet, a student must spend a little time in the classroom a few days prior to the time when the observation is to be made.)
Talk with a small group of children about an experience with growing things you had with them earlier (e.g., planting birdseed on a paper towel or beans on wet sponge). What questions did you raise? Record as much as you can of the conversation; underline the parts that indicate an awareness of change taking place on the part of the children.

Worksheet 19.3   Observing Relationships

As children classify objects or phenomena, they learn to observe and report their findings more accurately if they are encouraged to see the variety of categories that are possible. For example, leaves may be classified according to color, shape, or size; a rainy day may be classified as pouring, drizzling, or misty.

   Observe children classifying objects and record the different frames of reference from which their categories are derived; for example, texture, shape, color.

Objects classified	Categories

Worksheet 19.4   Problem Solving

Problem-solving processes may differ from person to person. Observe two children in the room to determine what their learning styles are. For example, does learning appear to be strictly trial and error, or does there appear to be a setting up and testing of an hypothesis (probably nonverbal)? Describe the problem-solving activities of each child, and indicate the processes that appear to be involved.

Child 1 (age)

Child 2 (age)

Worksheet 19.5   Problem Solving—Identifying a Problem

Problem solving is an important part of the learning process. One of the essential elements of problem solving is stating the problem. Children often set up their own problems and try to find ways to solve them.

Look around the room and see if you can find places where children are posing their own problems and attempting to find solutions. Describe them.

Area I

Area II

Area III

Worksheet 19.6   Formulating Hypotheses

As children work on a problem, they often predict possible solutions. "What will happen if I rub the point on the paper?" "What will happen if I hold the hammer this way?" Observe for fifteen minutes and describe as many situations as you can in which children appear to be formulating hypotheses (either verbal or nonverbal).

Ways in which the teacher has structured the environment to make hypothesis-forming possible.

1.

2.

3.

4.

5.

Make other suggestions.

1.

2.

3.

Worksheet 19.7   Testing Hypotheses

Making plans for and testing hypotheses are an integral part of any scientific process. Some of the simplest acts of children incorporate these activities. As they become more experienced, they verbalize their proposed solutions. ''We need a ramp to get the cars up. Maybe this board will do it. No, it doesn't work. Let's try this triangle.''

Observe children involved in two of the following activities: playing with puzzles, finger painting, block building, woodworking.

Evidence of making plans for testing hypotheses	Hypotheses that seemed to be involved

Worksheet 19.8   Methods of Measurement

In adult life we use measuring tools such as a ruler, yardstick, quart, and cup frequently. Each of these was developed in response to an immediate need, utilizing materials at hand (for instance, the length of the king's foot became our foot measure). Children, too, measure, using materials they find at hand. A child will measure the length of a nail against the thickness of the wood to see if it is the correct length; a child will stand next to another child to see if he is as tall as the other one.

Observe in the classroom for illustrations of ways in which children measure. What reason was there for measuring? What materials were used?

Need	Materials used

Worksheet 19.9   Recording Experiments

Children's experiments can be recorded, sometimes by the teacher and sometimes by the children themselves, who may paint a picture, dictate a story for a chart or book, or take a photograph. What can be recorded can be recalled, repeated, and elaborated on. It serves as a history of experience. Select one experiment that you observe a child engaged in and together record it or observe him recording it by himself. Indicate age of child. Describe the experiment.

What values might this recording have for the child?

Worksheet 19.10   Evaluation

Evaluation can be incidental or planned; in most classrooms for young children we expect to find both types. For example, as a child evaluates his art work, he exclaims, "Look what a glorious color I made!" or, "This didn't drip!" Or a teacher may ask, "How did you get this tall building to stay up?" List illustrations of formal and informal evaluations you have observed.

Formal evaluations	Informal evaluations

Worksheet 19.11   Conclusions and Generalizations

People are constantly making generalizations, but often these are based on too little data. The object of using scientific processes is to make data available from which to draw generalizations and make decisions. Observe children as they engage in various activities in a room. In which of the following areas do children seem to have been making generalizations, and what were the generalizations? Did the conclusions seem to be based on sufficient evidence or on overgeneralizing?

	Description	Evidence of overgeneralizing
Easel		
Finger painting		
Woodworking		
Block building		
Puzzles		
Manipulative materials		
Water play		
Dough		
Clay		
Other		

Worksheet 19.12   Attitudes and Appreciations

Children bring many interests with them, and their interests broaden and multiply as they come in contact with teachers, other children, and materials. Observe a teacher in a classroom and note what he says or does to intensify or broaden children's interests.

Description of children's interests	Description of teacher's behaviors	Other possible interventions

What did the teacher do to stimulate further interest?

What additional stimulation would you recommend?

Worksheet 19.13   Scientific Concepts

A child's world reflects many scientific concepts. His future learnings will be based on the concepts that he develops in his early years. As children have experiences with materials, concepts are clarified. Observe in a classroom to see what concepts can be developed. List in the appropriate boxes those scientific concepts that may be developed in this setting with the available materials.

Astronomy	Physics
Botany	Physiology
Chemistry	Zoology
Geology	Other

Worksheet 19.14   Changes

The phenomenon of change is an important part of science. Children themselves are growing and changing. They are surrounded by other things that change, such as weather and the seasons, and by chemical changes. Observe a child's awareness of the changes taking place around him and record them.

Nature of change	Child's apparent awareness or lack of awareness of the change

What roles might a teacher play in providing experiences in change?

Worksheet 19.15   Classification

Classification is fundamental in every scientific inquiry. As knowledge is ordered, new discoveries are made. List four types of materials (living or nonliving things) that lend themselves to classification.

I. Item:	II. Item:
How classified:	How classified:
What other classification possibilities are there?	What other classification possibilities are there?
III. Item:	IV. Item:
How classified:	How classified:
What other classification possibilities are there?	What other classification possibilities are there?

Worksheet 19.16   Equipment and Phenomena

Most science experiences for young children involve the materials and phenomena, such as the weather, growing plants, and rocks, that they come in contact with in their daily living. Occasionally, there are pieces of scientific equipment that may enhance the program if used with discretion; for example, a hand lens, a magnet, or a prism.

Observe in a classroom and on a playground for examples noted below.

1. Objects and equipment that encourage scientific investigation but are not considered to be scientific.

2. Objects and equipment that are ordinarily considered to be scientific.

3. Natural phenomena that stimulate scientific investigation.

Worksheet 19.17   Study Trips

Plan a study trip. Confine it to the school building or the adjoining grounds. In planning the trip for a small group of children (no more than three or four), be sure that all arrangements have been made ahead of time. Discuss with the children the purpose of the trip. The children will be encouraged to watch for landmarks so that they will know their way back to the room. For example, the teacher may ask, ''How will we know when to turn the corner?'' A child might observe, ''It's near the room that has the pumpkin.'' Take a trip with a small group of children. Answer the following questions.

What landmarks did the children select?

Were they able to point out the return trip accurately?

What questions did children ask when they reached their destination?

What values do you feel were introduced or reinforced through the trip?

Worksheet 19.18   Animals in the Classroom

(This observation can be made only in a classroom where there is a live animal such as a tortoise, a hamster, or a gerbil.)
Much excitement is generated if an animal is brought into a classroom occasionally and left long enough to observe its eating habits, changes, or a birth. Observe children responding to an animal in the room. What parts of the life cycle are observable during this time? What scientific processes are involved? Record concepts that the children verbalize.

Record other concepts that might be learned.

Worksheet 19.19   Children's Books

Look through a classroom library. Find five books that contain science concepts. List the names of the books and authors below and state the concepts involved.

Name and author	Concepts
1.	
2.	
3.	
4	
5.	

Select one of the above books and read it to a child or a small group of children. Record any conversation that occurs before, during, or after the reading.

Worksheet 19.20   Planting

(This worksheet must be used over an extended period of time so that a plant can grow.)
When children plant things in a classroom, they gain experience in all of the components of the scientific process. Prepare a planting experience with children and record your observations.

Components of scientific process	Description of experience in terms of the component
Identify problem	
Identify hypothesis	
Make plans for testing hypothesis	
Test hypothesis (include method of measurement)	
Record experiments	
Generalizations	
Evaluation	

Worksheet 19.21   **Sensory Experiences**

The whole being is involved in learning. Information is channeled into the being through the senses. The quality of observations that children make are dependent upon their use of the five senses. Observe a group of children. What opportunities do they have for sensory experiences? Describe the opportunities in the appropriate spaces below:

Smelling

Seeing

Touching

Hearing

Tasting

Worksheet 19.22   Role of the Teacher I

Much of what a teacher says indicates his awareness of scientific concepts. A teacher who recognizes this will attempt to be accurate in everything that he says.

Transcribe all of what a teacher says in a fifteen-minute period. Underline words that describe or indicate awareness of a scientific concept or processes on the part of the teacher.

Worksheet 19.23   Role of the Teacher II

The quality of an activity is largely related to the quality of the questions asked. A teacher needs to ask some questions; however, if he asks all the questions, children will lack this skill that is so important in inquiry. Observe a teacher with children. Record the questions asked by teacher and children. What was the nature of the response engendered by the questions?

Teacher's questions	Nature of response
1.	
2.	
3.	
4.	

Children's questions	Nature of response
1.	
2.	
3.	
4.	

Worksheet 19.24   Role of the Teacher III

Some of the behaviors we might see teachers engaged in in a classroom are listed below. Observe the teacher for fifteen minutes. Check the behaviors you observe and describe them.

Check	Behavior	Description
1.	Sets atmosphere	
2.	Gives information	
3.	Gives explanation	
4.	Gives direction: verbal	
	nonverbal	
5.	Gives opinions	
6.	Gives rationale	
7.	Organizes	
8.	Answers questions	
9.	Raises questions	
10.	Sets up goals	
11.	Summarizes	
12.	Evaluates	
13.	Supports	
14.	Accepts ideas	
15.	Others	

Which of these behaviors might encourage children to be independent? List them.

Which of them might cause children to become dependent?

Objectives	Behavior Indicators	Worksheets
To describe a classroom environment conducive to children developing mathematical concepts.	Complete Post Test 1 satisfactorily.	20.1, 20.2, 20.3
To identify the language of mathematics (including words) that will help children in their development of mathematical concepts.	Complete Post Test 2 satisfactorily. During participation, demonstrate an activity that is planned to help a small group of children to engage in experiences with mathematical concepts.	20.3
To identify the concepts of number and number systems that young children incorporate in their play.	Complete Post Test 3 satisfactorily.	20.4, 20.5, 20.6, 20.7, 20.8, 20.9, 20.10, 20.11, 20.12, 20.13
To identify the concepts of space that young children incorporate in their play.	Complete Post Test 4 satisfactorily.	20.13, 20.14, 20.15, 20.16.
To describe the concepts of measurement that children acquire as they explore the ideas of quantity and space.	Complete Post Test 5 satisfactorily.	20.16, 20.17, 20.18, 20.19
To describe the ways in which children use mathematical concepts in problem solving.	Complete Post Test 6 satisfactorily.	20.20, 20.25
To list the mathematical record keeping that can be used with young children.	Complete Post Test 7. During participation, prepare a record related to a child's activity.	20.22
To identify the ways in which mathematical concepts are used in social interaction.	Complete Post Test 9 satisfactorily.	20.23
To describe evidence of children's enjoyment and valuing of mathematical concepts and tools.	Complete Post Test 10 satisfactorily.	20.24
To analyze the relationship of the development of mathematical concepts and the enhancement of self-concept.	Complete Post Test 11 satisfactorily.	20.16, 20.21
To describe the role of the teacher in helping children develop concepts and skills in mathematics.	Complete Post Test 8 satisfactorily. During participation, demonstrate and have someone keep a record or videotape of each of the teacher behaviors listed on worksheet 20.25.	20.2, 20.19, 20.25

MATHEMATICS

Pre/Post Tests

1. Describe a classroom environment that would encourage children to learn mathematics.

2. List words and other symbols that would help children to learn mathematical concepts.

3. List concepts of number and number systems you would expect children to incorporate into their play.

4. Describe concepts of space you would expect children to incorporate into their play.

5. List instruments that children might create to measure the following: length, volume, weight, time, and temperature.

6. Select three areas of an early childhood classroom and describe three problems that might arise and be solved in each area.

7. Describe three kinds of mathematical record keeping that you feel would be suitable for young children.

8. Describe the role of a teacher in developing concepts and skills in mathematics.

9. Identify mathematical concepts that enhance the play of children.

10. Describe children's behaviors that indicate that they are developing appropriate attitudes toward mathematical learnings.

11. Describe the ways that the development of mathematical concepts contribute to the development of a positive self-concept.

Children are interested in numbers and will discover mathematical concepts for themselves if they are provided with a situation in which there are adequate materials and sufficient time for exploration.

Mathematical understandings are an integral part of all life. The meaning of number and number relationships is developed through concrete experiences. Almost any environment has materials that children may use in developing number concepts. These are not necessarily the materials that have been designed for the study of mathematics, either. "Are there enough crackers for four children?" "You have more juice than I do." "Is there enough space on the shelf for these long blocks?" What a thrill a child has when he sees a number relationship for the first time! "Look, these two blocks are the same size as this one! Two makes one." "Ooh, I have just enough brushes. Three brushes for three jars!" If a child is constantly shown these relationships, then he will never have the thrill of discovering for himself and valuing his ability to do so. As a child learns about quantitative and spatial relationships, he begins to use the language of mathematics, opening the way to mathematical thinking.

VOCABULARY

Even if a child's vocabulary contains many mathematical terms, this does not necessarily mean that he has comprehension of their meaning. He is probably imitating adult language. For example, a child can count to 100 without being able to comprehend the meaning five, or a child may chant, "One, two, buckle my shoe" because it is fun, without having any idea of the meanings of one or two. In a sandbox a child enjoys making equal mounds of sand. In the beginning, he counts by rote from one to five, but as he develops an understanding of one-to-one correspondence, the counting is related to the quantity, and he begins to realize that he really has five mounds. The practice of using the words with concrete materials eventually gives meaning to the language. When this is achieved, language can be used as a tool in exploring quantitative relationships.

COUNTING

When a child sees a row of three crayons, he understands that this crayon is one, and this is one, and this is one, and that the three ones together make three; then he has the comprehension to deal with mathematical ideas. He really knows what number is. In the beginning, a child would probably identify the second crayon in the row as two, without understanding the system of counting.

A child working at a peg board puts in one more peg, and one more, and then one more. Another child removes one bead at a time from a string of beads. At the clay table, one child breaks off part of his piece of clay to share with a friend. While building with blocks, a child stacks his blocks in piles of three. As children play, they lay the bases for computation. Adding, subtracting, dividing, and multiplying are number skills that a child will use many times in play.

CLASSIFICATION

Everywhere in the world, in all stages of life and in all aspects of living, people engage in sorting activities. It is a process that helps bring order to living. Much of what is done in mathematics is related to grouping and regrouping. Young children enjoy grouping all the red blocks in one pile and all the blue blocks in another one. They separate the round buttons from the square buttons. They put one yellow crayon beside another yellow crayon, matching color. They develop their own categories for classification. These may be color, shape, size, texture, odor, brightness, temperature, or weight. As a child becomes more and more fascinated by the process of classification, he invents systems that are his and his alone. As he engages in classification, a child often arranges sets, or collections of objects. Sometimes the sets are exactly alike (matching, equal, or the same sets). Sometimes they differ (unequal sets).

When children begin to separate the long red crayons from the short red ones, they are working with subsets. As they begin to put the colored cubes in the frame, they compare the number of green ones with the number of orange ones, and, by noting two equal rows, find they are the same.

MAKING COMPARISONS

Making comparisons is important in mathematical thinking. There are many materials such as buttons, shoes, containers that lend themselves to comparison. Sometimes children group a different way, placing in a row the half-unit, the unit, and the double unit blocks, or the biggest

spool, a smaller one, and a still smaller one. When a child separates the crayons into piles and then places them back in a box, a whole-part relationship is involved. When a large ball of dough is broken up into four smaller balls, a whole-part relationship is shown. While the terminology may not be used, the concept of fractions is operating. Four small balls are equivalent to the one large ball. A child building a house exchanges a quadruple block for four-unit blocks in order to make his door. He may not understand that the quantity is the same (the principle of conservation), but he is having a concrete experience with equivalency.

ORDINAL NUMBERS

Even though children are gaining understanding of cardinal numbers, it cannot be assumed that they have equal understanding of ordinal numbers, of first, second, third, etc. They probably understand what being first in line means, but they are less likely to understand the meaning of second or third. As a teacher calls attention to this ordering, children's awareness is sharpened.

SPATIAL RELATIONSHIPS

In order for a child to develop an understanding of spatial relationships, he needs to develop a sense of self in space.

A child tries fitting himself into many different kinds of space. It is great fun for him to see what he can do with himself. He is big but not so big. He can fit inside a box, behind a cabinet, or under a table. He sections off space for himself with blocks or in the sandbox, and confines himself to the area in which he plays. He runs the length of the yard, spanning a large area of space.

As a child sets challenges and tests himself, he develops an awareness of who he is. As he steps over his friend's structure, he is estimating distance and mastering his ability to control his movements. A child's activities are related to both three-dimensional and two-dimensional space. Moving through space or playing with blocks and other such materials involves him in three-dimensional space, and as he uses brush or crayon on paper he is exploring two-dimensional space.

GEOMETRIC FORMS

Shapes in wood, clay, and dough have volume. Shapes on paper cover area. Volume and area are both aspects of geometry. A child creates his own shapes and reproduces his version of other people's shapes. He makes various configurations and geometric forms. He matches one stroke with another, varying length and width. Having established his own order, he can eventually understand what order is and begin to comprehend and apply his knowledge to the ordering that constitutes the discipline of mathematics.

At the three-dimensional level, children are able to move around shapes and see them from different perspectives. Large hollow blocks, tables, and cartons provide this type of experience.

Additional experiences with shapes are possible as children paste circles, squares, rectangles, and triangles.

MEASUREMENT

Measurement is another aspect of mathematics that intrigues children. Sometimes they use their own bodies or parts of their bodies as instruments of measure. A child stands beside a post and measures his shadow against the shadow of the post. Distance takes on real meaning when expressed in terms of how many jumps it takes him to get from the door to the sink. He measures how deep a hole is with his thumb.

Sometimes he uses a stick or a block to do his measuring. "Last week the stem of the plant came up to here on this stick." A teacher places a new mark to indicate how much it has grown. Sometimes a ruler or a yardstick is introduced for linear measurement.

Often children measure weight according to what they can and cannot carry. "Help me carry the box of wood. It's too heavy for me." A teacher might suggest, "Maybe we can lighten the load by taking out some of the wood." "Now I can do it!" Although a child does not comprehend what a pound is, he speaks of his weight in terms of pounds and understands that he weighs more pounds now than he did the last time he was weighed.

Children find all sorts of objects to weigh and compare. A balance scale provides opportunities to compare the weights of objects. Because a balance scale can be made easily, commercial scales are not necessary.

A child's concept of time and time relationships differs from an adult's. Actual time measures that adults use (minute, hour, day, week) are not clear to children. Little by little they develop these concepts. "Your mother will be here soon." "We need to wash the paintbrushes because we will be going outside in a few minutes." "Today is Friday. We won't be coming to school for two days." Birthdays always interest children even before they understand what they mean. "My birthday is in three days. I'll be four years old."

Children are aware of changes in temperature. "I'm too hot to wear my hat." "The weather is cold."

Although a child may make exaggerated statements concerning money ("A coat costs ten cents"), that same child knows that forty cents in a machine will give him a can of soda. As children use play money, they are learning about the concept of exchange. The denominations of the bills and coins probably have little meaning in themselves.

WRITING SYMBOLS

There are occasions when number symbols are written. Children enjoy copying and identifying them. Some classroom doors have numbers. There are numbers on the telephone. The pages of a book are numbered, and there are numbers in the recipe for French toast.

As quantitative information is written, children become aware that information can be recorded, can serve as a reminder, and can be read by others. "October tenth is my birthday." A teacher may respond: "Let me record that so we won't forget." A teacher who is reading poems may say, "I will put the book mark at page 14 so that we can hear this poem again tomorrow." Records of children's heights may be recorded on a wall with strips of masking tape. When the heights of all the children are recorded next to one another, a graph is formed.

PROBLEM SOLVING

The problem-solving processes of estimating, predicting, and comparing can be identified at a child's level just as well as at an adult level. A teacher is helping children engage in problem-solving techniques as he raises questions such as "What do we want to find out?" "How can we find out about it?" "Did it work?" "How did you do it?"

ATTITUDES

Children develop and clarify mathematical concepts as they play. Mathematical concepts enhance the play. Dramatic play activities that incorporate the post office, the bakery, and bus rides are illustrations of this. Appreciation of and positive attitudes toward mathematical learnings as a part of living develop when children are encouraged to discover them for themselves and practice them in their play. As they have opportunities to discover, test, practice, and enjoy success with these concepts and tools, positive self-concept is fostered.

ARRANGEMENT

The arrangement of a room can contribute to or detract from children's mathematical explorations. Too many materials in a classroom can be overstimulating and can clutter a room. In a cluttered room, children cannot easily distinguish figure from ground. When a few carefully arranged materials are made available, each one takes on great importance for children. The way materials are stored can provide for a learning experience. Blocks should be arranged according to size and displayed on shelves so that the whole arrangement can be seen as well as the parts that make up the whole. This provides a valuable learning experience, as do woodworking tools silhouetted on a peg board. When trays are designed to hold a complete set of materials, the very arrangement suggests uses to the child, as well as a sense of order. For example, colored cubes fit into certain frames and beads are arranged according to color in a section tray.

When a teacher rearranges materials or replaces them, new interest is stimulated.

MATERIALS AND EQUIPMENT

A classroom for young children is a mathematical laboratory. A quick look around the room will reveal many pieces of materials and equipment suitable for mathematical experiences. The wood in the wood box has length, width, and thickness. There are nails to be sorted and counted, and selections to be made as to which nails will best hold two pieces of wood together. There are paintbrushes and containers to be matched at the easel, and paper to provide space for experimenting with shapes and different arrangements.

At a finger-painting table there is an opportunity for trial and error and the creation of many shapes in a short time, as well as a chance to repeat shapes over and over. Clay has volume and density. It can be divided, separated into parts, rearranged in space, and shaped. Dough can be cut, pulled, pressed, and pounded into many shapes. Cookie cutters may come in different geometric or representative shapes. Pulling a shape out of the dough after cutting provides experience with figure-ground.

Collage provides experiences with many types of shapes, both standard and nonstandard, which can be arranged in many patterns. Pegs, colored cubes, and beads can be sorted, classified, patterned, counted, and arranged in sets and subsets.

A table set for juice and crackers presents an opportunity for the creation of sets, both like and unlike. There are cups and napkins to be counted and arranged in a one-to-one relationship. There is estimating to be done as liquid is poured from the pitcher into the cups.

In a block area, a child learns about configuration and one-to-one correspondence as he stacks blocks by twos or threes, sorts according to size and shape, orders, rearranges, and changes shapes. The principle of equivalency is shown as the sides of a building are equalized.

Songs, chants, rhythmic instruments, and body movement all contribute to a child using his body in relation to experiences with numbers and direction.

Puzzles provide experiences with configuration, shape, and arrangement of space. Children find their own clues for solving puzzles.

Balance scales, egg timers, and old alarm clocks are additional materials to bring about mathematical experiences.

Mathematical explorations are numerous in a housekeeping area. Sets of dishes, arrangements of furniture, or classification of dress-up clothes provide opportunities for playing out many kinds of adult roles involving mathematics. Water in a sink or in a dish pan gives children a chance to explore volume and measurement of liquids.

ROLE OF THE TEACHER

The ways in which a teacher arranges the environment will determine the quality of the mathematical experiences that children will have in a classroom. This is one of many roles a teacher takes. An open classroom provides for individual differences by giving children the freedom to make choices. Some children may choose materials they are very familiar with. Because they know the material very well they do not have to be preoccupied with controlling it and can afford to experiment with it. Other children will choose materials that, even though strange to them, present a challenge. They may explore and test various possibilities and relate this new experience with experiences they have had with other materials. A child who has had many experiences with stringing beads may then begin to pattern the beads in color sets. Another child who has enjoyed organizing pegs, blocks, and cubes in rows may then use this organization when he plants seeds in rows.

A teacher who selects open-ended materials—those that can be used in may ways—gives children opportunities for responding in terms of their own levels of development and therefore they have a greater chance for a successful experience. As a teacher does his planning, he should assess the ways in which materials are being used and how much interest there is in them, before deciding which ones should be left out or put away and whether or not additional materials should be made available.

Some teachers have the idea that colorful, cleverly packaged kits are necessary for a good program. With only a few pieces of simple equipment such as pegs, paint, and blocks, an excellent program can be achieved. Preoccupation with materials can often destroy creative explorations.

Many children work by themselves and are attracted to activities because of their own interests. Less adventuresome children are often stimulated simply by the teacher's presence. Often he does not have to say a word. They feel his strong, silent support. His presence attaches importance to the activity and there is a feeling of security when a teacher is near.

Teachers are not silent all the time. They make valuable contributions to extend and enrich children's play. A teacher may introduce a new material, such as a piece of rope that could serve as a firehose. When he sees the play deteriorate, this material may serve to renew the children's interest. He may ask a question: "Is this hose long enough to reach the fire?" "How can you tell whether or not the rope is long enough?" Or, "We have three firemen and only one hat. How many more hats do we need?" Sometimes the teacher might incorporate mathematics vocabulary by saying, "Charles is first. Who will be second and then who will be third?" A teacher may give information. For example, the children have decided to make firemen's badges and are arguing about their shape. The teacher says, "Let's see if we can find out what shape they really are." The teacher finds several books in which firemen are wearing badges of different shapes. A teacher serves as a resource person and gives information to children. He knows where to find additional information as well. If a teacher is going to add information or give ideas, he needs to be aware of when he is enriching children's play and when he is really interfering with it. If a teacher interferes too often, children tend to become dependent and the teacher's role changes from facilitator to dictator.

ADDITIONAL RESOURCES

Leeb-Lundberg, Kristina. "The Block Builder Mathematician." In *The Block Book*, Elisabeth S. Hersch (ed.). Washington, D.C.: National Association for the Education of Young Children, 1974.

Leeper, Sarah Hammond; Skipper, Dora; and Witherspoon, Ralph. *Good Schools for Young Children.* 4th ed. New York: Macmillan, 1978. Chapter 13, "Mathematics," pp. 291–311.

Moffitt, Mary W., and Swedlow, Rita. "Dynamics of Play for Learning." In *Play: Children's Business.* Washington, D.C.: Association for Childhood Education International, 1974.

Rudolph, Marguerita. *From Hand to Head—A Handbook for Teachers of Preschool Programs.* New York: McGraw-Hill, 1973. Chapter 15, "Striving for Concepts in Preschool Education," pp. 141–148.

Spodek, Bernard. *Teaching in the Early Years.* Englewood Cliffs, N.J.: Prentice-Hall, 1972. Chapter 7, "Mathematics for Young Children," pp. 137–153.

Todd, Vivian Edmiston, and Heffernan, Helen. *The Years Before School.* 3rd ed. New York: Macmillan, 1977. Chapter 10, "Exploring Time, Space, and Numbers," pp. 376–408.

Film (16mm). *Foundations of Mathematics.* New York: Campus Films, 1977.

Worksheet 20.1   Concepts

(This worksheet is appropriate for use when only one observation is being made in this area.)
Children will develop mathematical concepts if appropriate situations are provided. Select one activity area
of the room. When a child is playing in this area, what experiences would be available that might lead to
the development of mathematical concepts? What concepts are involved (matching, classification, etc.)?

Area of the room selected:

Experiences	Concepts involved

Describe one incident that happened while you were observing.

Worksheet 20.2   Environment for Learning I

Through the arrangement of the environment, it is possible to encourage mathematical learnings. The
types of materials in a room have an influence on a child's explorations. Children need time to make
discoveries. The ways in which the teacher participates influence the type and quality of learnings.

    Observe children as they play in the classroom. What materials do you see that could contribute to
explorations of number, space, measurement, problem solving, etc., and what, if anything, does the
teacher do that might enhance the learnings? Describe indications of whether or not there was time
available for children to complete their activities to their own satisfaction.

Materials	Teacher role	Time
		(Indications of whether children did or did not have time to finish their investigations.)

Worksheet 20.3   Language

As one listens to a group of children talking, they are likely to make references to numbers. Nursery rhymes are filled with number words. Chants are often based on counting. Children sometimes move about counting in a rote manner from one to one hundred. Since there are so many words in most children's vocabularies related to numbers and number concepts, it would be easy to conclude that they comprehend these concepts. However, close observation will usually reveal that many of their number words are spoken simply for fun and purely by rote. What a child is able to count with comprehension may be limited to three, four, or five objects.

Observe the children in a classroom. Record examples of the use of mathematical language that appear to be merely rote or incorrect and those that appear to indicate comprehension.

Language that indicates rote use of mathematical words and numerals.

Language that indicates use of mathematical words and numbers with comprehension.

Look through a collection of children's nursery rhymes and a series of picture books. List those stories or rhymes that include number words.

Worksheet 20.4   Sets and Subjects

As children gather collections of objects, they deal with basic mathematical concepts of sets. There are many opportunities in a classroom for grouping and regrouping of objects. Sometimes children organize things in a given way just for fun. Other times there is purpose to their organization such as when they organize a set of items in a picnic basket or the ingredients for a cake.

Observe in the following areas of a room and describe activities of children in which they group materials into sets, indicating the characteristic(s) that make them sets.

Housekeeping	Blocks	Manipulative materials

Worksheet 20.5   Classification

Classification is important for all aspects of living. There is an abundance of packaged materials and kits intended to help children develop skills in classification. Teachers often develop exercises using buttons, rocks, and shells. A teacher who is aware of and makes use of the many opportunities for classification available in any classroom does not have to rely on specially prepared lessons. Given the opportunity, children will often create their own classification systems. The quality of the learning takes on depth when children themselves find opportunities for classifying and develop their own categories.

　　Describe the opportunities you see for classifying in the following areas. Place a check mark next to those activities in which you observe a child(ren) engaging in classification. Include age of child.

Activity	Description
Painting _____	
Clay (or dough) _____	
Book area _____	
Manipulative materials _____	
Blocks _____	
Housekeeping _____	
Other _____	

Worksheet 20.6   **One-to-One Correspondence**

An understanding of one-to-one correspondence is basic for developing skill in any mathematical program. Children enjoy repeating activities involving matching. They will also find their own materials and invent their own exercises. Observe children as they play and look for materials that lend themselves to the development of the concept of one-to-one correspondence.

Materials involved:

Look for some unusual material(s) that can be matched. Arrange it in the classroom. See whether children use the material(s) for matching as intended, or invent other ways of using it. Describe what happens.

Worksheet 20.7   **Basic Processes**

Children are constantly engaging in experiences in basic mathematical processes; they share crayons in a box, they add one block to the pile, they take away two spoons from the drawer, they give each child at the table two cookies. These activities help give meaning to arithmetic facts and processes. Observe children in a classroom and record activities in which they add, subtract, multiply, or divide.

What children did	Other activities in which they might engage
Adding:	
Subtracting:	
Multiplying:	
Dividing:	

Worksheet 20.8   Fractions

From a very early age, children have experiences with fractions. A cookie is divided into halves. A pie is cut into fractional parts. An apple is divided into half and then quartered. Observe activities in a classroom and describe experiences that children are having with fractions.

Plan an activity for this classroom in which a small group of children may have experiences with fractions. Write the plan in the space below.

Worksheet 20.9   Seriation

People are usually comfortable when there is order to the objects around them. However, there are many ways of ordering objects. One way that is used in mathematics, and which children frequently enjoy, is placing objects in a series according to length, height, volume, color, etc. Seriation is an important concept in mathematics.

Observe children with blocks and at a table with manipulative materials such as pegs, colored cubes, or beads. Observe the many ways in which children order the objects in a series. What is the frame of reference in which each seriation is done?

Block area:

Manipulative materials:

Other:

Worksheet 20.10   Part-Whole Relationship

As boys and girls play with materials in a classroom, they can develop the basic understandings of part-whole relationships upon which so much of mathematics is based. Observe in a classroom ways in which children experiment with part-whole relationships and with words and/or drawings. Describe the activities.

Clay or dough	Blocks	Food	Other

Write a short paragraph describing the ways in which such experiences contribute to mathematical understanding.

Worksheet 20.11   Exchange

Exchange plays an important part in daily living. Look for evidences of children having experiences in exchange in the housekeeping and the block-building areas.

Housekeeping area

Block-building area

Suggest other kinds of opportunities:

Worksheet 20.12   Systems

The number system in our culture uses base ten. A number system is only one of many systems that exist and new ones are constantly being developed in the world (e.g., a set of blocks contains many different sizes and shapes, and yet each one is carefully designed in relation to every other one according to length, width, and thickness). The sets of ten colored cubes are in a system of 100 colored table blocks. The rope, the wheel, and the container form systems for transporting small objects in the classroom.

   Observe in a classroom and describe the systems you see. Indicate which systems children were aware of. Were there any indications that children were creating their own systems?

Systems	Indication of children's awareness	Children's original systems

Worksheet 20.13   Patterning

Each person sees any material in his own way. It is important to respect and encourage this uniqueness. This means that before children get involved in copying the patterns of others, which they will be doing as they learn to write, they must have opportunities to create their own patterns. Having engaged in the process of patterning, they are then in a better position to understand the processes that have gone into the development of symbols used in adult communication.

   Observe a three-year-old, a four-year-old, and a five-year-old as each strings beads, arranges pegs in a board, and builds with blocks. Record with colored pencil the pattern each child makes.

	Three-year-old	Four-year-old	Five-year-old
1. Beads			
2. Pegs			
3. Blocks			

What differences did you notice?

Worksheet 20.14   **Shapes I**

A child's world is made up of shapes. So important is the understanding of the quality and function of shape that a whole discipline, geometry, is based on shape. As a child handles and uses shapes, he attaches meaning to many words such as circle, triangle, and rectangle. Observe children at the easel and with blocks. Examine a pile of children's paintings. Identify the shapes children have created. Be sure to include the unusual shapes as well as the basic square, triangle, circle, and rectangle. Count and record each of the times you find one of the basic shapes in the children's art.

Observe children at play with blocks. What shapes do they create? Sketch these shapes below, as part of your description.

Did the children at any time attach a verbal label to the shape? Explain.

Worksheet 20.15   **Shapes II**

Children not only create shapes, they work with them as well. Many manipulative materials such as cubes and balls are made in basic shapes. Art materials can also be shaped.

Prepare a collage tray with an assortment of basic and unusual shapes. Observe and record how children arrange them. If children have any conversation pertaining to shapes, record it.

Arrangement	Children's conversation

Worksheet 20.16   Exploring Space

Children seem to be intrigued with the idea of space. They see how far they can run. They throw the ball as high as they can. They move the blocks into patterns on the floor and then place them back on the shelf. A child steps over his structure without knocking it down; he can curl up small enough to get into the bed in the housekeeping area. As he engages in these activities, he is estimating and measuring distance and size at the same time, further developing a concept of himself in space.

  Look for behaviors like the above in a classroom or on a playground. Describe them and include any indication that these behaviors might extend the child's self-concept.

Describe any instances of children using some concrete way of measuring space (e.g., the child using his own body as a measure sees that the sandbox is two times as long as he is).

Worksheet 20.17   Measurements

It is very difficult for a child to understand the concrete—such as one inch or one-half cup—before he has developed an understanding of what it means to measure something and that things have sizes that can be measured.

  Everyday experiences in a classroom provide many opportunities for measuring. Observe at a table where food preparation is in progress. Describe the kinds of measuring or estimating involved.

What other opportunities do you see in the classroom for experiences in measuring?

1.   5.

2   6.

3.   7.

4.   8.

Worksheet 20.18   Time

At an early age many children can be shown how to tell time and can learn to do it reasonably well. But if a child has a variety of experiences related to time before he learns the mechanics, he is more likely to have a real comprehension of the concept. Children are living in time and must relate to experiences that have gone on in the past and will go on in the future. It is very hard to understand what time is, prior to understanding the relationship of "before" and "after" to the present.

Observe and record the ways in which a teacher uses time or speaks about it. This might include reference to calendars, clocks, and schedule of activities, or it might include such phrases as, "when we come in," "as soon as we are ready," "before snack time," or "after play."

Write a paragraph in which you explain at least one understanding that you feel is being developed with a child or children.

Worksheet 20.19   Weight, Temperature, and Volume

Boys and girls are constantly surprised at how light cotton is and how heavy a magnet is. They check the temperature before they decide what clothing to wear outdoors. They feel the temperature of the water before they wash their hands. They become aware of volume when they find that all of the wood does not fit in the box. Two small blocks take up the same amount of space as one larger one.

Observe in some area of a room to identify evidences of measurement and the role of the teacher.

	Evidence of measurement	Was measurement with or without an instrument?	Role of the teacher
Weight			
Temperature			
Volume			

Worksheet 20.20   Problem Solving I

As children become skilled in handling materials, they create new challenges for themselves. These often lead to interesting and sometimes very complicated problem-solving tasks. Observe in a block-building area. What problems in construction develop as the children play? In what way does each child attempt to solve his problem—trial and error, estimating, or asking for help? Illustrate by sketching a construction.

Problem	How solved

Describe other problems that did not arise in this observation but could easily develop.

Worksheet 20.21   Self-Concept

Children enjoy making discoveries for themselves. A discovery that a child makes for himself has a long-lasting effect both in terms of mathematical learnings and positive feelings. "What a worthwhile person I am. I can find out for myself." A classroom in which children have time and materials with which to explore number concepts also affords opportunities for enhancing self-concept.

Observe in an area of the room where you feel there are possibilities for children to develop number concepts and positive self-concepts. Describe them.

Possibilities for number concepts	Self-concepts

Worksheet 20.22   Record Keeping

There are ways of keeping records that help children to recall the measurements they have made (e.g., "the plant is as tall as the string," "these pieces of masking tape on the wall indicate our heights," "we put the recipe for soup on a chart"). Observe measurement in a classroom. Select one activity, prepare a record, and share it with the child(ren) involved.

Plan:

Evaluation of the project:

Worksheet 20.23   Social Interaction

Mathematical understandings are an integral part of activities that take place in both small groups and larger groups, in school and outside. As children play together, they share concepts that some of them have already developed and become aware of new ones. These concepts give depth and meaning to their play. Observe a group of children. What evidence do you find that social situations contribute to mathematical understandings?

What evidence do you find that mathematics contributes to the social interaction of boys and girls?

Worksheet 20.24   Valuing

Children take pride in putting the right number of paintbrushes into paint jars, and in putting the appropriate place settings on a table for a snack. They enjoy finding the nail that will be just the right length for holding two special pieces of wood together.

Describe situations in which children show a positive attitude toward mathematical understandings.

How do you know?

Worksheet 20.25   Role of the Teacher

Many teachers interrupt children by raising questions or offering solutions too often and too soon; there are times, however, when it is appropriate for a teacher to intervene. Intervention need not necessarily mean verbal communication. Through her presence alone, a teacher can encourage children to continue explorations and even to engage in more risk-taking behaviors in search of a solution. Observe a teacher in a classroom and describe evidences of the following behaviors:

Teacher support (nonverbal):

Questions about materials:

Questions about the process involved:

Encouragement (verbal):

Encouragement (nonverbal):

Suggestions (verbal):

Suggestions (nonverbal):

Other:

Objectives	Behavior Indicators	Worksheets
To describe the processes involved in planning—long-range, weekly, daily.	Complete Post Test 1 satisfactorily.	21.1, 21.2, 21.3, 21.4, 21.5, 21.6, 21.7, 21.8, 21.10
To draw a diagram of a room arrangement and state the criteria for the arrangement.	Complete Post Test 2 satisfactorily.	21.9
To list materials and equipment that might be found in a well-equipped classroom. To state the criteria for selecting each item.	Complete Post Tests 3 and 4 satisfactorily.	21.11
To identify the provisions a teacher must make to maintain standards of good health.	Complete Post Test 5 satisfactorily.	21.12, 21.13
To identify the provisions a teacher must make to maintain standards of safety.	Complete Post Test 6 satisfactorily.	21.14, 21.15
To identify the provisions a teacher must make to create a social climate that fosters positive attitudes toward eating.	Complete Post Test 7 satisfactorily.	21.16, 21.17, 21.18
To describe the provisions a teacher must make for a rest period that encourages children to relax.	Complete Post Test 8 satisfactorily.	21.19
To describe the arrival and departure of children and to identify the objectives of each phase.	Complete Post Tests 9 and 10 satisfactorily.	21.20, 21.21, 21.22
To describe the goals for cleanup time and the provisions necessary for carrying them out.	Complete Post Test 11 satisfactorily.	21.23, 21.24
To define the purposes of assessment in a classroom for young children, and describe the ways in which they can be implemented.	Complete Post Test 12 satisfactorily.	21.25, 21.28, 21.30
To list the kinds of records that are important for an early childhood teacher to keep. To state why the records should be kept and how they can be implemented.	Complete Post Test 12 satisfactorily.	21.26, 21.27, 21.29

Other(s).

PLANNING AND MANAGEMENT 21

Pre/Post Tests

1. Name some of the factors a teacher should consider when making: long-range plans, weekly plans, daily plans?

2. Draw a diagram of a room arrangement. State the criteria used.

3. List the permanent equipment that might be found in a well-equipped classroom. State the criteria used for selecting each item.

4. List the expendable materials that might be found in a well-equipped classroom. State the criteria used for selecting each item.

5. Identify five provisions a teacher might make to maintain standards of good health.

6. Identify six provisions a teacher might make to maintain standards of safety.

7. Identify five provisions a teacher must make to create a social climate that fosters positive attitudes toward eating.

8. Describe four provisions a teacher must make for a rest period in which children will be encouraged to relax.

9. Describe suitable arrangements for children's arrival at school and identify the objectives for such arrangements.

10. Describe suitable arrangements for children's departure from school and identify the objectives for such arrangements.

11. Describe goals for cleanup time and provisions necessary for carrying them out.

12. Describe the kinds of records that are important for an early childhood teacher to keep. State why these particular records are important and describe how they should be kept.

LONG-RANGE PLANNING

There is no one way to manage a classroom. Planning for any classroom depends upon the philosophy on which a program is based.

If a program is to be more than a collection of experiences, then long-range planning is essential. A careful rethinking of the philosophy is basic to long-range planning. The goals have to go beyond keeping children busy and happy. When overall objectives are clear, there is continuity of activities and processes. In any school the activities in each room may be different while the overall philosophy is the same.

A teacher must keep his eye on the overall growth of a child as he develops skills, knowledges, and attitudes. Provisions must be made for physical, cognitive, emotional, and social long-range planning. A teacher should look at the materials in the room in relation to the philosophy and the children's development and select those materials that make it possible for children to make choices and develop their own ways of working. For example, if a teacher is aware that young children are continually solving problems, then the arrangement and selection of materials (blocks, paint, clay, etc.) should be such that children will have many opportunities to grow in their approach and ability to solve problems.

In making long-range plans, a teacher should build-in opportunities to study children during the day. Through this study, he can learn about the children and plan activities for them. In the planning, provisions should be made for interactions with both materials and other children. Long-range planning allows teachers to get materials together and think through room arrangements that would be most suitable for realizing overall goals.

WEEKLY PLANNING

It is always important for teachers to make weekly plans, but it is particularly important when more than one adult is in a classroom. Planning may take many forms. It is wise to set aside time after school hours for planning because it is difficult to judge the length of time a good planning session will take. The teacher must consider the observations that have been made of children and evaluate the classroom arrangement. A teacher should examine the roles he has taken and consider possible changes in those roles in light of these observations. It is important to check weekly planning in relation to overall goals so that there can be meaningful continuity that goes beyond mere activity building. Individual children need to be considered when materials are selected.

DAILY PLANNING

No matter how carefully weekly plans have been drawn, there has to be a reassessment at the end of each day. Materials must be laid out, some things require cleaning, and provisions must be made for immediate needs. It is also necessary to provide for unexpected interests that may have developed.

There are different ways of planning a schedule. Planning for large blocks of time gives flexibility to the program. Since each child has unique needs, children work at different rates and have different interests. Given a large block of time, children can stay with an activity for a long period of time, or move from one activity to another. This gives them opportunities to gain independence. When planning, a teacher must take into account routines and transitions from one phase of the program into another.

Other members of the school staff must be considered because such things as the ways in which food is prepared, cleanup, use of outdoor space, and other shared areas directly influence the program.

ROOM ARRANGEMENT

The way a teacher arranges a room indicates what is being emphasized and what the teacher's priorities are. Arrangement is influenced by the size and shape of the room, the location of doors and windows, and the provision for sinks and toilets. While children need spaces for privacy and enclosure, they also need room to move about without climbing over furniture. Care must be taken to provide for children with special needs, for example, blind or deaf children, or children with prostheses.

When there is movable equipment, it is possible to have a flexible arrangement. Rearrangement can be done as needed. Low, open shelves permit children to help themselves to materials. Bulletin boards should be placed at children's eye level. When materials are carefully arranged on shelves, they can distinguish figure from background. It is easier for children to make choices if there is order to the arrangement on the shelves. A teacher needs a private place for his resource file, a place to put materials not intended for children's use. When children eat breakfast or lunch, enough tables and chairs are needed so that all can be seated at once. Under other circumstances this may not be necessary. Chairs should be stacked or stored when not in use in order to provide more space. Even though the school has a maintenance staff every teacher should be responsible for the orderliness, neatness, and cleanliness of the room and materials.

MATERIALS

When selecting materials, emphasis should be on those which have multiple uses rather than a single purpose. There are times, however, when single-purpose materials are appropriate. Pegs or colored cubes can be used in many different ways, whereas a sorting box has a more limited range of possibilities. Clutter can be distracting and disorienting for children, but it is essential to have a variety of materials for children to make choices.

A teacher should be very aware of the quality of the materials he chooses. The least expensive item is not always the most practical one in the long run. Durability is important, particularly when a piece of equipment is to be used many times.

There are attractive materials that would be useful in a classroom but are not necessary. It is important, particularly on a limited budget, to consider the amount of use a material will have before purchasing it. Parents can build or repair easels, cubbies, climbing apparatus, and storage facilities.

HEALTH

A teacher has responsibility for maintaining a healthy environment. He is equally responsible for helping children to develop positive attitudes toward health and to recognize their responsibilities in maintaining their own good health.

Health records should be kept up to date. In most schools children are required to have a medical examination before entering and a health record is usually on file for each child. It is important for a teacher to be aware of contagious diseases to which children in the neighborhood may have been exposed. He should be on the lookout for watery eyes, flushed faces, sore throats, and other symptoms. Skin infections require a doctor's care. Parents should be encouraged to keep children home when they are ill.

A teacher should be aware of school regulations concerning the administering of first aid for minor cuts, bruises, scratches, and scraped knees. Any serious injury or illness must be reported to the parents or to the persons designated by them. A child must be cared for until a parent arrives. Most schools maintain a cot in a special area where a child can be isolated.

A box of tissues should be available in every classroom. Children feel very important when they learn how to blow their noses. The attitude that a teacher takes toward the health needs of children will influence the children's attitudes.

Toilet procedures are important experiences for young children. They may need help as they learn to fasten their own clothes. Some may need help in learning to flush the toilet. When the toilets are low, children are more comfortable about getting on and off them. A child is less likely to be fearful of being left alone on the toilet if he can handle the situation himself.

If equipment is set up so that a child can wash his hands easily, he enjoys becoming self-sufficient, and washing his hands after using the toilet becomes a habit. When the height of the sinks is appropriate for children, they cannot only gain independence in washing their hands, but they have opportunities to become familiar with the qualities of soap and water; these become media for learning. Many children have pet words for urination and defecation. If a teacher uses the correct terminology, children will soon use it as well. If boys and girls use the same facilities, there is less mystery attached to toileting. When a child's earlier experiences cause concern about such matters, a teacher must respect his privacy.

Some children may wet their clothes during the day. They may spill water on them, or in their excitement they may urinate. A relaxed teacher will avoid anxieties. It is essential for each child to keep a change of clothing at school so that he will not have to stay in wet clothes.

A teacher often cannot control the temperature in the classroom, but it is very important to provide proper ventilation. It is also important to be sure that radiators are covered so that children will not be burned accidentally.

SAFETY

Safety is a necessary consideration in any classroom. There are many potentially dangerous materials on hand. Blocks can fall, saws are sharp, hammers can be used with great force, scissors are lethal weapons, as are the knives used to cut vegetables. Climbing apparatus brings children to heights that they may not be able to climb down from. Even shoelaces, when untied, are a hazard.

However, this does not mean that these materials should not be used. They simply require teacher supervision and the establishment of basic rules.

When children are busy with their block constructions, accidents are rare. If a teacher sees a tall structure that is tottering, he can offer a suggestion for making the foundation more firm. In some situations, children are not permitted to build structures higher than themselves; this denies them an opportunity to explore space upward. It is very satisfying to children to build something taller than themselves.

Because children do not understand the sharpness of a saw or the power of a hammer, a workbench requires careful supervision. As these materials are introduced, each child should become familiar with a few basic rules. Tools must remain at the workbench. The number of children at the workbench should be limited so that there will be good distance between children. Children are not to point tools at others. A teacher should help a child to learn where to place his hand so that he will not smash it.

Scissors and knives should not be carried around the room but should be used only at the specified area.

Climbing apparatus is designed for climbing, and most falls occur when it is used for other purposes. Children automatically exercise caution when climbing. When a child climbs, he will stop when he feels insecure. He establishes a relationship between himself and the ground. When a child is pushed beyond his own goals, then anxieties are likely to develop. Accidents occur when he has not yet learned the necessary cautions and when his balance and coordination are not matched to the challenges. When climbing apparatus are stationed in sand or grass, there is no need for additional protection on the ground. When they are located on a concrete or asphalt surface, movable mats or a commercially produced rubberized playground surface are recommended.

Equipment should be kept in good condition. Wood should be sanded before it splinters. When equipment is repaired, it is important to check for sharp edges. The playground itself should always be cleared of debris.

Some schools maintain a supply of wheel toys, including tricycles, scooters, cars, and wagons. Traffic areas need to be designated so that these vehicles do not interfere with other areas of play.

When cooking is done in a classroom, special care must be taken. Arrangements should be made for electric cords and hot plates to be out of reach. When a pot is steaming, children should be far enough away to avoid burns, and the teacher should be present. Electric hot plates and electric frying pans should be used only when the teacher can supervise the entire activity. An electric frying pan is particularly dangerous because the whole pan gets hot and children are tempted to come up close to it in order to see what is happening.

While a teacher is developing a safe environment, it is important that children develop responsibilities for their own safety. It is important for children to follow whatever rules a teacher has set up. However, there is more to safety than a blind following of rules. Young children are beginning to understand their own limitations and to develop rules for themselves according to their own awareness of what the dangers are. When a child grows up, he will be responsible for his own safety. He needs experiences in developing inner controls in order to begin to develop his own judgment in risk taking.

A teacher needs to be alert and ready to intervene when a child is in danger. If a teacher is not overly anxious, then children accept suggestions concerning safety in a positive way. A teacher may redirect the activity to less dangerous channels. Sometimes her presence is supportive to children, as she anticipates when they are about to go beyond their limits. If a teacher considers safe behavior as one of her educational goals, then it is incorporated into the whole program, and children develop an awareness of its importance. In this type of environment a necessary routine such as a fire drill becomes a learning experience rather than an incomprehensible game.

FOOD

Teacher attitudes apply to eating habits and nutrition as well. During snack and lunch, children learn to enjoy many kinds of foods. They become aware of a healthy diet as they experience well-planned meals. A teacher cannot usually determine the menu but she can make eating together a happy learning experience. Children learn how to sit at a table and talk together.

Many doctors feel that eating problems arise because of anxieties adults have about food and the pressures they place upon children about eating.

In many nursery-kindergarten schools, a snack is served at mid-morning and mid-afternoon. This may consist of milk or juice with a cracker or freshly cut vegetables. Whether a snack is served to a whole group in a formal setting or informally at one table, a teacher's presence sets the tone. This does not mean that a teacher manages the entire process. Children enjoy being independent and can be encouraged to pour their own milk or juice and help themselves to other foods. A snack period can either be a routine for children, or it can be a worthwhile learning experience.

REST

It is possible to determine a teacher's attitude toward rest by how restful a room is during the formal rest period. When a teacher sees it as an unnecessary daily routine or as a punishment, there is likely to be a roomful of resentful, restless children. If a teacher values the period as a time for complete relaxation of mind and body, and sees it as a time when children can withdraw from outside stimulation and come to terms with their own thoughts and feelings, then the whole atmosphere of the room is calm.

A good rest period does not just happen accidentally. Children are more likely to fall asleep if the activity prior to the rest period has been a quiet one. Whether cots or mats are used, care must be taken that children are physically comfortable. They should have an opportunity to go to the toilet and have a drink, if necessary, before they lie down. Most teachers encourage children to remove their shoes.

Cots should be arranged and separated so that children are not so close together that their natural movements disturb one another. Sometimes dividers provide privacy. Children do not need to be perfectly still in order to rest. It is the quiet atmosphere in the room that helps them relax. In many classrooms two-thirds of the children will go to sleep. Others may remain quiet with their eyes open throughout the entire period. A darkened room adds to the restful atmosphere, as does a teacher who sits in a relaxed position. A teacher who walks about the room, talks with another adult, works on records, or prepares materials not only disturbs the children but negates the objective of a rest period. A teacher who is interested in a child's inner relaxation does not want this time disturbed by music, toys, or books.

When a rest period is over, folding blankets can be an important learning experience. Some children want the help of the teacher. Others try to devise their own systems of folding and putting blankets away. Some children help others with shoes and shoelaces.

ARRIVAL AND DEPARTURE

Greeting parents and children is part of a teacher's role. A staggered arrival is helpful not only because it gives the teacher an opportunity to see each parent but also because it gives the parents and children some leeway in getting to school in time. When a teacher takes time to say a few words to the parents in the morning, she keeps communication open between home and school. This communication should be a two-way process. It provides an opportunity to find out what is going on at home and how a child is feeling. It also provides an opportunity to let parents know that the teacher is ready for their children and really cares about them.

Departure is an equally important time in which to develop continuity between the home and the school. An unrushed departure gives a child time to make the transition and also gives a parent the opportunity to find out what has been going on during the day and over a longer period of time so he can see how the child has grown and developed.

CLEANUP

If a teacher enters into the cleanup process in a wholehearted manner, fully appreciating its educational value, children will enjoy it too. The model an adult sets determines whether it will be a pleasing or a distasteful process. Routines play an important part in giving order to a child's life. A child has little concept of time but he begins to understand sequence of time in terms of "before lunch," "after rest," and "as soon as we clean up." She begins to see herself as a useful and capable person.

The teacher should not impose adult standards when children engage in cleaning up the room. Children need more time for cleanup than adults do. If a teacher understands the learnings involved in the process, he does not impatiently take over and complete a task for a child. However, a teacher does participate in the cleanup process with enthusiasm. When a teacher undertakes a job, children will usually join him. When appropriate cleanup materials such as sponges, brushes, brooms, dustpans, and carpet sweepers are available, children enjoy using them. Applying soap and water to a finger-paint table can be fun.

Adequate storage space and an orderliness in the arrangement of materials foster independence. Drying paintings is often a problem. If spread out on the floor, they may get stepped on. A collapsible clothes rack is often used. Some schools use a cabinet with sliding shelves so that paintings and other art materials can be left to dry flat and out of harm's way.

Some children have difficulty stopping an activity abruptly, especially if their work has meaning for them. A warning a few minutes in advance is helpful.

ASSESSMENT

A teacher constantly assesses his program. Very often he does this in a casual or informal manner. A teacher is assessing the day's program when he says, "The morning went very well," or, "We're going to have to change our schedule because there is entirely too much confusion during cleanup." A teacher is assessing children as he comments about how involved Charles was with the blocks today, or notices the difficulty Cathy has in entering the room.

While this is one form of evaluation, a teacher cannot rely solely on such random observations. He is responsible for planning programs that will promote the growth of young children. He is concerned with their physical, emotional, social, and intellectual development.

Although final evaluations have a place in the program, assessment is an ongoing process. Monthly or even weekly evaluations are not enough.

Whatever evaluations are made should be in relation to goals that have been carefully thought through. In planning for program evaluation, it is important to consider social, emotional, and physical development as well as intellectual growth.

Some parts of evaluation a teacher does himself. Other parts he performs with other members of the staff, such as the nurse, another teacher, or an aide. Children also make evaluations of both their work and their interactions with others. "I like it." "I have two friends."

RECORD KEEPING

While many evaluations are done in an informal manner, it is important to record information so that it can be referred to as needed. Some teachers keep running records of what happens. Others keep short daily accounts in a diary. Still others record critical incidents. When children have problems that a teacher wishes to record, he may do time or event sampling. Videotapes or audiotapes provide immediate and retrievable feedback by which a teacher can assess her own behavior, her interactions with others, and children's behavior.

There are simple and complex category systems that teachers can use to assess their own behaviors, each other's behaviors, and children's behaviors. There is ample evidence that feedback from such checklists based on such category systems contributes to the improvement of teaching behaviors.

For each child, there should be on file a cumulative record containing medical information, family information, conference reports, and progress reports.

ADDITIONAL RESOURCES

Cohen, Dorothy H., and Rudolph, Marguerita. *Kindergarten and Early Schooling.* Englewood Cliffs, N.J.: Prentice-Hall, 1977. Chapter 18, "Classroom Management," pp. 343–370.

Cohen, Dorothy H., and Stern, Virginia. *Observing and Recording the Behavior of Young Children.* New York: Teachers College Press, 1970.

Gross, Dorothy Weisman. "Equipping a Classroom for Young Children." In *Ideas That Work with Young Children,* Katherine Read Baker (ed.). Washington, D.C.: National Association for the Education of Young Children, 1972.

Harms, Thelma. "Evaluating Settings for Learning." In *Ideas That Work with Young Children,* Katherine Read Baker (ed.). Washington, D.C.: National Association for the Education of Young Children, 1972.

Hess, Robert D., and Croft, Doreen J. *Teachers of Young Children.* 2nd ed. Boston: Houghton Mifflin, 1972. Chapter 9, "Crisis in the Preschool," pp. 264–290, and Chapter 10, "The Challenge of Evaluation," pp. 291–322.

Hildebrand, Verna. *Introduction to Early Childhood Education.* 2nd ed. New York: Macmillan, 1976. Chapter 4, "Setting the Stage," pp. 66–88, and Chapter 16, "Program Planning and Evaluating," pp. 394–421.

Leeper, Sarah Hammond; Skipper, Dora; and Witherspoon, Ralph. *Good Schools for Young Children.* 4th ed. New York: Macmillan, 1978. Chapter 10, "Planning for Learning," pp. 196–225; Chapter 17, "Health and Safety," pp. 376–379; and Chapter 21, "Recording the Development of Children," pp. 485–498.

Pfluger, Luther W., and Zola, Jessie M. "A Room Planned by Children." In *Ideas That Work with Young Children,* Katherine Read Baker (ed.). Washington, D.C.: National Association for the Education of Young Children, 1972.

Schmidt, Velma E. *Early Childhood Development.* Dallas, Texas: Hedrick-Long, 1976. "Nutrition, Health and Safety," pp. 49–58.

Spodek, Bernard. *Teaching in the Early Years.* Englewood Cliffs, N.J.: Prentice-Hall, 1972. Chapter 11, "Organizing for Instruction," pp. 219–239, and Chapter 15, "Evaluating Education in the Early Years," pp. 305–326.

Todd, Vivian Edmiston, and Heffernan, Helen. *The Years Before School.* 3rd ed. New York: Macmillan, 1977. Chapter 5, "A Preschool Group," pp. 152–199, and Chapter 6, "Health and Safety," pp. 203–247.

Wills, Clarice Dechant, and Lindberg, Lucile. *Kindergarten for Today's Children.* Chicago: Follett, 1967. Chapter 20, "Keeping Healthy and Safe," pp. 278–289; Chapter 21, "Working and Playing in Groups," pp. 290–299; Chapter 22, "Toward Better Mental Health," pp. 300–311; Chapter 23, "Problems of Classroom Management," pp. 312–322; and Chapter 24, "Evaluating Pupil Progress," pp. 326–334.

Yamamoto, Kaoru. *The Child and His Image.* Boston: Houghton Mifflin, 1972. Chapter IV, "To Fathom the Self: Appraisal in School," pp. 80–120.

Worksheet 21.1   Planning and Management

(This worksheet is appropriate for use when only one observation can be made in this area.)
Planning is essential to good programs. In long-range planning, the overall philosophy of a program should be considered. Weekly planning includes the selection of activities according to the needs of children. Daily planning consists of adaptations of the weekly program, incorporating any unexpected needs. Observe in a classroom and indicate evidences of each of the types of planning listed below.

Long-Range Planning: Do you see evidences that there is a prevailing philosophy upon which the program is based? Describe:

Weekly Planning: Do you see evidences that the selection of materials appears to be related to children's needs? Describe:

Daily Planning: Do you see evidences that there was planning in preparing the environment for the day's activities? Describe:

Worksheet 21.2   Individual Differences

Materials should be arranged so that each child can use them in his own ways, thus making it possible for him to use his ingenuity. Observe three areas of a classroom. In each area, observe more than one child and describe the ways in which different children use the materials. Include the amount of time each child participated.

	Child 1	Child 2	Child 3
Activity I			
Activity II			
Activity III			

Worksheet 21.3   Charting Utilization of Space and Materials

In order for a teacher to plan effectively, he or she must know which areas of a room are being used and what the traffic is in any given area. Chart the utilization of the areas listed below by marking how many children are in each area at five-minute intervals.

Time	Blocks	House-keeping	Paint	Clay	Collage	Books	Music	Wood-working	Food	Other

Worksheet 21.4   Daily Record

If a teacher keeps a daily record of the materials used, the activities, the participants, and the nature of the teacher-child interactions, he gains information that can be used in the management and planning of a classroom. Observe in a classroom and complete the record below.

	Check if used	Description of activities	Participants	Role of the teacher
Painting				
Clay				
Paste				
Dough				
Crayon				
Other art materials				
Blocks				
Housekeeping				

	Check if used	Description of activities	Participants	Role of the teacher

Music:
  Singing
  Chanting
  Rhythm
  Other				

Movement				
Reading stories				
Telling stories				
Making books				
Outdoor activity				
Puzzles, pegs, cubes, etc. (specify)				
Indoor climbing equipment				
Other				

Worksheet 21.5   Daily Observation

A teacher needs to make provisions for individual children. While she cannot observe each child on a given day, she can observe three or four and then incorporate her findings in subsequent planning.

Checklist	Child 1	Child 2	Child 3	Child 4
Name and Age				
Child's Entrance into Room				
Entered room willingly				
Entered room reluctantly				
Clung to parent				
Reaction to Environment				
Freely explored				
Curious but hesitant to move out				
Reluctant to explore				
Relationship to Others				
Sought contact with other children				
Sought contact with teacher				
Remained apart from group				
Rejected advances made by others				
Aggressive toward others				
Response to Materials				
Chose materials freely (specify)				
Needed help in selecting materials				
Able to complete a task				
Exhibited a reasonable span of attention				
Behavior seemed to lack direction				
Handled materials well				
Followed directions				

Worksheet 21.6   Children's Needs

There are many lists of children's needs in the literature. As part of long-range planning, it is helpful for a teacher to list children's needs as he sees them. Below is a list of needs one teacher had in mind:

1. Activities that provide for individual differences in terms of development and experience.
2. As active learners, children need firsthand experiences.
3. Opportunities to engage in activities that enhance self-concept.
4. Opportunities to make use of their own experiences in a planned setting.

List areas of a room below. Beside each one, note the needs listed above (1–4) that might be met.

Worksheet 21.7   Teacher Interaction

When a teacher is planning, it is important for him to know the kind of interactions he engages in. Observe in a classroom. Indicate the nature of the interactions, the results, and with whom the interaction took place.

Teacher interaction (with whom)	Nature of interaction	Results of interaction (if possible)

Worksheet 21.8   Social Development

All children are different. They develop at different rates. In planning a day's schedule, it is helpful for a teacher to understand these differences, focusing on the social development of boys and girls. Find illustrations of each of the following kinds of play. In your description, give the name of the child or employ some other code.

Isolate play	Parallel play	Associative play	Cooperative play

Worksheet 21.9   Room Arrangement

There is no one way to arrange a classroom. However, in determining a room arrangement, there are certain criteria to be considered (e.g., painting near water, using books in a well-lighted area, working with blocks and woodworking out of the line of traffic, and the need for quiet areas). Draw an arrangement of a classroom for young children.

List the criteria you used below.

Worksheet 21.10   Daily Schedule

Every classroom has some kind of a daily schedule. Some are worked up according to small blocks of time, while others are more globally defined. Ask the teacher for the daily schedule. Copy it in the space below.

Examine the schedule according to the following criteria:

1. Times in which children can make choices.

2. Opportunities for small-group activities.

3. Balance between quiet and strenuous activities.

4. Provision for cleanup.

5. Provision for toileting and handwashing.

6. Opportunities for both indoor and outdoor activities.

7. Other.

Worksheet 21.11   Materials and Equipment

Materials and equipment do not in themselves determine the quality of a program but they do play an important part in implementing it. While classrooms are filled with both materials and equipment, some of these are more essential than others. Construct a priority list of materials and equipment. Place a star (*) next to those that are essential, an (O) next to those that are helpful but not essential, and an (X) next to those that are not necessary. Give reasons for placing each item in its designated category.

Items	Reasons

What criteria did you use in selecting priority items?

Which of these criteria would you discuss with parents to aid them in selecting toys and other materials for use in their homes?

Worksheet 21.12   Health

Children learn health practices early in life. They follow the rules and practices set down by adults. It is important that, along with this, they develop attitudes about their own responsibilities for good health so that these attitudes become a way of thinking and a part of the whole process of living. Observe in a classroom and find evidences of sound health practices.

Evidence that the teacher is making provisions for the following:	Evidence that children are developing appropriate attitudes concerning the following:

Sound eating practices

Sound hygienic practices
(e.g., washing hands, toileting)

Dress appropriate to weather

Adapting to environmental conditions

Worksheet 21.13   Handwashing and Toileting

A teacher's attitude toward handwashing will be reflected in the way he sets up the procedure. Children do or do not develop independence and positive attitudes toward body care, depending upon the teacher's values. Describe the physical provisions made for handwashing and toileting (including location of facilities, manner of dispensing soap, height of facilities, etc.).

Describe how handwashing and toileting are incorporated formally and informally into the program. Describe the teacher's role.

Watch one child wash his hands. Describe the entire process.

Worksheet 21.14   Safety I

Children are developing habits of safety, so it is important for them to understand what safe behavior means. Providing for a safe classroom and teaching the safe use of materials and equipment are important parts of a teacher's responsibility. In addition, each child must be allowed to work out for himself ways of coping with the environment.

Observe places in a classroom where there is potential danger (e.g., a workbench or a climbing apparatus). Indicate the choice of materials, evidence of care, and arrangements that have been made for their safe use.

Teacher	Children
Evidence of care in selection, arrangement, and limitations of materials and equipment.	Ways in which children use the materials that help develop risk-taking, judgment, etc.

Worksheet 21.15   Safety II

Two key aspects of safety in a classroom are providing for a safe room and teaching the safe use of materials and equipment. Observe children in a classroom and indicate ways in which teacher and children practice safety rules.

Name of child	Activities	Child's role	Teacher's role

Identify materials you consider potentially dangerous.

Were any special arrangements made for children with handicaps?

Worksheet 21.16   Lunch I

(To be used in a school where lunch is served.)
When children sit down to eat together, there are opportunities for them to socialize, to become familiar with food, and to learn to enjoy many types of foods. They gain independence as they pass plates, serve food, and help clear the table. Observe a group of children having lunch. Describe the health habits and attitudes, social interactions, and routines you observe during lunch.

Health habits and attitudes	Social interactions	Routines

Describe the roles of the teacher in each of these areas.

Worksheet 21.17   Lunch II

There are differences of opinion as to whether or not an early childhood program should include lunch. After observing lunch in a classroom, give reasons to justify each point of view in the spaces below:

1. Lunch program

2. No lunch program

Worksheet 21.18   Snack

Most early childhood settings provide a snack time for children, which can involve the learning of both social and nutritional values. Observe children having a snack and describe the following:

What was served?

Where was the snack served?

How was the snack served?

What value did you see in the snack period?

Worksheet 21.19   Rest Period

(To be used in a setting where children have a formal rest period.)
Rest should be an integral part of any program for young children. It becomes especially important in any kind of all-day school. The way in which arrangements are made and the type of supervision given are significant in determining what the quality of rest will be.

Observe in a classroom during a rest period. Find a spot in the room where you will be as inconspicuous as possible. Use the questions below as a guide for your observations.

1. What provision for physical facilities was made to enhance the quality of rest?

2. What behaviors do boys and girls engage in?

3. What does a teacher do to develop a proper atmosphere for rest?

Worksheet 21.20   Arrival I

As each child arrives, note how the child enters the room and which activity area he goes to. (Since you may not know the names of all the children, designate them by describing clothing, hair, etc.)
Record your observation.

Name of child	Mode of entry	Activity

Were there opportunities for parents and teacher to share their concerns?

Worksheet 21.21   Arrival II

The way in which the day begins will often determine how the rest of the day will go. Greeting children and parents upon arrival is an important part of a teacher's role and is also an important part of the day's program. Observe and record provisions made for children's arrival.

What evidence is there that the teacher is ready for the children's arrival?

Was there an opportunity for the teacher to talk with the parent (even to say a word or two)?
   In terms of getting information about the child?

   In terms of giving or getting information about the school?

Worksheet 21.22   Departure

There should be continuity between home and school experiences in a child's life. By taking the time to say a few words to a parent about the day, a teacher is acknowledging the parents' roles in the child's life and is developing continuity between home and school. Observe departure procedures in a classroom. What did the teacher say?

What other things might you, as a teacher, communicate to parents? How might you word them?

Worksheet 21.23   Cleanup Procedure I

When teacher and children work cooperatively at cleanup, children enjoy it. Not only do they develop habits of orderliness and a sense of responsibility, but they gain other learnings that can be as important as those acquired in other portions of the program. Cleanup is a vital part of the educational process. Observe cleanup activities in a classroom and describe the possible learnings.

Activity	Possible learning

Worksheet 21.24   Cleanup Procedure II

Cleanup procedures vary from room to room. Some teachers expect each child to complete a task by cleaning up when he is finished. Others feel that this procedure may discourage a child from using materials. However, they do consider cleaning up as an important habit and a vital learning experience. Observe in a classroom. Which of these points of view did the teacher appear to follow? Describe the cleanup process that led you to your conclusion.

Describe the role of the teacher.

Worksheet 21.25   Assessment

If a program is designed to meet the needs of children, there must be continuous assessment of materials, equipment, and social interactions. Observe in the classroom and determine what kinds of information you could gather that could help in assessing the materials used, the arrangement of materials and equipment, and the quality of interaction with children and teacher.

Materials:

Arrangement:

Interaction (child-child):

Interaction (teacher-child):

Child growth (affective):

Child growth (cognitive):

Worksheet 21.26   Record Keeping I

In order for a teacher to make an assessment of the program in relation to children's needs, it is important to keep records. The kind of records a teacher keeps is determined by the kinds of information he will need to make the assessments. Ask the classroom teacher for sample copies of the records he keeps. Examine them. Describe each record and the information sought that will help the teacher assess children's growth.

Worksheet 21.27   **Record Keeping II**

Records of children's behavior, which serve an important function in program planning, take many forms.

Select a child to observe and fill out the form below as completely as you can.

Directions: Write legibly in ink or type. Summarize the facts you have observed about the child. Include examples to illustrate the points made. Longer anecdotal records may be written on a separate sheet and attached.

INDIVIDUAL CHILD RECORD

Child: _____   Date: _____

Age: _____   Recorder: _____

1. *Physical Growth* (description of child, general characteristics of his activities, large and small muscle coordination, eating, dressing, toilet habits, rest):

2. *Social Adjustment* (attitude toward other children: ability to lead and follow; special friends, social techniques used with other children: sharing, cooperation, etc.; attitude toward adults: regular teachers, student teachers, visitors):

3. *Mental Growth* (attention span and persistence; reasoning and problem solving; comprehension; abstract concepts; memory; imagination; language, including vocabulary and ability to express needs and ideas):

4. *Emotional Growth* (adjustment to change and new situations; ways of expressing anger, fear, frustrations, affection, joy, pleasure):

5. *Interests* (activities preferred; favorite toys; ideas expressed in play; interest in stories and books; uses of art materials; interest in music; experiences in science and other areas):

6. *Summary of Abilities and Needs:*

7. *Teacher Recommendations:*

8. *Outline for Parents' Conference:*

9. *Teachers' Comments after Parents' Conference:*

Worksheet 21.28   Teacher Movement

The way a teacher moves around a room indicates his priorities. If a teacher will have someone chart his movements from time to time, information gained can be used in modifying plans. Draw a diagram of the room using a different colored pencil for each teacher (if there is more than one), and chart each teacher's (and student teacher's, if any are present) movements with arrows to illustrate how he moves about in the classroom.

Ask someone to chart your own movements during a half hour of your participation. What guidelines were you considering that influenced your movements? (Use a carbon of the room diagram to chart your movements.)

Worksheet 21.29   **Record of Child Behavior**

In order to plan programs for children, careful observations should be made of each child's behavior. Observe a child and note your findings, using this form.

Date: _____ Age: _____ yrs. _____ mos.   Name: _____

                                                  Recorder: _____

1. Physical characteristics

   Description of child

   Coordination

2. Separation from parent

3. Child-teacher relationship

4. Child-child relationship

5 Adjustment to routines

6. Uses of materials

Check with the teacher to see to what extent your impressions coincide with hers.

Worksheet 21.30   Self-Assessment

While a teacher expects to be supervised by an outside person or persons, it is important for him to be able to assess his own performance. Although videotape, audiotape, and category systems provide objective feedback, they are not always available. Here is another form of self-assessment. Using this as an instrument for self-assessment, answer the following questions.

TEACHER'S SELF-EVALUATION GUIDE
(equally suitable for students)

1. *School Policies*
   Do I work within policies and procedures established by the school?

2. *Theoretical Knowledge*
   a. Do I make use of knowledge and understanding of child development and curriculum in early childhood education?
   b. Do I keep informed of new developments?

3. *Supervising a Group of Children*
   a. What are my relationships with individual children?
   b. How do I manage small and large groups?
   c. Do I use good judgment?
   d. Do I plan for appropriate blocks of time indoors and outdoors?
   e. Do I make good use of indoor and outdoor space?
   f. Do I provide appropriately for transitions and routines?
   g. Do I maintain an attractive classroom?
   h. Do I keep equipment in good condition?
   i. Do I consider health and safety factors in planning my activities?

4. *Curriculum*
   a. Do I offer a wide range of experiences so that children can make choices according to their interests and needs?
   b. Do I look for signs of growth and adjust the program when these signs are evident?
   c. Do I allow for various levels of ability among children?
   d. Do I know how and when to ask questions?
   e. Do I talk too much?
   f. Do I make adequate provision for music, language, science, graphic art, dramatic play, block building, woodworking, and modeling activities?

5. *Work with Co-teacher or Teacher Aide* (where applicable)
   a. Do I see myself as a member of a team?
   b. Do I coordinate my efforts with those of my coworkers?
   c. Do I work out suitable division and exchange of responsibilities?
   d. Am I able to assume full responsibility in the absence of coworkers?

6. *Staff Meetings and Workshops*
   a. Do I participate in these activities?
   b. Am I able to transfer concepts from theoretical discussions at staff meetings and workshops to action programs in my own teaching?

7. *Other Staff Relationships*
   Do I find ways to help children understand the roles of other adults at school?

8. *Work with Parents*
   a. Do I maintain good professional relationships with parents?
   b. Do I recognize the importance of seeing the child as a member of the family?
   c. Do I share a child's experiences with his parents?
   d. Do I bring appropriate information to parents' attention in a helpful way?
   e. Do I know when to refer a parent's or child's problems to an appropriate person?
   f. Do I interpret my program to parents?

9. *Record Keeping*
   a. Do I experiment with systems of notetaking to assist in planning, to evaluate growth, and to form the basis for written records of individuals and groups?
   b. Do I use information in record folders appropriately?

10. *Professional Activity and Use of Community Resources*
    a. Am I a member of at least one professional organization in the field?
    b. Do I attend meetings conducted by professional groups?

Worksheet 21.31   Parents' Meetings

(This worksheet is appropriate for use when it is possible for a student to attend a parents' meeting.)
There are different kinds of meetings planned for parents. Workshops often give parents opportunities to become familiar with the curriculum. Lectures and films cover specific topics of interest. Attend a parents' meeting and record your observations.

Time of meeting:

Location of the meeting:

Way in which parents were notified:

Description of the meeting:

Number of parents in attendance:

List ten topics for discussion you would consider appropriate for a group of parents of young children.

1.

2.

3.

4.

5.

6.

7.

8.

9.

10.

INDEX